JESUS

JESUS

EDUARD SCHWEIZER

TRANSLATED BY DAVID E. GREEN

JOHN KNOX PRESS
Richmond, Virginia

Library of Congress Catalog Card Number: 76-107322
International Standard Book Number: 0-8042-0330-X
Printed in the United States of America

Translated from the German *Jesus Christus*
published by Siebenstern Verlag, Munich, 1968

First published 1971
Translation © SCM Press Ltd 1971

SCM Press Ltd
Bloomsbury Street London

John Knox Press
Richmond, Virginia, U.S.A.

CONTENTS

ABBREVIATIONS

ASNU	Acta Seminarii Neotestamentici Upsaliensis (Uppsala: Gleerup)
ATANT	Abhandlungen zur Theologie des Alten und Neuen Testaments (Zürich: Zwingli)
BevTh	Beiträge zur evangelische Theologie (München: Kaiser)
BJRL	*Bulletin of the John Rylands Library* (Manchester)
BZ	*Biblische Zeitschrift* (Freiburg)
BZNW	Beihefte zur *Zeitschrift für die neutestamentliche Wissenschaft* (Berlin: Topelmann)
EvTh	*Evangelische Theologie* (München)
FRLANT	Forschungen zur Religion und Literatur des Alten und Neuen Testaments (Göttingen: Vandenhoeck & Ruprecht)
NEB	New English Bible
NovT	*Novum Testamentum* (Leiden)
NTD	Das Neue Testament Deutsch (Göttingen: Vandenhoeck & Ruprecht)
NTL	New Testament Library (London: SCM, and Philadelphia: Westminster)
NTS	*New Testament Studies* (Cambridge)
RGG³	*Die Religion in Geschichte und Gegenwart*, 3rd ed. (Tübingen: Mohr, 1956–62)
SBT	Studies in Biblical Theology (London: SCM, and Naperville: Allenson, First Series, 1950–66; Second Series, 1967ff.)
SUNT	Studien zur Umwelt des Neuen Testaments (Göttingen: Vandenhoeck & Ruprecht)
TDNT	*Theological Dictionary of the New Testament* [Eng. trans. of *TWNT*], trans. and ed. G. W. Bromiley (Grand Rapids, Michigan: Eerdmans, 1964ff.)
ThB	Theologische Bücherei (München: Kaiser)

TLZ   *Theologische Literaturzeitung* (Leipzig)

TU   Texte und Untersuchungen zur Geschichte der altchrist-
             lichen Literatur (Berlin: Akademie)

TWNT   *Theologisches Wörterbuch zum Neuen Testament,* ed. G. Kittel
             (Stuttgart: Kohlhammer, 1933ff.)

WMANT   Wissenschaftliche Monographien zum Alten und Neuen
             Testament (Neukirchen: Erziehungsverein)

ZNW   *Zeitschrift für die neutestamentliche Wissenschaft* (Berlin)

ZTK   *Zeitschrift für Theologie und Kirche* (Tübingen)

Biblical quotations are normally taken from the Revised Standard
Version of the Bible.

I

THE NEW TESTAMENT

INTRODUCTION

In recent years, biblical studies have taught us a new way of understanding the Old Testament: as a book that always remains open to the future. Time and time again Israel experiences its history as a new intervention on the part of God. He revives ancient promises, but fulfills them in a way completely different from that which an earlier generation expected. Or he may refocus them so that they point to a fulfillment still awaited in the future. Each time, there is also a certain process of selection: statements once central become peripheral or vanish entirely; others, which were hardly noticed, come to occupy center stage. Thus the Old Testament is a historical book *par excellence*, reminding us that God seeks to encounter us quite outside the realm of speculative thought, in his actions within history.[1]

Should not this also be our starting point for an elucidation of the New Testament? If what we have just said holds true also for God's acts in Jesus Christ—and that in the most radical sense—then the unity binding the manifold interpretations of the New Testament rests in this very act of God. This should make us always ready to rethink our ideas and arrive at a new understanding. It becomes clear at the same time how open to the future the New Testament is also. In new situations, confronting new dangers, and in a new language that allows completely new ideas to be expressed, the church must keep retelling what God has done in Jesus Christ. This continual movement, which is permanently committed to the congregation of Jesus Christ, also runs through the centuries of church history. It will not end until God's sovereignty is established and the entire history of

---

[1] G. von Rad, *Old Testament Theology*, trans. D. M. G. Stalker (Edinburgh: Oliver & Boyd, and New York: Harper, 1962–65) II, pp. 319–26, 357–8.

the human world, as of the world of nature, is brought to that goal where God will be all in all (I Cor. 15.28).

Then, of course, we can see that the New Testament is not simply a collection of revealed truths that faith has only to adopt *en masse* in order to know everything necessary. Obviously faith must allow itself to be borne along by the witnesses of the New Testament, and must in each new situation (e.g., Europe 1968) allow them to bring it to the place where it can learn to understand what God's acts in Jesus Christ mean for it.[2] Of necessity, therefore, faith will allow many statements to recede into the background, while attaching such importance to others that they begin to determine its entire conduct. Luther, for instance, allowed this to happen to the Bible's statement concerning the righteousness of God. Such selectivity is wrong only when it becomes petrified but is still maintained—in other words, when the New Testament is no longer permitted to live and to speak afresh to a new age. Then people repeat the statements of the fathers without noticing that God does not want to battle with enemies long defeated, but enemies that live today.[3]

This establishes a completely new relationship between us and the New Testament. It means that we must get used to the fact that it is not simply an arsenal full of inspired truths and demonstrated facts concerning salvation, which we need only take up to be armed against all dangers. It demands much more of us. In a completely new way the witnesses of the New Testament engage us in dialogue and set us in motion. We must renounce the whole idea of finding guarantees for unimpeachable saving events and infallible theological propositions that need only be repeated verbatim. But this is how it must be. There can be guarantees—more or less—for the durability of a new steel bridge, for the truth of a mathematical proposition, for the washability of a fabric. But there can never be guarantees for the things that really matter in human life—for the beauty of a picture, for the enthralling power of a sonata, for a woman's true love. A

---

[2] Cf. Jesus' use of parables, below, pp. 26–30.

[3] In Romans 9—11, Paul uses Israel as an example to show what the grace of God means. One can therefore say that the theme of these chapters is the superiority of God's free grace over all human actions. If, however, during the period of National Socialism in Germany, with its persecution of the Jews, a preacher had preached on these sections by discussing only the superior grace of God without saying anything about the problem of Israel, he would have exhibited a complete lack of understanding about Romans 9—11, even about what these chapters say concerning God's grace.

husband who wants guarantees of his wife's love may have her shadowed by private detectives. Even if at the end of a year he has accumulated 365 spotless reports, he will still not be sure, though one thing will be: he is on the brink of destroying his marriage. And the other husband, who will admit no questions and shuts his eyes tightly to the facts, will worship all his life an idealized image of his wife, and perhaps not even notice that he does so; but he will never come to know his real wife, and there is once more great psychological probability that his marriage will be destroyed by repressed questions on his part and a sense of not being understood on the part of his wife. How could it be any different with God? Faith means not less but much more than encounter with a fellow human being who confronts us as an individual. A faith that wants guarantees or closes its eyes to scientifically unmistakable facts is in mortal danger. When faith really comes upon us, we are taken upon a course that can never reach its end until the final coming of God's kingdom. It will instead lead us ever onward to new questions and answers, new defeats and victories, new experiences of temptation and strength.

The purpose of this small book is to help the process a bit. What has just been said should make it clear that some mental effort will be required of the reader. On the other hand, the book is in many ways a modest undertaking. In the first place, I wrote it in the fall of 1966, during the first weeks of my service in Japan, when, besides the text of the New Testament, I had at my disposal considerable leisure but not much literature. So I attempted to summarize the most important conclusions I had drawn from my reading. Then, in the winter of 1967–68, I went over what I had written critically in a series of lectures before an audience drawn from all the departments of the University. As a consequence of this procedure, I expanded my material at many points and added various bibliographical references, especially at those points where my views differ from those of most modern scholars.[4] This may account for a certain lack of uniformity.

[4] An asterisk * is used in the notes to designate works written more for the general reader, which do not demand special grounding in theology or the Biblical languages. The apocryphal writings of the Old and New Testaments, i.e., those writings not accepted as Scripture, can be found most easily in R. H. Charles, ed., *The Apocrypha and Pseudepigrapha of the Old Testament* (Oxford: Clarendon, 1913 [reprinted 1963]) and E. Hennecke and W. Schneemelcher, *New Testament Apocrypha*, ed. R. McL. Wilson (London: Lutterworth, and Philadelphia: Westminster, 1963–65). The documents from Qumran (a monastic Jewish sect that lived near the Dead Sea) are available in several English translations, including A.

Technical and foreign terms that are used frequently are explained at their first occurrence.[5] And so I hope that this unpretentious survey of what has been important and meaningful to me will help some readers to come to love the New Testament and the Lord to whom it bears witness.

SOURCES FOR THE LIFE OF JESUS

The man who has put his stamp on nearly two thousand years of history did not leave a single written word. It is also clear that the accurate preservation and transmission of his words meant nothing to him.[6] This is in itself a remarkable fact. It shows that encounter with Jesus cannot be replaced by a mere acceptance of his words. It can only be mediated by persons who have really encountered him themselves and borne witness to this encounter.

Now it is impossible for any historian to write history without personal involvement. Whoever narrates a historical event must choose between what is important to him and what appears to be of secondary importance. To do so he must understand to some extent what the events were all about. If I want to describe a battle, I must recount what was important in bringing about victory for one army and defeat for the other; but I do not have to describe the lovely weather or the way the fauna of the region live. On the other hand, such involvement must not obscure the view. For instance, I must not look for only those events that contribute to the glory of the first army

---

Dupont-Sommer, *The Essene Writings from Qumran* (Oxford: Blackwell, and Cleveland: World, 1962); T. H. Gaster, *The Scriptures of the Dead Sea Sect* (London: Secker & Warburg, and Toronto: Doubleday, 1957); and G. Vermes, *The Dead Sea Scrolls* (revised ed.; New York: Heritage, 1967). For the Bible itself, a good modern translation like the New English Bible or the Jerusalem Bible is recommended.

[5] Cf. "apocalyptic", p. 18; "Didache", p. 56, n. 7; "glossolalia", p. 60, n. 15; "indicative" and "imperative", p. 108; "parousia", p. 54, n. 4; "Q" or "sayings-source", p. 124; "Synoptic Gospels", p. 6.

[6] B. Gerhardsson, *Memory and Manuscript* (ASNU 22, 1961), pp. 324–35, maintains that Jesus had his disciples learn certain statements by heart, after the fashion of a Jewish rabbi. It is impossible, however, to overlook the divergent forms of even such crucial utterances as the Lord's Prayer or the words of institution of the Lord's Supper (cf. Matt. 6.9–13 with Luke 11.2–4, of Mark 14.22–25 with 1 Cor. 11.23ff.). Furthermore, we can still observe new corrections and revisions of Jesus' words being made half a century after his death, for instance when we compare the reformulations of Matthew or Luke with their original form in Mark.

and the disgrace of the second. My involvement must itself be determined by what I am describing; the event itself must involve me. Such involvement becomes more necessary when a historical event claims to address me personally.

The example of a theatrical performance will help clarify what I mean. If I want to share in this event after it is over, I have to rely on people who participated in the experience. An uninvolved witness would report with complete neutrality everything he observed, for example, that the curtain took thirty-five seconds to rise, that the make-up on this performer was visible, but scarcely noticeable on another, etc. He would, however, be incapable of mediating to me any sense of what actually took place. Another spectator might report only his own experiences: "I tell you, tears came to my eyes in the second act, and in the third act my heart was beating so that I almost thought I would have to leave." Such a man would be of no more help to me than the first. Between these two extremes fall various stages of reporting, in all of which the report of what took place must be linked with personal involvement in the play. One man may give his report in such a way as to presuppose a knowledge of the play but show how this performance gave him new insight into its meaning and significance, while illustrating by means of occasional examples how one scene or another was played by this or that actor in a new and unusual way. Another may give his report in such a way as to recall the general outline of the action, while emphasizing the things he found crucial and omitting details of minor importance. Both methods are legitimate, and both allow the listener to participate in what took place. Applying our analogy to the events surrounding Jesus, we might place Paul, for example, in the first category, and Mark in the second.

But there is one more crucial factor. If I am properly to describe a battle or even a theatrical performance, I have to be involved in such a way as to understand what it was all about; but I do not have to give or refuse my assent. I can depict the positions and goals of both armies without myself becoming a partisan in a conflict resolved long ago, even if I personally regret or rejoice in the outcome of the battle. I can even understand and reproduce what a dramatist is trying to say while still leaving the question open as to whether he will finally be proved right or not. I can even feel that the play has a personal message for me but admit to others that they may see it differently.

Toward Jesus one cannot remain neutral. Of course I can encounter him with an open-minded attitude that is not yet faith. In a sense, faith never reaches its final goal, and is therefore always open to new encounters. But this is an openness that at bottom acknowledges that Jesus can be master over me. Neutrality is in any case impossible as a definitive attitude, for his summons is such that whoever seeks to remain neutral has already rejected him. Therefore even Mark, who formally merely recounts the life and death of Jesus, is obviously writing as a witness on Jesus' behalf. For this reason he omits everything that, interesting as it might be to the historian, is irrelevant to what the believer finds in Jesus: for example, Jesus' youth and early development, details concerning his appearance, his age, his education, his profession, his family, his marital status (it is extremely unusual for a Jew of Jesus' time to be single). At most, we are given bits of such information in passing.

Even today not all New Testament scholars agree on the relative historical value of the sources.[7] Most, however, have accepted the so-called two-source theory, which has stood up for over a century. According to this theory, Mark is the earliest Gospel, probably written towards the end of the sixties. Matthew and Luke were acquainted with it, as well as with an additional collection of Jesus' sayings, called "Q" (from the first letter of *Quelle*, the German word for "source"). There is as yet no agreement concerning the amount of this tradition that was extant in written as opposed to merely oral form, or whether Luke had before him this same source or an altered version of it. Both Matthew and Luke, furthermore, made use of additional special traditions. These three evangelists, who often agree almost word for word when dealing with material from Mark or Q, are for this reason called the "synoptics" ("sharing a common perspective"). Even before Mark, isolated stories or sayings of Jesus were brought together to form minor collections, and obviously the origin of the individual sections goes back even further.

With the help of scientific methodology, we can in large measure distinguish the sayings and acts of Jesus from the interpretation of

[7] For a survey of opinions see, for example, W. Marxsen, *Introduction to the New Testament*,* trans. G. Buswell (Oxford: Blackwell, and Philadelphia: Fortress, 1968), pp. 113ff.; Paul Feine, *Introduction to the New Testament*, founded by Paul Feine and Johannes Behm, completely reedited by Werner Georg Kümmel, translated by A. J. Mattill, Jr. from the 14th ed. (Nashville: Abingdon, and London: SCM, 1966), pp. 33ff.; Edward P. Blair, *Jesus in the Gospel of Matthew* (New York: Abingdon, 1960), pp. 18–26.

later writers, including Mark and the other evangelists.[8] It is therefore possible to make an estimate of the extent to which a story reproduces accurately the course of events and to what extent it does not, or to determine which sayings were spoken by Jesus and which were later placed in his mouth. It is by no means true, however, that everything that does not go back to Jesus is necessarily unimportant or even of lesser importance. It is even possible to claim that only a believing witness can tell us what really took place in the story of Jesus. A newsreel with sound from Jerusalem, depicting the crucifixion of Jesus, could have provided us with many historical details; but it could not have told us what actually happened there, whether we were witnessing the execution of a harmless fanatic or an ambitious nationalist, or whether God himself was giving us his final word. Only a witness, whom we can believe or not, can tell us this. Let us consider three examples that illuminate this point:

1. Matthew 8.5-13 and Luke 7.1-10 tell how Jesus *in absentia* healed a centurion's servant at Capernaum. According to one account, the centurion himself comes to Jesus; according to the other, he remains at home, merely sending some elders and later some of his friends. In Luke 7.6b, 7b-8, these emissaries say almost word-for-word the same thing that the centurion himself says to Jesus in Matthew 8.8-9. The responses of Jesus likewise agree, except that the second portion (Matt. 8.11-12) is assigned to another occasion by Luke 13.28-29. Although the possibility that Jesus said the same thing on two different occasions could explain this phenomenon, it is impossible for the healing of the centurion's servant to have taken place twice, with the centurion coming in person once, but sending his friends the next time and having them say exactly the same thing. When a story is being retold, however, it is quite natural for details that are irrelevant to the point of the story to change, so that, for example, what the centurion has his friends say to Jesus is described in the retelling as his own request to Jesus, while the friends, who are irrelevant to the story, are left out. This example shows that the words of the person making the request, as well as the words of Jesus, are preserved more carefully than the story in which they are set. It is quite conceivable that Q preserved in writing only these words with a brief indication of the setting, while everything else was transmitted orally. If so, we are dealing with a simple instance of the law that

[8] Cf. E. Schweizer, *Good News according to Mark* (Richmond, Va.: John Knox, 1970; London: SPCK, 1971), especially pp. 12ff.

applies to all oral tradition: non-essentials change in the course of transmission without any specific intention on the part of the narrator.

2. Our second example is more significant. According to Mark 11.1ff., Jesus goes to Jerusalem and enters the temple, but returns at once to Bethany when he has seen everything. The next morning he curses the fig tree, returns once more to Jerusalem, drives the merchants and money-changers from the temple, and leaves the city that evening. The next day, the disciples discover the withered fig tree, and Jesus speaks with them concerning the power of prayer. Matthew 21.1ff. places the cleansing of the temple on the day of Jesus' entry into Jerusalem. As a result, the cursing of the fig tree comes to coincide with its withering, so that the curse is fulfilled immediately. Finally, John 2.13ff. transfers the ejection of the merchants from the temple to the beginning of Jesus' ministry. Although Jesus might conceivably have cleansed the temple at both the beginning and conclusion of his ministry, it is impossible for him to have done so in the same fashion and with the same words on two consecutive days. It is likewise impossible for the cursing of the fig tree and discourse on the power of prayer to have been repeated on two different days. If we ask what seems the most likely historical possibility, we have to say that at least the beginning of the account in Matthew carries the most conviction. It would indeed be strange if Jesus' entry into Jerusalem led up to nothing more than his visiting the temple like a tourist and then returning to Bethany to spend the night.

But why does Mark shape his account in this fashion? All three Synoptics tell how Jesus called the temple a "house of prayer" in contrast to a "den of robbers"; Mark, however, cites Isaiah 56.7 more completely than do the others: "a house of prayer for all the nations". This shows us how Mark understood the cleansing of the temple. To him it is a sign given by Jesus himself that the purely Jewish cult has come to an end and that all nations can henceforth worship God. For this reason he places the story of Jesus' cleansing of the temple in a framework that begins with Jesus' cursing of the fig tree that bore no fruit and concludes with the fulfillment of the curse. For Mark, this barren fig tree is the symbol of an exclusivistic Judaism that will not open itself to the nations of the world, and whose time is past. At the same time, he uses the discovery of the miracle the next morning to develop the theme that worship of God is the true "cult", thus providing a transition to what follows.[9] In this case, then, the desire of the

---

[9] Cf. Schweizer, *ibid.*, ad loc.

evangelist to make a specific point has consciously or unconsciously influenced his manner of presentation, and has probably altered the actual course of events in his account. But is this phenomenon avoidable? Mark and the community before him would not have preserved the story at all if it had not acquired significance for them. What Mark does is simply this: he shows us why he considers this story so significant, lets us see how Jesus encountered him in this story and affected his life. Of course we can still ask whether he (or the community before him) understood Jesus correctly, and we will discover that he places greater emphasis on something that was only implicit, in fact almost hidden, in Jesus' actions. For he is living in the post-Easter period, when the advance of the gospel through all nations was an accomplished fact and men could see what had actually taken place in Jesus. Suppose, however, that we were even more cautious, reaching the conclusion (erroneous, in my opinion) that Jesus' actions gave no hint of anything of this sort. We should still have to ask what really happened when Jesus drove some merchants from the temple—or, to be completely critical, what really happened when Jesus took such a negative attitude toward the temple (which then led to the story of the cleansing of the temple). How could we answer this question without hearing the evidence of Mark and the other witnesses? Even if we should finally have to formulate a different opinion, we could not do so without drawing on the services of these witnesses. The matter is therefore clear: Mark is not at all interested in recounting the train of events in purely historical fashion; historically speaking, either his account, or that of Matthew, or both, must be inaccurate. His overriding interest is presumably to attest for us what really took place: according to his interpretation, the end of the purely Jewish cult and the beginning of God's worship among all peoples. This response springs of course from his faith, so that the reader is at once confronted with a question: can he say, with Mark, that this is the crucial event that then took place?

3. A third example is perhaps even clearer. According to Mark 15.25, 33–34, Jesus is crucified at the third hour, i.e., about nine o'clock. The darkness over the cross of Jesus begins at the sixth hour, i.e., about noon. Jesus dies at the ninth hour, i.e., about three in the afternoon. According to John 19.14, however, Pilate does not condemn Jesus until the sixth hour, i.e., about noon. Historically speaking, at least one of these chronologies must be incorrect. The question is whether both Mark and John are not trying to make the same true

point, and whether this truth is not all that matters. What it boils down to is this: according to John, Jesus dies on the eve of Passover; according to the Synoptics, he dies on the day of Passover itself. Now in the Jewish system of reckoning time, each day begins in the evening. According to John 19.14, Jesus dies late in the afternoon preceding the Passover meal, which took place after sundown; he dies, therefore, at the very hour when the Passover lamb is being slaughtered. John 1.29, 30 and especially 19.36 make it quite clear that this association is intentional.[10] According to Mark, however, Jesus' last supper with his disciples was the Passover meal. Mark is thinking of another Old Testament passage, Amos 8.9, according to which the sun will set at noon and darkness will cover the earth at midday on the Day of the Lord, i.e., the Day of Judgment. According to Mark's chronology, the sun sets precisely at noon on the day of Jesus' crucifixion, and darkness lasts from noon until three p.m. This precise hourly chronology of events, elsewhere unparalleled in Mark, also emphasizes the fact that on this day everything takes place, hour by hour, according to God's will. With this chronology, Mark is therefore trying to say that this day marks the fulfillment of time, that on this day, hour by hour, God's will was done. What the prophets had been expecting on the day of God's fulfillment of his purpose has taken place. John and Mark are therefore using two different modes of presentation, which cannot be reconciled historically, to say the same thing: in the death of Jesus the expectations of the Old Testament finally reached their goal.

The purely historical question can no longer be answered with certainty. Mark's chronology seems more likely with regard to the hour, John's with regard to the day. The real question, however, is whether they are both right in seeing this day as the fulfillment of God's will, as had long been stated in Israel's history and the witness of the prophets. Whether they are right—not, of course, in their exegesis of individual Old Testament texts, but in their fundamental perspective—can be decided only by one who has encountered Jesus in the historically contestable testimony of these two witnesses.

If so, however, the question arises whether we should not be content with the witness of the evangelists to their faith, making no

[10] Psalm 34.21 may be the original source of this view, as C. H. Dodd suggests (*The Interpretation of the Fourth Gospel* [Cambridge: Cambridge University Press, 1953], p. 428, n. 1). John himself, however, surely is thinking of the instructions for preparing the Passover lamb found in Exodus 12.10 (LXX), 46 and Numbers 9.12.

attempt to distinguish a historical picture of Jesus' ministry from that shaped by the faith of the post-Easter church. There is much to favor such caution. The disciples themselves did not really have their eyes opened so as to know who Jesus was until after Easter. According to all accounts, the crucifixion of Jesus was such a shock to them that we can make out only the collapse of their faith and its complete restoration through the appearance of the resurrected Lord. When we distinguish what can with some assurance be ascribed to the earthly Jesus of Nazareth from what the post-Easter church placed in his mouth or added to the accounts of his actions, we do not do so in order to limit the authority of a saying or a story. How could the words of the resurrected Jesus, speaking to us through his disciples, have less authority than those of the earthly Jesus?

We must, however, keep both sides of the argument in mind. On the one hand, only a post-Easter witness speaking in faith can testify to us concerning what really took place in the life and death and resurrection of Jesus, as he recounts them. Only such a witness can tell us that Jesus is the *Christ*. On the other hand, the disciple knows from the very outset that he is saying these things about Jesus, in other words, about the man from Nazareth whom he accompanied, to whom he listened, and whose ministry he saw. He knows, in other words, that *Jesus* is the Christ. The former tells us who the man Jesus is, namely, he through whom God himself would speak to us; the latter tells us who this Christ of God is, namely, the man from Nazareth who died on the cross, not the national hero who drove out the Romans and established a kingdom of Israel to rule the world. It is therefore impossible to understand the testimony of the post-Easter community—that this is God's Christ—without knowing that the community is speaking of a man who was crucified, that this identification is based not on worldly success and military victory, but only on what God has said and done. The new insight that Easter gave the disciples was an insight into Jesus.

These are the basic considerations, but there is a further point. We of today have to think historically in a way that Jesus' immediate disciples did not if we are not to find ourselves in a completely different culture and way of thinking when we consider certain questions, e.g., religious questions. As men of the twentieth century we cannot help asking historical questions when we read the Gospels.

In seeking to reconstruct as much as possible of the historical Jesus of Nazareth, we do not claim that this alone could show what he really is and what he signifies. What we mean is that the statements proceeding from the faith of the post-Easter community would be misunderstood if they were not thought of as statements about this man Jesus. For we shall also see how the witness of the post-Easter community kept trying to redescribe and proclaim the mystery of Jesus in new terms, while at the same time submitting to correction by reminiscences of Jesus' ministry and preaching.[11] Because of this necessary reciprocal interaction, we shall begin our account with Jesus of Nazareth.

[11] See below, p. 22, n. 18.

II

JESUS: THE MAN WHO FITS NO FORMULA

THE CLAIM OF JESUS

Who was Jesus?[1] He might have considered himself (1) a *Messiah*. "Messiah" (Greek: "Christ") means "the anointed one". The king in particular was anointed in Israel; so were the priests and occasionally the prophets (1 Kings 19.16–17). Israel expected the eschatological king to come and deliver the people from all distress. This was true especially after the Babylonian exile, when the hereditary succession of the Davidic kings finally ceased. As a rule, the Messiah was expected to conquer the Gentile nations and restore Israel. This expectation was usually linked with fantastic ideas of world domination by Israel (to which all the nations would be subject), the end of sin and godlessness, and occasionally the renewal of nature and the restoration of paradise on earth.

Argument has raged for decades over whether Jesus himself thought he was the Messiah. The earliest Gospel makes the strange statement that Jesus usually forbade people to spread the word of his miracles. Wrede showed that this is a fiction on the part of Mark; it cannot possibly correspond to the actual course of events in Jesus' ministry. The same holds true for Jesus' refusal to let Peter repeat his confession, "You are the Messiah", and for the theory that the parables were intended to conceal the truth that Jesus was proclaiming. Wrede suggested that Mark's purpose in using this fiction was to explain why Jesus was not recognized and hailed as Messiah until after Easter. In

[1] On the epithets "Christ", "Son of God", and "Son of Man", see E. Schweizer, "Gottessohn und Christus", "Menschensohn", in Claus Westermann, ed., *Theologie: VI x 12 Hauptbegriffe** (Stuttgart: Kreuz, 1967), pp. 67–77. The same work contains additional relevant material by Schweizer (pp. 94–6) and Heinrich Ott (pp. 206–10).

fact, according to Wrede, Jesus never claimed to be the Messiah, and was certainly not hailed as the Messiah during his life on earth. Although this explanation cannot be maintained,[2] one thing remains certain: Jesus' strange refusal to let his deeds be proclaimed and the remarkable theory about the parables do not go back to Jesus himself. Did he then think of himself as the Messiah or not?

There can be no doubt that Jesus accomplished all sorts of healings. It is also clear that Jesus spoke to tax collectors, who were excluded from the people of God because of their frequent contact with pagans and questionable business conduct, summoning them to fellowship at his table and thus to fellowship with God; in other words, he offered forgiveness as though he stood in the place of God.[3] It is also certain that he promised men the kingdom of God as though he had authority to grant it. It is certain that he did not begin, like the prophets of the Old Testament, by saying, "Thus says the Lord", or like the rabbis, by saying, "Thus it is written". In short, he did not refer his own words to any other authority. Quite the contrary: among the sayings of Jesus that are most likely to be genuine are such unprecedented statements as the "But now I tell you" passage (Matt. 5.21–48), in which laws of the Old Testament are abrogated and the "I" of Jesus speaks in the place of God. And when Jesus says, "It is by the finger of God that I cast out demons" (Luke 11.20), he is equating his finger with God's. If Sodom and Gomorrah will be better off at the last judgment than the cities that reject Jesus (Matt. 11.21–24), if Jesus is greater than Solomon and Jonah and John the Baptist (Matt. 11.11–14; 12.41–42), then who is he?

Neither the Old Testament nor Judaism ever expected such talk from a Messiah; Jesus' actions and words burst the bounds of all messianic expectations. Nevertheless, there is not a single genuine saying of Jesus in which he refers to himself as the Messiah.[4] It is

[2] See William Wrede, *Das Messiasgeheimnis in den Evangelien* (3rd ed.; Göttingen: Vandenhoeck & Ruprecht, 1963), pp. 214ff.; E. Schweizer, *Beiträge zur Theologie des Neuen Testaments* (Stuttgart: Zwingh, 1970), pp. 11ff.; idem, *Good News according to Mark*, pp. 54f.

[3] Ernst Fuchs, "The Quest of the Historical Jesus", in his *Studies of the Historical Jesus*, trans. A. Scobie (SBT 42, 1964), p. 22.

[4] The word "Christ", which occurs more than five hundred times in the New Testament, is found only a few times in sayings attributed to Jesus: Mark 9.41 (where Matthew 10.42 probably preserves the earlier form of the saying, in which the title does not occur); 12.35 (where the title may not refer to Jesus); 13.21 (which, like Matt. 24.5, speaks of false teachers who will appear); Matthew 23.10

conceivable that Jesus meant an affirmative answer to the question asked by the High Priest (Mark 14.61); here, however, the title is applied to him by someone else, and is substantially corrected by the statement concerning the "Son of Man", which follows immediately (14.62), as well as by the fact of Jesus' execution. None of the disciples were present at the trial, however, nor could Jesus himself give an account of it later; the accuracy of the tradition is therefore especially doubtful at this point. Peter's confession at Caesarea Philippi is harder to evaluate. Since Jesus could not possibly have announced the details of his passion and resurrection (Mark 8.31) in the form recorded—if he had, the complete confusion of the disciples on Good Friday would be incomprehensible—many scholars have suggested that Jesus' sharp rebuke of Peter (8.32–33) historically followed directly after the latter's statement, "You are the Messiah". This would mean that Jesus completely rejected the title. In my opinion, the original form was a simple reference to the rejection of the Son of Man, and Peter is rebuked not for his confession but for his caution in advising Jesus to avoid the suffering. Even if this is so, however, it remains clear that, according to the earliest Gospel, Jesus was not at all happy about Peter's statement. At the very least, then, Jesus exercised the greatest reserve and considered the title of "Messiah", if not false, at least unsuitable for public acknowledgment.

Perhaps the entry into Jerusalem should also be taken into account. Here there is no mention of the Messiah by title, or, originally, even of the Son of David (who is of course identical with the Messiah); we do, however, hear an echo of Davidic and messianic expectations.[5] We can no longer determine whether the description corresponds to the actual course of events; in any case, the title is here, too, applied to Jesus by the people, and here, too, these expectations were substantially corrected by his unprepossessing entrance—every farmer rides home on his donkey after a day working in the fields—whether or not we have here a deliberate reference to Zechariah 9.9.

Jesus might also have considered himself (2) the *Son of God*. The

(which already presupposes the offices of the Christian community); Luke 24.46 (after Easter); and the appropriate parallels. In all these passages the title "Christ" can probably be traced back to the Christian community. Even in John, who usually preserves a late form of the tradition, the title is used by Jesus only in 17.3.

[5] The salutation in Mark 11.10a was given to every devout pilgrim; only verse 10b indicates expectation of a Davidic kingdom. The title "Son of David" does not occur until Matthew 21.9, 15; cf. Luke 19.38.

meaning of this title would have differed little from that of "Messiah". In 2 Samuel 7.13–14, God speaks through Nathan, promising David that he will maintain the throne of David's son or offspring for ever: "I will be his father and he will be my son" (NEB). Israel has ever since been waiting for the son of David who will reign for ever as king of the last age, adopted by God as his own son. Did Jesus consider himself the Son of God in this sense?

Jesus called God "Father" in a way that was completely new and unexampled. There are no parallels to this usage. It is very rare to find God addressed as "Father" in Palestinian Judaism, and never with the more intimate expression "Abba" (Mark 14.36). Further-more, although Jesus uses the expression "my Father" and "your Father", he never includes himself among the disciples by saying "our Father".[6] This suggests that Jesus felt his own relationship with his Father to be unique, and only later let his disciples share in it. It is therefore wrong to say Jesus merely got men to realize that all are obviously God's children; this had long been the faith of pagan religions outside Israel. What is new is not that Jesus taught men to call God "Father"; it is that a people more sensitive than any other to the distance between God and man, between God and the world, were granted the freedom to say "Abba". They therefore found this free-dom to be a miracle, an incomprehensible gift. Only this one man, only Jesus, had the right to say "Father"—that is why it is so astound-ing for other men to share this form of address.

There is not a single genuine saying of Jesus, however, in which he refers to himself as the "Son of God".[7] The parable of the vineyard and its tenants in Mark 12.1–9 may possibly go back to Jesus himself, but it was more probably produced by the Christian community, which knew of Jesus' death. In any case, the meaning of the image is only that the significance of Jesus surpasses that of the prophets. Jesus himself may conceivably have formulated Mark 13.32 and Matthew 11.27; but this is unlikely, because the absolute expression "the Son" is almost impossible to reproduce in Aramaic, Jesus' mother tongue.

[6] The original invocation of the Lord's Prayer is simply "Father". Furthermore, according to Luke 11.2 and Matthew 6.9, Jesus does not say the prayer with his disciples, but recites it to them as a model for their own prayer.

[7] The expressions "Son of God" and "the Son" must be carefully distinguished. The former is a title of majesty, standing in contrast to "Son of Man". The latter, which stands in contrast to "the Father", stresses subordination. Apart from the statement by the mocking onlookers in Matthew 27.43, John is the first to use the former title in sayings ascribed to Jesus.

In the case of Matthew 11.27, one might at most think in terms of a general statement such as "Only the father knows the son, only the son knows the father" which would then also apply to the special relationship between Jesus and his Father.[8] In this case, however, it too would not be a direct statement made by Jesus, but an image borrowed by him. If Mark 13.32 really did go back to Jesus, it would nevertheless refer not to the majesty but to the subordination of the Son. It would therefore have nothing to do with the title of dignity "Son of God", but would be similar to the designation of Israel as God's son (Exod.4.22). The emphasis would be on the obedience of the Son. In this case, too, however, we must reckon with the possibility that the Christian community produced this saying, at a time when the Last Day seemed further off than Jesus' words had been taken to indicate.

Jesus might have considered himself (3) the *Servant of God*. Once again it is David or his successor who is occasionally referred to as the "Servant of God", even in God's address to the future Messiah (Ezek. 34.23–24; 37.24–25; Zech.3.8). A more important figure, however, was the Servant of God mentioned in Isaiah 40—55, especially Isaiah 53. Here we have the Servant sent by God, who willingly accepts all the suffering God imposes on him; for the benefit of many he is despised by all, but exalted by God. Israel, of course, did not interpret these passages as referring to the Messiah, but to any righteous man who suffers. For example, a pre-Christian Jewish document tells how men despise and reject the virtuous man, even condemning him to a disgraceful death, because he considers himself the servant and son of God; at the Last Judgment, however, he will be exalted by God and confront his enemies (Wisd.2.10—5.5). Did Jesus then consider himself the "Servant of God"?

No reasonable historian can doubt that the Romans executed Jesus on the cross. It is certainly also true that one of his disciples betrayed him, that all the others fled, and that the women stood quite a distance away, so that Jesus had to endure his death agony alone, while the spectators mocked and scoffed at him. The earliest and most reliable account tells us that Jesus died with a loud cry; and if any of the seven last words is genuine, it is the only one known to Mark: "My God, my God, why hast thou forsaken me?" (Mark 15.34). Not only, then, did Jesus die at the hands of pagans, not only did he

[8] This is the conclusion of Joachim Jeremias, *The Prayers of Jesus* (SBT II 6, 1967), pp. 45–52.

die forsaken by his closest friends and relatives, he also died without the spiritual calm of a man who knows that he is completely at peace with God. In other words, he died in physical and spiritual anguish. This exceeds all the expectations of the Old Testament and Judaism concerning the suffering of the "Servant of God". Terrible accounts were written of the deaths of the Maccabean martyrs and later of the prophets; but the dying are depicted as more or less impervious to all torment, going to their deaths praising God and strengthened by him. The prosaic account of Jesus' death is shocking; it will not fit the pattern of the righteous sufferer and the "Servant of God" as found in Judaism. Once more, however, there is not a single genuine saying of Jesus in which he refers to himself as the "Servant of God" promised in the Old Testament or awaited by Judaism.[9]

Are there any other titles? We simply do not know. In the Old Testament, the phrase "Son of Man" refers simply to an individual human being (cf. Ps. 8.4.) The expression assumes great importance in the Book of Ezekiel, who is so addressed by God about sixty times as he is summoned into service on behalf of Israel. The vision in Daniel 7.13–14 depicts "one like a son of man" who approaches God's throne. As 7.18, 22, 27 explicitly state, however, this image represents the chosen people of Israel, who are raised to God's presence after the time of persecution and will there be vindicated. Since the other kingdoms were previously represented as animals, and since in Hebrew or Aramaic "Son of Man" means nothing more than (an individual) human being, the image is apposite. In Ethiopic Enoch and 2 Esdras, however, the Son of Man appears as a heavenly figure dwelling in God's presence or as a supernatural figure endowed by God with miraculous powers. Both books are clearly Jewish; the latter, however, was not composed until the end of the first century of our era; the chapters in the former that mention the Son of Man can so far not be dated. We therefore do not know whether in contemporary Judaism "Son of Man" was some kind of title applied to a divine deliverer. There is no trace of such a title elsewhere; there is no reference to it among the Qumran community by the Dead Sea. At best, then, the term "Son of Man" in this sense was known to a narrow circle of Jews with markedly apocalyptic outlook (i.e. looking forward to the imminent end of the world), if it did not instead origin-

[9] The title occurs only in Matthew 12.18 (a quotation from Isa. 42.1–4 cited by the evangelist); Acts 3.13, 26 (with echoes of Isa. 53); and Acts 4.27, 30 (in parallel with David, who represents not the suffering but the royal "Servant of God").

ate among Christian apocalypticists, from whom it was borrowed by Jewish compatriots and made to refer to the Jewish Messiah. Did Jesus then refer to himself as "Son of Man?"

The phrase occurs about eighty times in the New Testament (about forty-five if the Synoptic parallels are not counted). It is always placed in the mouth of Jesus except in Acts 7.56, where there is some doubt concerning the text. Certainly not all these words were spoken by Jesus himself; the situation is completely different, however, from the case of the titles "Christ", "Son of God", or "Servant of God", which are seldom if ever used by Jesus himself. Three possible reasons for this situation have been suggested.

(a) "Son of Man" was already a familiar title. Jesus spoke of the coming of the Son of Man; in doing so, however, he was not referring to himself but to another, who would finish the work begun by Jesus.[10] This solution appears highly improbable, if only because Jesus would hardly have assumed a secret title known only to apocalyptic circles while in all other respects exhibiting great reserve towards all apocalyptic expectations. Furthermore, the sayings of Jesus cited on p. 14 above make it hard to conceive that Jesus expected the coming of someone greater, namely the Son of Man. Finally, Jesus' resurrection would then merely have convinced his disciples that he was a true prophet and that they must therefore certainly await the greater figure to come, the Son of Man. It would not have induced them suddenly to equate Jesus with the Son of Man.

(b) Others think that this title, like the rest, was given to Jesus by the Christian community, and that all the sayings about the Son of Man came into being after Easter and were later ascribed to Jesus.[11] This is conceivable; the only difficulty is that "Son of Man" occurs so frequently and almost exclusively in sayings of Jesus, not in sayings of the community about Jesus. This circumstance may be explained by the suggestion that this title was introduced by early Christian

---

[10] This is the line followed by Heinz Eduard Tödt, *The Son of Man in the Synoptic Tradition*, trans. D. M. Barton (NTL, 1965), pp. 32ff., 222–3; Ferdinand Hahn, *Christologische Hoheitstitel* (FRLANT 83, 1963), pp. 13ff.; A. J. B. Higgins, *Jesus and the Son of Man* (London: Lutterworth, and Philadelphia: Fortress, 1964), pp. 135–209.

[11] This is the view of Philipp Vielhauer, *Aufsätze zum Neuen Testament* (ThB 31, 1965), pp. 55–91; and Hans Conzelmann, "Jesus Christus", in *RGG³* III, cols. 630–1; also Norman Perrin, *Rediscovering the Teaching of Jesus* (London: SCM, and New York: Harper, 1967); R. A. Edwards, "The Eschatological Correlative as a *Gattung* in The New Testament", *ZNW*, LX (1969), pp. 9ff.

prophets, speaking in the name of the exalted Jesus.[12] This too, however, is an unsatisfactory solution.

(c) The third possibility is that Jesus did in fact refer to himself as the Son of Man. This would explain why the expression occurs almost exclusively in his own sayings and those later ascribed to him, but did not form part of the vocabulary of the Christian community. Contemporary Judaism never spoke of the coming of the Son of Man at the end of time, but of his exaltation then, to be visible in God's vindication of him, in his victory over all his foes, and in his judicial rank.[13] We must therefore reckon seriously with the possibility that Jesus expected to be exalted, bringing all the ways of God to fruition. This of course does not mean that he spoke of his return.[14] Jewish expectations never mention such a hope. Above all, a man addressing his listeners here on earth could speak of his return only if he declared at the same time that he would first die and rise again or ascend into heaven. Never do we find sayings concerning Jesus' return associated with sayings concerning his death and resurrection. Probably, however, he could express hope for his exaltation and parousia, i.e., the revelation of his exaltation as judge. The extent to which this was in fact the case is still a matter of debate. One thing is sure: this being the case, "Son of Man" was not an actual title, but rather described Jesus' destiny and work; furthermore, the sayings concerning the Son of Man who has no home, is despised for associating with tax collectors, and will be handed over to men (Luke 9.58; 7.34; 9.44), as well as those that speak of his intercession at the Last Judgment on behalf

---

[12] See below, pp. 60f.

[13] See Dan. 7.13–14; 2 Esdras 13; Eth. Enoch 37—71; August Strobel, *Kerygma und Apokalyptik* (Göttingen: Vandenhoeck & Ruprecht, 1967), pp. 45ff. A similar suggestion is made by Horst Robert Balz, *Methodische Probleme der neutestamentlichen Christologie* (WMANT 25, 1967), pp. 61ff.; Matthew Black, "The 'Son of Man' Passion Sayings in the Gospel Tradition", *ZNW*, LX (1969), pp. 1ff.

[14] Mark 13.26 cannot possibly be a genuine saying of Jesus. It occurs in a passage that merely assembles Old Testament quotations (vs. 24 = Isa. 13.10; vs. 25 = Isa. 34.4; vs. 26 = Dan. 7.13; vs. 27 = Zech. 2.10. [6]); all these quotations follow the Greek translation, and the last could only be used in the form of the Greek Bible, since the Hebrew text speaks rather of dispersion in all directions. It is not so easy to decide about Mark 14.62; here we read first of the coming of the Son of Man on the clouds of heaven, and only afterwards of his sitting at the right hand of God. Did the verse then at one time refer to the exaltation of the Son of Man, as is true also of Daniel 7.13 and other Jewish passages? Mark, of course, makes it refer to Jesus' return, as the parallel formulation in Mark 13.26 shows. For further discussion, see below, p. 61.

of those who confess Jesus (Luke 12.8), can certainly go back to Jesus himself. The only question is whether he borrowed the image of the Son of Man as used especially in the Enoch corpus and even there associated with Enoch, the archetype of the righteous man in the Old Testament,[15] or whether "Son of Man" was merely a periphrastic way of saying "I", as we find, for example, in 2 Corinthians 12.2, and as was presumably also possible in Aramaic.[16] In the former case, Jesus' expectation bore an apocalyptic stamp from the very outset, but included the humble path of the righteous man unrecognized and rejected by others. In the latter case, the dominant image was that of the righteous sufferer who could expect recognition from God. The former involves the difficulty that Jesus would be using and presupposing an image that was probably familiar only to a narrow circle and seems to have been unknown to the Judaism of the Pharisees and Qumran. The latter involves the difficulty that the concepts of the Son of Man and the righteous sufferer are not associated anywhere else; neither can the exaltation of the righteous sufferer be simply equated with the exaltation of an Enoch or Elijah to the status of witness or even judge at the judgment.

In any case, Jesus did not assume any current title with an exalted meaning. On the contrary, even if he was looking forward to his exaltation and his future role in the judgment, he carried out his ministry in association with the tax collectors, sharing the life of the homeless poor, rejected by men. The reference to the Son of Man is therefore not an answer but rather a question, asking the listeners just who Jesus is.[17] Jesus does not use the title "Servant of God", "Messiah", or "Son of God" to indicate his significance; neither, in all

---

[15] This is suggested by Strobel, *op. cit.*, p. 62.

[16] This is the view espoused by E. Schweizer, "Der Menschensohn", *Neotestamentica* (Zürich: Zwingli, 1963), pp. 56–84, and "The Son of Man Again", *ibid.*, pp. 85–92, and in his *Erniedrigung und Erhöhung bei Jesus und seinen Nachfolgern* (ATANT 28, 2nd ed., 1962), §3. The first edition of the latter work is availllabe in English as *Lordship and Discipleship* (SBT 28, 1960). For a similar view, see Matthew Black, "The Son of Man Problem in Recent Research and Debate", *BJRL*, XLV (1962/63), pp. 305–18; Morna Hooker, *The Son of Man in Mark* (London: SPCK, and Montreal: McGill University Press, 1967). For a recent discussion of the linguistic problems, see G. Vermes, "The Use of נשׁ בר/נשׁא בר in Jewish Aramaic", in Matthew Black, *An Aramaic Approach to the Gospels and Acts* (3rd ed.; Oxford: Clarendon, 1967), pp. 310–28; R. E. C. Formesyn, "Was There a Pronominal Connection for the 'Bar Nasha' Self-Designation?" *Nov T* VIII (1966), pp. 1–35; H. R. Balz, *op. cit.*, 63–4.

[17] Cf. Eduard Schweizer, "Menschensohn", in C. Westermann, *op. cit.*, pp. 73ff.

probability, does he use a familiar apocalyptic title of honor. His refusal to use these titles shows that he fits none of these formulas. Repetition of a pre-existing title, assent to some definition of Jesus' nature, cannot dispense a man from real encounter with him.[18] The way God uses Jesus represents the culmination of all the Old Testament hopes concerning the Messiah, the Son of God, and the Servant of God. But Jesus keeps all the possibilities open; he refuses to use titles, which of necessity define and delimit, to make God's free action an object of human thought, placing it at the disposal of the human mind.[19] By his very act of avoiding all common labels, Jesus keeps free the heart of the man who encounters him. He wants to enter into this heart himself, in all the reality of what he does and says, not as an image already formed before he himself has a chance to encounter the person.

THE COMING AND THE PRESENT KINGDOM OF GOD

John the Baptist proclaimed the imminent coming of God's kingdom. Soon the last judgment will break forth, destroying all the unrepentant but giving those who repent entrance into final glory. Jesus went to John to be baptized, thereby affirming John's message. It is clear that he never protested against or disagreed with the Baptist or the movement that grew up around him except on the question of fasting (Mark 2.19). This in itself makes it extremely likely that Jesus, too, took as his point of departure expectation of the coming kingdom of God. Jesus is not an enthusiast. He does not overlook harsh reality. The poor and the starving and the sorrowful cannot simply turn into ecstatics denying the reality of poverty and hunger and tears. But in the kingdom of God they will be satisfied and happy. The coming of the kingdom of God is such a foregone conclusion that both versions of the Beatitudes (Matt. 5.3–10; Luke 6.20–21) link it with a verb in the present tense: "Theirs is the kingdom of heaven", while all the

[18] When someone knows that another man is a clergyman, his image of a clergyman can shut him off from a real encounter. On the other hand, after a good conversation he can say, "That's a real clergyman!" The impression made by the personality he has encountered gives new meaning to what was for him the obsolete notion of a "clergyman". In the same way, after Easter a disciple can proclaim Jesus as Messiah, Son of God, Servant of God, and Son of Man; but when he does so, the name of Jesus does as much to define these concepts as the concepts do to suggest what Jesus is.

[19] See above, p. 1, and G. von Rad, *op. cit.*, II, 382–4.

other promises are made in the future tense. However the parables of growth (Mark 4.3–9, 26–32; Matt. 13.24–30) are interpreted, they certainly imply a basic difference between the present time and the future to come. Jesus' ministry itself, his association with tax collectors, his occasional healings—which seem a mere drop in the bucket compared to the ocean of suffering in the world—would be nothing but the completely inadequate endeavors of a fanatic or a kind of wonder-worker's propaganda if they were not signs of a coming redemption by God.

But this does not bring us to the heart of Jesus' message. Here, too, he does not fit the formula of a Jewish apocalypticist, who expects everything in God's future.[20] We may notice at once how cautious Jesus is whenever he speaks of what is to come. For the most part he uses parables and images that induce the listener to share in the joy and hope of the future. Above all he uses the image of a banquet to describe the coming age of God. At the same time, all of this is being realized in Jesus' daily life; this is a crucial point, and will be considered below. Jesus does not go beyond such hints, which draw the listener along a path but do not furnish him with specific knowledge of a world to come; he does not describe the bliss of the elect or the torments of the damned. There is no trace of calculations to determine the time when God's rule will begin, such as occur frequently in Jewish apocalyptic works from the time of Daniel on. Either approach might tempt the listener to take an indifferent attitude and look upon himself as viewing the kingdom of God from outside. In this case he would know about every conceivable detail, and could consider whether or not the prospect pleased him. He might, as a man of another age and another culture, have to conclude that this paradise, described so accurately, did not appeal to him at all.[21] He would then know the date when this kingdom would come; and, even if the calendar were calculated to leave little time, even if the great transformation were expected imminently, he would still have the chance to remain an outsider, unconcerned with the kingdom for at least a short while.

[20] It is more likely that the Qumran community shared a similar perspective (Heinz-Wolfgang Kuhn, *Enderwartung und gegenwärtiges Heil* [SUNT 4, 1966], esp. pp. 181–8); their understanding of the presence of salvation is not, however, the same as that of Jesus.

[21] Cf., for instance, the expectation that in the kingdom of God women will be able to bear children every day, without a word about the angels that assist in the education of these children (Hermann Strack and Paul Billerbeck, *Kommentar zum Neuen Testament aus Talmud und Midrasch* [München: Beck, 1922–28], IV, 957).

Who could tell whether, in the very next moment, something might not happen that would place this man's "yes" or "no" to the kingdom of God in a completely new perspective?

This reticence on Jesus' part may have struck people as strange but it was understandable. What shocked them was that he spoke and acted as though this coming kingdom of God were already in effect as though it had already come upon the companions of Jesus. When Jesus healed the sick, were not the words of the prophets concerning the last days fulfilled, could people not catch their first glimpse of the glory to come (cf. Matt. 11.2–6 and Isa. 29.18–19; 35.5–6; 61.1) Jesus seems to have done nothing to extinguish such hopes. There is even a very strange saying of his that as much as asserts the presence of this coming kingdom of God: "But if it is by the finger of God that I drive out the devils, then be sure the kingdom of God has already come upon you" (Luke 11.20). And is there not another saying of Jesus that means the same thing: "The kingdom of God is among you"? (Luke 17.21)?[22]

More important than these individual sayings is the general import of Jesus' talk and actions. In the parables of Jesus, the kingdom of God comes to those who attend; it comes into being wherever someone allows Jesus to take him along the way illustrated in the parable The living seed falls on the waiting earth, the prodigal son is met by his father with open arms, the pearl of great price lies ready for purchase. Wherever Jesus heals someone, the coming kingdom of God is revealed and the power of the enemy is broken. When Jesus sits with tax collectors and calls fishermen to be his disciples, there is the kingdom of God (Mark 1.16–20; Matt. 11.19 [cf. Deut. 21.20]; 21.31–32 Luke 7.36ff.), there men live once more in full fellowship with God

Here, too, Jesus differs from the Jewish apocalypticists who concentrate everything in the glorious future God will bring about. For Jesus, this world is not simply doomed to destruction without further qualification. Of course Jesus is not a nature-worshipper: sparrow fall to the ground (Matt. 10.29) and thorns choke the grain (Mark 4.7). This is even more true for the human world: a tower falls, burying eighteen people; an authoritarian tyrant massacres a crowd of

---

[22] This saying is not easy to interpret. The Greek word could mean "within you" but this is impossible in a saying directed to Jesus' enemies. The meaning may conceivably be "yours", i.e., "up to you", the presence of the kingdom of God rests on your decision. The most likely meaning, however, is that the kingdom of God encounters them in Jesus himself, is "among" them.

pilgrims (Luke 13.1–5). That's the way the world is. But it is still a world upon which God causes his sun to shine and his rain to fall, on the good and on the bad alike (Matt. 5.45); in which God himself feeds the sparrows (Matt. 6.26), although they will one day fall to the ground; and in which the glorious lilies bloom, more splendid than Solomon, although they will some day be burned (Matt. 6.28–30). Nature and the world are neither gilded over with a sentimentality that ignores reality, nor are they blackened with the smoke of a coming apocalyptic conflagration.[23] Even John the Baptist did not call upon men to withdraw from the evil world, although he himself went into the desert, adopted food and clothing that set him far apart from the civilization of his contemporaries, and taught his disciples to fast (Mark 1.6; 2.18). Jesus has even less to say about withdrawing from the world. He issues a strong warning against the danger of letting one's heart be captured and hardened by the lust for wealth (Matt. 6.19–21, 24); but Jesus does not fast like John, nor does he withdraw to the desert, and his sayings involve his listeners in their marriages and families, in their social contacts and their work in the fields (Mark 10.1–12; Matt. 13.44–46; etc.). The coming kingdom of God is therefore the goal that makes it impossible to treat this world and its treasures as the last word, beyond which there is nothing that could really place any constraints on life. At the same time, however, the kingdom is already so embedded in this world that the world does not pale into insignificance before it or become merely a temptation from which one can at best flee to the desert and to mortification of all natural desires.

This was Jesus' message that shocked all his contemporaries. They would have understood and tolerated an ascetic who wrote off this world for the sake of the future kingdom of God. They would have understood and tolerated an apocalypticist who lived only for hope, completely uninterested in worldly affairs, in politics and culture. They would have understood and tolerated a Pharisee who urgently summoned people to accept the kingdom of God here and now in obedience to the law, for the sake of participating in the future kingdom of God. They would have understood and tolerated a realist or sceptic who took his stand in this life with both feet on the ground, declaring himself an agnostic with respect to any future expectations. But they could not understand a man who claimed that the kingdom

[23] Günther Bornkamm, *Jesus of Nazareth,** trans. I. and F. McLuskey with J. M. Robinson (New York: Harper, and London: Hodder & Stoughton, 1960), p. 117.

of God came upon men in what he himself said and did, but nevertheless with incomprehensible caution refused to perform decisive miracles; healed individuals, but refused to put an end to the misery of leprosy or blindness; spoke of destroying the old temple and building a new one, but did not even boycott the Jerusalem cult like the Qumran sect to inaugurate a new, purified cult in the cloister of the desert; who above all spoke of the impotence of those who can only kill the body, but refused to drive the Romans from the country; who left all these matters to God, knowing that God would one day honor the promises and commitments now made by Jesus. And on this point, too, Jesus follows in the tradition of the Old Testament, which more than any other document shows the torment of the man to whom God is hidden, and yet places every hope in this very God.[24]

But was there any reality to this kingdom of God? Where was it to be found?

THE PARABLES OF JESUS

Jesus did his teaching in parables; so much is certain. That he should do so is not self-evident, but a remarkable fact. Of course Jesus did not invent the parable. Others in Palestine and in Greece, both before him and contemporary with him, used parables. In the sayings of Jesus, however, parables occur more often than any other rhetorical form. This is not merely a quantitative difference; it is absolutely basic to the manner of his preaching.

A few banal examples will make this clear. A simple statement like "departure time 9.30" can be merely heard and noted. It can also be translated directly into other languages, even by a machine. Metaphorical expressions such as a mother might use in talking to her child cannot be translated literally into other languages. When a mother calls her child "midge", we have to allow ourselves to be touched by her feelings to some extent if we are to grasp the full import of the word. If we had no inkling of what the love of a mother for her child involves, we would not be able to understand—on the basis, say, of our knowledge of zoology—what the word expresses.

The same holds true, though in a very different way, for a fully developed parable. For us to hear it and take note of it means nothing. We must let it speak to us directly if we are to understand it at all. We must allow ourselves to be moved so as to know what the speaker of the parable is getting at. In fact, a parable is intended to produce

[24] Cf. von Rad, *op. cit.*, II, pp. 374–8.

interaction between the speaker and the listener. The speaker uses the parable to bring the hearer to a new realization or to confront him with a decision he has not yet made. Whether the attempt is successful does not depend on the speaker. The listener can hear the whole parable, hear it so well that he could repeat it word for word; he could even agree completely with what the parable says in itself, without allowing himself to be moved to see where the verdict of the parable speaks to his own situation—in other words, without really understanding the parable. But there is more: because the speaker wants his parable to bring about a change in the misery or the inertia or the blindness of the listener, he must tell it in such a way as to enter into the situation of the listener, in such a way that he can count on the listener's assent.[25] He must therefore himself enter deeply into the listener's situation and, as it were, go the whole way with him, from the listener's present condition to the point where the speaker would like to bring him. In telling his parable, he must proceed in such a way that it is possible, and in fact inevitable, for the listener to follow.

For this reason there is an essential difference between a man who, like most of the rabbis, uses an occasional parable to illustrate or prove a statement that he has made and a man who uses parables as the very content of his message, without even putting into words the statement toward which the parable is leading. This is so typical of Jesus' parables that sometimes two different listeners have to formulate this statement in different ways, even though both have correctly understood the parable as Jesus intended.[26] Jesus is therefore not simply a good school teacher who adapts himself to the limited intellectual capacity of his pupils by using metaphors and illustrations so as to drum a rather difficult proposition into their heads better. Of course the difference between Jesus and other Jews or Greeks who used parables is not absolute. The situation to which Jesus addresses himself, as it were, provides the statement to which the parable leads up. Neither is it impossible that Jesus occasionally put this statement into words (Luke 17.10, etc.), just as there are parables apart from

[25] Cf. Eta Linnemann, *The Parables of Jesus,** trans. J. Sturdy (London: SPCK, and New York: Harper, 1966), pp. 23–7.

[26] For Luke, the parable of the lost sheep (Luke 15.4–7) depicts the way God seeks after men, a search that has become real in Jesus; for Matthew (Matt. 18.12–14), however, in his different context, it illustrates the solicitude with which a member of the community goes after his brother who threatens to go astray. In a new situation the parable begins to take on a new life.

Jesus' preaching that do not formulate their content in a statement
that might be taken as a summary. Nevertheless, quite different demands are placed on the speaker who leads the way with his parable
and the listener who follows him when the parable is not merely a
decorative addition to what is being taught, but becomes the structure
itself. Finally, this use of parables means that God is not the subject of
an academic lesson. It means that a man encounters him when he
allows himself to be led beyond the realm of specific statements subject to logical manipulation (which can only be learned by rote) and
brought to a living and changing situation in which he encounters
God—or rather in which God encounters us and carries us along, so
that the clear and necessary statement comes not at the beginning, but
at the end.

In the parable of the prodigal son, Jesus does not appear. But it is
wrong even to speak in terms of whether he "appears" in the parable
or not. A parable cannot be treated like an allegory, with each of the
characters representing something specific; the father cannot be
equated with God, or the younger son with the sinner. A parable has a
single goal: to lead the listener along a certain path. Of course there
must be certain correspondences, so that the listener can see that the
parable is dealing with him and his situation, but never in such a way
that he can make simple identifications: this stands for this and that
for that. The listener is to allow himself to be caught up in the joyful
celebration over the finding of him who was lost—he himself, but also
all the others, in whose company he might not necessarily want to be
seen. Does Jesus then appear in this parable? Certainly not—and yet
the joy that the parable seeks to have us share is found only where
Jesus imparts the presence of God to men. According to Luke 15.1–2,
it is Jesus' companionship and celebration with the tax collectors and
sinners that provoked the question of what he was doing, to which this
parable gave the answer. Historically speaking, Luke was probably
right in maintaining that Jesus' attitude toward the tax collectors
provides the background for this parable. Whether an attack on the
part of Jewish theologians was really the immediate cause is more
doubtful. In any case, Jesus explains his conduct toward the tax
collectors with a parable that tells how the kindness of *God* operates.
With an assurance that must have struck his hearers as unexampled,
he equates God's merciful conduct with his own conduct toward the
tax collectors.[27] Who but Jesus could venture to describe such in-

[27] Cf. E. Linnemann, *op. cit.*, pp. 87–8.

credible and absolutely unexpected conduct on the part of the father towards his windbag of a son? Who but Jesus would have the authority to assume the role of God himself in his parable and proclaim a celebration on behalf of the sinner who has been restored to fellowship with God? Those who nailed him to the cross because they found blasphemy in his parables—which proclaimed such scandalous conduct on the part of God—understood his parables better than those who saw in them nothing but the obvious message, which should be self-evident to all, of the fatherhood and kindness of God, meant to replace superstitious belief in a God of wrath.

But Jesus identifies himself so with the cause of God that he dies for the truth of his parables. When Jesus tells the parable of the mustard seed, which is smaller than all other seeds but still grows up to be a tree (Mark 4.30–32), he is not speaking of himself but of the kingdom of God, which lives and grows, even though it appears so insignificant and wretched. And only where Jesus speaks the parable to his listeners is the seed sown; only there is the kingdom of God present in its insignificant and wretched form as a living and growing thing. The parable of the sower (Mark 4.3–9) could practically be called the parable of the presence of the coming kingdom of God in the wretched and controverted words of Jesus. The toiling farmer laboriously tries to sow his seed in his tiny field, where success is threatened from all quarters; all of his experiences are paralleled in what happens to Jesus.[28] Here again, however, it would be wrong to allegorize. The parable tells about a farmer, not about Jesus. Of course, to him who has ears to hear, it tells what the kingdom of God is like: despite all failures; despite all opposition; wretched, insignificant to the outside observer, it still continues to grow, producing a miraculous harvest that surpasses all human expectations. And the man who tells this parable can tell it only because he speaks with the authority of God, and so identifies himself with God and God's kingdom that he completely shares their fate, culminating in the cross and the resurrection that lies beyond death.

Who is this teller of parables? Is he a rabbi, standing in the traditions of his people? Is he the founder of a new sect, preaching a new

---

[28] This is the interpretation of Joachim Jeremias, *The Parables of Jesus*, trans. S. H. Hooke (Revised ed.; London: SCM, and New York: Scribners, 1963), pp. 50–1; E. Schweizer, *Good News according to Mark*, p. 91. For another interpretation, see B. Gerhardsson, "The Parable of the Sower and Its Interpretation", *NTS* XIV (1967/68), pp. 186–91.

doctrine hitherto unknown? Is he a combination of both? None of
these categories fits him. Jesus' preaching is in the form of parables—
it cannot be classed as conservative teaching or liberal, as rabbinic or
sectarian. What happens in these parables is this: someone dares to
stand in the place of God himself and, as he tells his parables, to lead
the way along a path on which he wants his listeners to follow. Only
in some of the Old Testament prophets, and there only occasionally
and provisionally, do we find anything like it (2 Sam. 12.1–7a; Isa.
5.1–7; cf. Ezek. 4.1–3; etc.). But Jesus dares to do this with such authority that he himself continues along the path, far beyond the end
of the parables he tells, ending at the cross and his resurrection from
the dead. Thus the kingdom of God, which will come to pass one day
in the future, is already present among those who listen to Jesus.

JESUS' AMBIVALENCE TOWARDS THE LAW

It is clear that Jesus lives in the realm of the Old Testament. From
the Old Testament he knows the Creator, who causes his sun to shine
and the rain to fall (Matt. 5.45). From the Old Testament he knows
the God who is not indifferent to the spiritually poor, the sorrowful,
those of gentle spirit, those who desire to please God (Matt. 5.3–6).
From the Old Testament he knows the good master who expects
obedience from his servants (Mark 10.17–19). From the Old Testament stems his hope for the coming kingdom (Mark 4.32); his confidence, which sees the coming of God where human eyes can still
make out nothing (Mark 4.26–29); his obedience, which holds fast to
God even when God brings him into inconceivable suffering (Mark
5.3–4); his prayer to him whose name and dominion stand infinitely
beyond us, but whom we can still call upon as Father (Luke 11.2).

It is therefore only to be expected that he should also look upon the
law as God's great gift to Israel, transcending everything else. On
this point all the parties constituting contemporary Judaism were
agreed. Even the Qumran sect by the Dead Sea, which had ostentatiously separated from the "false priests" in Jerusalem, continued to
remit their offerings for the temple cult because the law so directed.
When Jesus submitted to John's baptism of repentance, he acknowledged that the law and its requirements were the guiding principles
for a life that would be righteous before God. And once when a lawyer
asked him about the way to eternal life, he replied by asking the in-
quirer about the Ten Commandments, with which he was familiar

(Luke 10.25–28). This is the automatic assumption of a Jew who has grown up in Palestine.

It can be seen at once, however, that Jesus is not content with precise exegesis of the law and the various interpretations of it given by the rabbis. He demands radical obedience far transcending mere observance of the letter of the law. The Sermon on the Mount contains a whole series of sayings formulated according to a single pattern: "You have heard that it was said to the men of old, . . . but I say to you: . . ." (Matt. 5.21ff.). The law says, "You shall not kill"; but Jesus declares that even an angry word or animosity is a transgression of this commandment. It is therefore not enough for us to observe the law the way we observe a police regulation. When the speed limit is set at thirty-five, we might like to drive faster, but observe the limit because of the potential penalty. At the same time, we use as much as possible of the freedom left us, i.e., driving thirty-five miles per hour. We would like to drive faster and do drive at the maximum speed permitted, but in no sense does this represent a transgression of the law. Jesus, however, says that the murder forbidden by God begins in the human heart with the desire to kill, and that the commandment is not fulfilled when we go as far as we can without passing the limit, when we merely beat our enemy bloody. In similar fashion, Jesus finds a lustful glance to be a transgression of the commandment against adultery; finds a properly arranged divorce to be a transgression of God's will; finds all oaths, not just false ones, to indicate an attitude reprehensible to God; finds resistance to evil and restriction of love to friends and compatriots to be conduct contrary to God's purposes in his commandments.

This radical approach permeates all Jesus' preaching. "Whoever of you does not renounce all that he has cannot be my disciple" (Luke 14.33); in fact, "He who loves father or mother more than me is not worthy of me" (Matt. 10.37). "Leave the dead to bury their own dead . . ." he says to a man who would proclaim the kingdom of God; for "no one who puts his hand to the plough and looks back is fit for the kingdom of God" (Luke 9.59—62). Therefore the city that rejects Jesus will suffer a worse fate than Sodom and Gomorrah (Luke 10.12). The Sermon on the Mount closes with the parable of the man who built on sand, whose house eventually collapsed. He resembles the man who hears Jesus' words and finds them attractive, but does not act upon them (Matt. 7.24ff.). This is far from the kind of fanatic enthusiasm we might expect from a man who, no matter what happened, expected the end of the world and the onset of the kingdom of God in the immediate future. Quite the contrary: a follower of Jesus must consider very calmly and thoroughly what he is undertaking, must be well aware what he is risking and what he seeks to gain. A man who wages war must compare the strength of his armies very closely with that of his foes, and a man who wants to build a tower must calculate precisely, so that he is not forced to leave the tower half finished and become the laughing-stock of all (Luke 14.28–32).

Is Jesus then to be understood as a rigorist? Does he belong among those who would like to see the law radically enforced? Should he be ranked with the strictest party of the Pharisees, like that represented later by Shammai, or, better, the monastic order of those Jews who lived at Qumran beside the Dead Sea? This possibility is ruled out by the remarkable carelessness with which Jesus quotes the commandments when speaking to the man who asked about the way to eternal life (Mark 10.19). Almost as though by chance a couple of the most important requirements are mentioned, neither their sequence nor their wording agreeing with that of Scripture. Jesus, in absolute contrast to the interpretation of the law at Qumran or among the Pharisees, obviously is not interested in the exact wording and a literal fulfilment of the commandments. But he goes still further: there are even places where Jesus annuls not only the Jewish interpretation but the Old Testament law itself. When Jesus replaces the commandment "Love your neighbor" with another, "Love your enemy", for which there is no parallel in all the Jewish writings of his day, his action could be understood as a mere tightening up of the law; there are later rabbis who could certainly come close to this statement. But when he goes on to say not to resist evil, the requirement of "an eye for an eye, a tooth for a tooth" found in the Old Testament is in fact abrogated. The same holds true for the Old Testament commandment that a divorced woman be given a note of dismissal, which Jesus finds totally inapplicable because divorce is itself contrary to God's will (Matt. 5.32). Although it is possible to ask whether the last two instances really go back to Jesus himself, there can be no doubt that Jesus, through his entire conduct, again and again ostentatiously transgressed the Old Testament commandment to observe the Sabbath and had little concern for the Old Testament laws relating to ritual purity.

Was Jesus then a liberal reformer, who wanted to temper the rigor of the law and eliminate antiquated commandments no longer suited to the age he was living in? Should he be ranked with the more moderate party of the Pharisees, like that represented by Hillel, or like that which was typical of the more hellenized Jews, especially outside of Palestine? The radical demands of which we have already spoken show that this label, too, will not fit Jesus. Who then is Jesus and what is he trying to accomplish?

When a lawyer asked him which commandment was the greatest, Jesus cited the commandment to love God with all one's heart, and one's neighbor as oneself. There is nothing out of the ordinary here; according to Mark 12.28–34, the questioner went on to praise Jesus, and Jesus told him that he was not far from the kingdom of God. According to Luke 10.25–28, in fact, the lawyer himself cites these two commandments, and Jesus agrees that in this way he will find life. When Jesus does this, he is of course not attempting to summarize the totality of the law in one basic formula, or even to rank the many commandments—all of which should be kept—insisting at least on the all-important requirement of love for God and for one's neighbor as the minimum observance for everyone. This is shown by all Jesus' statements concerning the law, both those that increase its rigor and those that annul it. On the contrary, this law of love shows the unity of both these groups of statements made by Jesus on the question of the law. If I must love God with all my heart, all my soul, all my mind, and all my strength, and my neighbor as myself, then my heart is required. Then I can no longer fulfill the law the way I fulfill police regulations, taking the utmost advantage of the freedom left me. Then I know that murder of my neighbor begins with hatred of him in my heart, and I know that rejection of God begins when other things crowd into the foreground and begin to hide him—though it be the honoring of a living or the burial of a dead father (Matt. 5.21–22; 10.37; Luke 9.59–60). At the same time, however, the God who expects such love from me frees me from all obedience to the letter. When God commanded "an eye for an eye and a tooth for a tooth" as a bar to unrestrained tribal feuding and to protect the enemy tribe from an unlimited war of revenge, he did not intend that I should have to carry out the letter of the law. If love is demanded of me, I can only respond by forgoing all revenge and all retaliation.

But I cannot even fulfill Jesus' own commandments by following them to the letter. When a small child hits his mother in a tantrum, it might be much more convenient not to resist evil or even to turn the other cheek. But a mother who loves her child as herself will probably have to pull herself together and take a much more difficult course, resisting the child and setting him straight by means of warnings or punishment so that he will understand why his actions are wrong. In similar fashion, we are not keeping the Sabbath commandment if we literally do no work and keep our sons and daughters, manservants and maidservants, cattle and guests from working (Exod. 20.8ff.). With magnificent freedom Jesus disregards all regulations when love for his neighbor requires him to heal even on the Sabbath (Mark 3.1–5). To use the Sabbath to free myself for God and for my neighbor who needs me could demand much more from us than any pedantic observance of the regulations governing rest. Even Old Testament prophets like Amos were familiar with this notion (Amos 5.21–24; 8.4–6).[29] But Jesus carried this freedom with its radical demands to the very limit. On behalf of all of us, he defended the position that even literal fulfillment of the commandments does not result in doing God's will, that his will demands much more of us and for this very reason gives us a much larger area of freedom, in which we can breathe and live and rejoice. On behalf of all of us, he defended this position without giving an inch. On behalf of all of us, he thereby defended the reality of the living God, although he was reviled and condemned as a transgressor of God's law. On behalf of all of us, he defended this position until his last outcry dying on the cross.

LIFE UNDER THE TWOFOLD LAW OF LOVE

But what does it mean to live by the principle of love? It means first of all to live in such a way that I can no longer calculate what God owes me or anyone else. The parable of the prodigal son (Luke 15.11ff.) has an ending that shocks us. It admits no doubt that the younger son is a good-for-nothing who squanders his father's property on prostitutes. It also admits no doubt that the elder son always obeys his father, and at some cost to himself. At its conclusion, however, the parable remains open; the one who is still standing outside, the one to whom the question of the parable is addressed, is the obedient elder son, while the younger son sits at a banquet in his father's house. What keeps the obedient son out of his father's house is his calculation. He points out to his father that he has not even received a kid in return for his obedience, while a calf has been slaughtered for his good-for-nothing brother. Thus he stands beside his father, yet miles

29 Cf. von Rad, *op. cit.*, II, pp. 388ff.

distant from him. He sees what is going on—the dancing and singing, the eating and drinking. He sees what his father and his younger brother see. But his perspective is completely different. He calculates, and he compares what he has earned with his reward. The younger brother understands that what is important here is not the reward for what he has earned, but unfathomable and undeserved kindness. He can therefore see the dancing and singing, the food and the wine, as his father sees them. But the father remains helpless when he confronts the elder brother. He can only try to touch his son's heart when he speaks: "It was fitting to make merry and be glad, for this brother was dead and is alive; he was lost and is found" (Luke 15.32). The father's power over his son does not extend beyond this. Just as he did not have his younger son shipped home, so also he does not compel his elder son to come in. His only power is in his words, and these he gives to his son. Here the parable ends. Whether the words penetrate the heart of his son we do not know. The possibility remains open, a question addressed to the person listening to Jesus.

The same point is made almost more forcefully in the parable of the laborers in the vineyard. Those who have worked for only an hour receive the same wages as those who have worked through the heat of the day, doing twelve times as much (Matt. 20.13–15). Here the idea of wages is specifically mentioned, only to be abolished.[30] Jesus' opposition to all legalistic religion could hardly be expressed more pointedly: how can I conceive of "wages", the ultimate eternal "wages" of heaven, except in relationship to my own effort?

Are we then to think of Jesus in modern terms as a precursor of the idealism that finds the total reward in the moral action itself and refuses to inquire further? Once again, however, Jesus does not fit the formula. Jesus speaks quite unaffectedly of wages and reward—of the future reward, given by God, that will surpass all human conception: "Your Father who sees what is done in secret will reward you" (Matt. 6.4).[31] Jesus clearly does not mean that man is to be left to himself, to be content and satisfied with his own morality.

[30] Heinrich Julius Holtzmann, *Lehrbuch der neutestamentlichen Theologie* (Sammlung theologischer Lehrbücher, 2nd ed., Tübingen: Mohr, 1911), I, 261; Johannes Weiss, *Die Predigt Jesu vom Reiche Gottes* (3rd ed.; Göttingen: Vandenhoeck & Ruprecht, 1964), p. 77; Paul Feine, *Theologie des Neuen Testaments* (8th ed.; Berlin: Evangelische Verlagsanstalt, 1951), p. 77; Günther Bornkamm, "Der Lohngedanke im Neuen Testament", in his *Studien zur Antike und Urchristentum* (*Gesammelte Aufsätze* 2, Bev Th 28, 1959), pp. 81ff.

[31] Cf. Matthew 5.12; 25.34–5; Mark 10.21, 28–30; Luke 6.38; etc.

What, then, are we to think? Reward or no reward—which is it to be? The first point to understand is this: if we could calculate what God owes us, he would not be God. He would not be a person confronting us. He would be like an automatic vending machine where you put your dime in the slot and get the corresponding candy bar down below. Man would in fact be lord over such a god, because he can consider whether the investment is worthwhile. Even to emphasize that the merchandise provided is worth a hundred times the investment would not basically change the situation. A person could still sit back and compare the investment with the potential gain and debate whether or not to take the risk. This would reduce God to something like a predetermined course of destiny, in which a good deed would be followed by reward, an evil deed by punishment. Thus when a person thinks he has some claim to a reward, he has deposed God, because God's future action is now determined entirely by man.

On the other hand, a god who made demands but showed no concern for what we did, or at most punished our transgressions, would be a blind tyrant. According to the words of Jesus, God does not even forget a cup of cold water that we have given to a traveler (Mark 9.41). According to the words of Jesus, God takes man so seriously that he also takes seriously everything man does, even the insignificant, almost automatic "normal" reaction towards a thirsty traveler. A man who would find all his satisfaction in his own good deed and renounce all reward would be giving the cold shoulder to the God who would stand by him and participate in the giving. Such a man would be a Prometheus, forging alone his own happiness and no longer willing to live from the gifts of others. When Jesus speaks of "reward", he is not inviting us to maintain the attitude of the elder brother in the parable, but to allow him to confer gifts on us. We understand this only when we realize that, according to the words of Jesus, the same God who makes demands of us is always the God who gives, and that man can really live only from what is given him. It is therefore also among God's gifts that he makes demands of us and does not leave us to our own devices—without a task, without a goal, without a purpose.

But what kind of demands does God make of us? We have already seen that he does not demand literal fulfillment of the law. Neither does he demand legalistic fulfillment of Jesus' teaching. In its present context, the parable of the man who built on sand because he heard what Jesus said and applauded it, but did not act on what he heard, follows upon another surprising statement made by Jesus: at the last judgment, men will recount before him all they have done in his name, telling how they have prophesied and cast out devils and performed many miracles. Whoever suffers the weakness and impotence of his Christian life could well be envious of such demonstrations of the spirit and of power. But Jesus will say to them, "I never knew you" (Matt. 7.22–23). In like fashion Paul states in one passage that a man can dole out all his possessions or even surrender his life, but it would avail him nothing if it were not done out of love (1 Cor. 13.3). Even in the context of the concluding parable of the Sermon on the Mount, the two buildings are externally indistinguishable. Only the storm—or, to drop the metaphor, the judgment of God—will show which house will collapse and which will stand.

What then does God require? In the parable of the prodigal son, the father expects one thing only of his son: that he be able to rejoice in his father's kindness. The call to rejoice occurs in Jesus' message with remarkable frequency. The dominant images are those of a wedding (Mark 2.19; Matt. 22.2; 25.10), of a banquet (Luke 14.15–24; 22.15–18, 30), of a happy gathering of friends (Luke 15.6, 9, 23), of discovering a treasure (Matt. 13.44), or of unexpectedly high wages (Matt. 20.9). Nowhere do we find the desperate efforts of a penitent to achieve salvation described in favorable terms: the farmer sleeps, gets out of bed each morning, and lets the seed grow without worrying about it (Mark 4.27–28). In his little story Jesus omits any suggestion that the farmer might put up scarecrows or do some weeding or dig some irrigation ditches. When we live in joy, there can be no calculation. Joy sees the gifts of the father. Joy can therefore look forward to what the father will give in the future. Joy, therefore, is never without a future, without hope, without the prospect of something to come. But joy cannot calculate, not even future reward. If it did, it would not be joy.

This is the childlike character and sincerity that Jesus has in mind, in which every "yes" is simply "yes" and every "no" simply "no", without the need for any embellishment, in which the eye is so clear that the whole self shines through it without concealment (Matt. 5.37; 6.22; cf. James 5.12), in which every prayer comes forth so spontaneously that it speaks the depths of a man's heart, concentrating on God and not on the man who prays, and trusting that this God will do what is best for the petitioner (Luke 11.2–13).

According to the words of Jesus, then, this is faith; in other words, the life that in all its manifestations takes God more seriously than it takes its own riches or its own need, its own power or its own failures. This is the life to which we must be summoned; this is the demand that must be made. For how could we live in this fashion when wealth or poverty, power or impotence, confront us time and time again, crowd in upon us, and seek to push all else aside? We must be summoned to this life by Jesus, who takes us with him on the way, in whose presence we can learn to have this faith. Of course this spells the end of all religious frenzy, all religious anxiety, and all religious avarice. A man who has learned to trust himself to God—how could he omit God himself from his trust? How could he seek to reach God by his own frenzied efforts? How could he set so low an estimate on God and God's gifts as to let his own sins and failures take center stage and focus all his attention on them? How could he turn God's gifts into his own personal property and consider his prayers or acts of love to be a treasury of good works? What Jesus has in mind is the childlike heart that finds God's gifts so great and so important and takes them so seriously that it receives them with an easy joy, trusting in God's care for us. Thus are we to understand Jesus' strange references to his disciples as "little ones" (Mark 9.42; Matt. 10.42; 18.6, 10, 14; cf. Matt. 5.3–12; Mark 9.35; 10.15–16).

When this faith is given to a man, he is also given the childlike characteristic of love that no longer calculates. When an act of love is performed as a moral exercise, it becomes charity and the other party becomes a recipient of charity, becomes a mere object, while the subject of the action earns a reward. In this fashion, too, the starving are kept alive and the sick tended; the moral act of love is not to be despised and decried. But this is not the love that Jesus has in mind. Only when a man has become free of himself, free of anxieties and frenzies, even free of the religious accumulation of merit, does he really live for his neighbor. Only the man who himself lives on God's infinite[32] love can and must be the channel of this love towards his neighbor (Matt. 18.21–35).

This does not provide a principle or law of love. The one who matters is always the one who happens to be approaching me. The Samaritan sees the man lying at the side of the road and does what is necessary, competently and skilfully, calmly and in a businesslike

---

[32] The sum in Matthew 18.24 is utterly fantastic when one considers that the total annual income in the kingdom of Herod the Great amounted to only ninety thousand talents.

manner; he does not spend more than is necessary, but provides generously to take care of the emergency. All that he does shows that his heart is alive and has not grown hardened (Luke 10.30–35). In like manner Jesus would open us to those whom he would send to us along the way. Such love does not count its acts, and does not seek an accounting either with God or with the brother who has been helped. Those for whom the gift of the kingdom of God is prepared will not know at the last judgment that they have done anything out of love for Jesus. Only then will they discover that he encountered them in beggars and prisoners, in the sick and the oppressed (Matt. 25.31–46). God's gifts so pass our comprehension that the kingdom of Heaven will be given to those who, like little children, received God's gifts and passed them on to others.

Even in the Old Testament, albeit as one idea among many others, we find the expectation that God himself will renew men's hearts that they may obey him. Even there a priest, or Moses, or the Servant of God can appear as a mediator.[33] But Jesus made this hope the radical basis of his life, for he, who called men to this faith, ended his life on the cross. In the parable it remained an open question whether the elder brother could still learn to renounce his claim to being his father's son without calculating how much more he had accomplished with his obedience and toil than his worthless brother. There was still a chance that his father's words might persuade him to rejoice in his father's boundless goodness and mercy, which included his younger brother. In the life of Jesus, the question did not remain open. He had to end his life on the cross because for our sakes he would not deny that we must not total up our accomplishments before God, but hope instead completely in his gifts and rejoice in his joy. "He trusts in God and says he is God's Son. Well, then, let us see if God wants to save him now!" Shouting these words at him, men brought him to a wretched death (Matt. 27.43).

THE CALL TO DISCIPLESHIP

It is certain that Jesus called disciples to follow him. The concept of discipleship is completely transformed in the New Testament. Greek thinkers are familiar with the notion, but they speak only in terms of following God, or nature equated with God. What they mean is to

---

[33] Cf. von Rad, *op. cit.*, II, pp. 425–32.

imitate God's virtues or the behavior of nature. Jewish teachers, too, speak of following as disciples, and their pupils practice it literally, walking at a respectful distance behind their teacher. But the teacher never calls a disciple: the disciple offers himself to the teacher. On the other hand, Jesus never holds discussions with his disciples like a rabbi, and he never brings them to a classroom or has them study the law. No disciple of Jesus would think of becoming the Son of Man, while a Jewish student quite naturally follows his teacher so that later he may become a teacher himself. And a Jewish teacher would hardly tell one of his students that the student's eternal life depended on whether or not he followed the teacher, as Jesus does according to Mark 10.17–22 or Luke 9.57–62.

We know nothing of the details of how Jesus called his disciples, and little about the different occasions. The stories that we have are stylized; that is, in the course of transmission all features have been dropped that seemed out of place or unimportant to the later community, until finally, as in a woodcut, only the crucial lines remain that still held meaning for those who read the Gospel.

What happens when Jesus calls a man to follow him? All the accounts agree that Jesus takes the initiative. He "sees" his disciples long before they notice that something is about to happen to them (Mark 1.16, 19; 2.14; 10.21; Luke 19.5; John 1.48), just as in the Old Testament God "sees" those whom he would encounter in a special way before he calls them or intervenes on their behalf (1 Sam. 16.1; Ezra 5.5; Zech. 12.4). Jesus even initiates the call itself; the disciple would not think of offering himself to Jesus or even yearning for his message. Four fishermen were called in the midst of their daily work; none were called from the group of people that gathered around Jesus of their own accord to hear his message (Mark 1.14ff.). Levi is called, who sits at the customs booth and is completely cut off from ordinary preaching and from the ordinary worshippers, who wrote him off long ago (Mark 2.14). This makes it clear that the call as such is an act of grace, that it restores fellowship that has been broken, that forgiveness takes place here without anyone mentioning it and without any confession or penance or act of faith on the part of the person forgiven, because they are all implicit in what Jesus does. Therefore, too, the person's response is told as though it were self-evident, without any mention of thoughts and reservations, difficulties and decisions on the part of the disciples. The response is already given to them in the call of Jesus. Indeed, according to Mark 1.17, it is Jesus who will give future obedience to those he has called and transform them for the purpose of their calling.

But what is the purpose of their calling? A passage in Mark formulates it strikingly: "to be with him" (3.14). But this is precisely what is meant by following Jesus. The phrase must not be taken in a spiritual sense; it means that the disciples walk with him, eat and drink with him, listen to what he says and see what he does, are invited with him into houses and hovels, or are turned away with him. They are not called to great achievements, religious or otherwise. They are invited as companions to share in what takes place around Jesus. They are therefore called not to attach much importance to themselves and what they accomplish or fail to accomplish, but to attach great importance to what takes place through Jesus and with him. They are called to delegate their cares and worries and anxieties a little to the one to whom Jesus bears witness in all he does and says.

Is that all there is to say? But what more could one say? When a person can become so free towards God in Jesus' company, then he also becomes free towards his neighbor who needs him. We can say, therefore, that while the disciples walked with Jesus they were more and more entrusted with a commission, and that this commission filled lives that were empty, gave purpose to lives frittered away in daily routine, gave meaning to lives condemned to be meaningless. But when we ask specifically what Jesus calls these men to do, it is hard to answer.[34] He takes them with him for a few months of living as wanderers, away from their families (Mark 1.19–20) and their places of business (Mark 1.17–18); and yet in the course of these very wanderings they hear Jesus call them to a stubborn loyalty within the human circle in which men are placed, towards wife or guest or neighbor (Mark 10.1ff.; Matt. 5.28, 37, 42, 44–45; Luke 10.29–37). He makes them "fishers of men" (Mark 1.17); but they are to "fish" for these men with absolute consistency on behalf of God, not on behalf of their own group or church. For who really belongs to this new community? There are the twelve, with whom Jesus eats the last supper; but on one occasion Jesus' family appear to fetch him home like someone not of sound mind, and Jesus says with almost shocking severity, "Here are my mother and my brothers", including in a single sweep of his arm all who are sitting about him (Mark 3.34).[35]

[34] The goal is never mere imitation of Jesus (for example, of his celibacy).

[35] Verse 35 was presumably appended by the Christian community, even though it may be a genuine saying of Jesus spoken on a different occasion in a different situation.

He does not even ask whether they have faith or not, whether they have come out of genuine desire or out of curiosity, deliberately or completely by chance. They are all mother and brothers to him. It is impossible to derive a rule. Then who belongs to him and who does not? A man who wants to follow Jesus as soon as he has buried his father is bluntly rejected: "Leave the dead to bury their own dead" (Luke 9.60); a man who wants to follow him at once out of gratitude and is ready for anything is sent back to his family (Mark 5.20); and a man who isn't even thinking of religion and doesn't even know Jesus is called to intimate companionship (Mark 2.14).

This is completely in line with Jesus' remarkable conduct, which repeatedly shocked observers. Unlike all the movements in Judaism, from the groups of Pharisees to the circles of the apocalypticists, Jesus does not gather a group of followers around him. Those who fall under his spell, who walk beside him for a time or until his death, receive nothing to keep them together, not even a new name, much less a rite, a sign, a creed, or even a place where they can meet Jesus or even assemble as a body. They are not even given a title with which they can properly address Jesus or which they can pass on to others.[36] One could almost say that Jesus does everything in his power to avoid success.

But behind this strange and incomprehensible attitude, which can only lead to failure, stands an obstinate and inflexible will that seeks to comprehend all Israel. Jesus does not seek out a religious elite, those who hunger after God; neither does he seek out those who are "interesting", open to the world. His desire is not merely for a "remnant of Israel", as described by the prophets, but for all Israel, without exception, without restriction, and nothing less. So strong is his desire to call all men to God that even the limits of Jewish nationality and Jewish religion are not absolute limits for him (Mark 7.15, 29; Matt. 8.11–12; etc.). The idea that slowly gained the upper hand in the Old Testament, contending against opposition and competing with other ideas (as in Deutero-Isaiah [Isaiah 40ff.]), was namely the realization that, as the chosen people of God, Israel could never be an end in itself but only a representative and emissary for the entire world —this idea is embodied uniquely and astonishingly in Jesus.

No movement is born in this way, no new sect is founded, no proof of success is demonstrated. Jesus' death on the cross is almost to be

[36] Cf. above, pp. 21f.; for a discussion of the whole topic, see M. Hengel, *Nach-folge und Charisma* (BZNW 34, 1968).

expected. A whole series of movements had first to hope that Jesus would be their advocate, or even their leader; all were disappointed by him because he did not fit any of their formulas, however much he might have in common with them. Jesus died, but the divine miracle for which many still hoped did not come to pass; he ended his life ignobly, with a loud cry, spelling the end to all hopes, all expectations, all formulas by which men sought to comprehend him.

THE MIRACLES OF JESUS

But did Jesus not perform miracles, and do they not paint a completely different picture?

There can be no doubt that Jesus performed acts of healing, even though we can no longer determine the extent of this activity or the degree to which it is susceptible to psychological "explanation". However that may be, men experienced in him the phenomenon of authority and felt power emanating from him that continued to have effect even in the corporeal realm. Can Jesus then be understood as a miracle worker? Many sought to interpret him as one, and even in the time of Paul there was probably a large movement that saw in Jesus primarily something like a resurrected "man of God" in the Old Testament sense, who demonstrated through his amazing miracles and authoritative preaching that God's power was at work in him. But even before Good Friday it was plain enough that Jesus could not be described in these terms. Even if the explicit prohibitions against publicizing the miracles could hardly have been spoken by Jesus himself in the form we now have them,[37] it is clear that he never used his healings for propaganda purposes, and was obviously very cautious about performing his healings in public. There were never any mass healings such as occur at ancient or modern shrines, either pagan or Christian. Mighty and important as the healings were for those concerned, they appear trifling in comparison to all the misery and suffering upon earth. Most important, however, is the fact that such miracles are repeatedly *subsidiary* to what Jesus considered the focal point of his ministry. Whenever someone demands a miracle of Jesus, he refuses (Mark 8.11–13, etc.). Mark can even report that at Nazareth Jesus "could do no mighty work there, except that he laid his hands upon a few sick people and healed them" (6.5). This does not mean that such acts of divine authority are unimportant. It means that we

[37] Cf. above, pp. 13f.

cannot understand Jesus on this basis. They are "signs", i.e., acts that point away from themselves to something else that they signify.

Toward what, then, do they point? In Luke 17.11–19, a very interesting story is recounted. We do not know whether it is an account of something that actually took place, but it certainly captures the essence of what really happened in the presence of Jesus. Ten lepers are healed and sent to the priest, who declares them clean again and hence restored to human society. One returns and gives thanks. To him Jesus says what he says elsewhere to people whom he heals (Mark 5.34): "Your faith has made you well." The nine others have also been restored to health, and the same could be said of them; but here it is said only to the one whose healing led him to give thanks. It is possible, in other words, to experience God's miracles in one's own body but to experience nothing of God. In another story, Luke tells of a prostitute who dares to push her way into the midst of a company of men, where she simply weeps hysterically and anoints Jesus' feet (Luke 7.36–50). To her Jesus says the same thing. No miracle has taken place, there has been no visible healing. It is therefore possible not to see any miracle at all and still experience God.

Jesus' miracles are not nearly as self-evident to us today as they were to earlier generations. We know how miracles are embellished, exaggerated, and altered in the course of transmission; we know that much that seems incomprehensible can be explained psychologically. In consequence, we are perhaps closer to the reality of Jesus' miracles than earlier generations were. It is clear that Jesus did all this, not to abuse his power for the sake of proof, but to hint at something quite different that awaits us beyond the miracles. Such hints are not to be despised; in them God's word to us takes on form, perhaps a strange form that does not completely satisfy us. But neither are such hints to be confused with the thing itself.

We have already seen[38] that proofs do not create faith, but rather make it impossible. Proofs can lead me to an absolutely certain conclusion, where I risk nothing because the result is unequivocal. They cannot, however, lead me to an encounter through which I am addressed, moved, set on a new path. But this is precisely the nature of faith: it brings me before God and lets me encounter him. It is therefore impossible to be certain about God (as it is also impossible to be certain about the love of another person) except by living with him, with all that that implies. Therefore Jesus took his disciples with him

[38] See above, pp. 2f.

as companions. God can no more be proven than he can be taught. But he proves himself wherever a man dares to rely on him and live with him.

Because Jesus' purpose was to give faith and not record success for his own movement, he had to refuse miracles when they were demanded for proof. Because he wanted to keep the way of faith open to us, he was executed. This, too, takes up a theme already suggested in the Old Testament. Nowhere in the surrounding world was the "demythologization" of God so radically carried out as in Israel. In Israel, all magical ceremonies, all conjurings of tutelary spirits, all guarantees secured through divine power were taken from man; nature, as the creation of God, became profane, purified of all indwelling spirits. In Israel, man was left more helpless before God than in any of the surrounding cultures; he could not influence God's miracles or conjure them up, but could only pray, hope, and believe for them. Of course the Old Testament is far from maintaining this perspective throughout. Again and again man's yearning for divine miracles that he can call on at will for proof comes to the surface.[39] In Jesus, however, man's lack of control over God was seen in such absolute form that no one understood it, not even Jesus' own disciples. It is even possible that Judas betrayed Jesus only in order to make him finally prove his divine power and conquer the Romans, establish the kingdom of God in Jerusalem, and smite his enemies. In any case, it was the immense disappointment of all who hoped for the miraculous sign, who expected that he would finally intervene with God's flaming sword, that brought him to the cross. There above all and for the last time the miracle did not take place. "Let the Christ, the King of Israel, come down now from the cross, that we may see and believe" (Mark 15.32), they shout. And they kept on shouting while he perished in misery. And the miracle, boldly demanded, secretly expected, devoutly hoped for, ardently prayed for, did not take place.

EASTER

Easter was the sign by which God said "yes" to this path taken by Jesus. The disciples had ceased to understand his path. For them, the crucifixion was a shock that put an end to their faith. But God raised Jesus from the dead, so that he encountered his disciples once more as

---

[39] On the first point, cf. von Rad, *op. cit.*, II, p. 361; on the second, see the lovely story in 1 Kings 22.

the living Jesus. What no one could believe any more was in fact true
God had been with Jesus, even and especially in his final failure on the
cross. Was this then the demonstrative miracle that had not taken
place on Good Friday?

That something decisive happened at Easter cannot reasonably be
doubted even from this purely historical point of view. Intimidated
disciples who had taken flight when their master was arrested were
transformed into a company of men who proclaimed Jesus in Jerusalem and soon throughout the known world, going to prison and death
for their message. But what actually took place? As soon as we seek
to penetrate more closely and find out details, our sources fail us. Paul
still knows that Jesus appeared to Peter; then to the Twelve; then to
over five hundred of the brethren; to James and all the apostles, who
must therefore constitute a larger circle than the Twelve; and finally
to Paul himself (1 Cor. 15.5–8). Here, too, there is no reason to doubt
for in these verses we have an account based in part on first-hand
experience, in part on what Paul learned from those directly affected.
He goes on to emphasize that most of the five hundred are still alive.
In this case, too, however, we do not know what actually took place.

We must first of all recognize that the Gospels themselves exhibit
no more knowledge than this of the resurrection, except for the appearance of Jesus to the eleven disciples. According to Luke 24.34, to be
sure, the disciples in Jerusalem still speak of an appearance to Peter
but this very passage shows that only a formula was known: "The
Lord has risen indeed, and has appeared to Simon!" Nothing more
could be said. Even weightier is the evidence of Matthew, according
to whom the appearance took place in Galilee. This must have been
the first appearance, since the disciples still doubted; it was clearly
also the only appearance, since no other is mentioned and the concluding verse already anticipates the Gentile mission. According to
Luke, however, this appearance took place in Jerusalem on Easter
Sunday, and the disciples were expressly forbidden to leave the city
before Pentecost. The same holds true in John's account, albeit Jesus'
appearance is described in quite different terms, with a repetition a
week later in Jerusalem and later still in Galilee. But there are still
more difficulties. Paul clearly thinks all the appearances were like
the one he himself experienced, that is, appearances from heaven.
This is also the case in Matthew's account, where the first words
of the risen Lord are: "All authority in heaven and on earth has been
given to me". Furthermore, the final statement, "I am with you always

o the close of the age", makes no distinction between the presence of the risen Lord that the Christian community will always experience and that which the disciples now experience. Matthew himself probably pictures the scene as taking place on earth, for he has added, "Jesus came and said to them". It is clear, however, that this is Matthew's own interpolation into the tradition he received. This phrase occurs some thirty times in the New Testament, and only in Matthew, where it is used in similar fashion; one can often show how it has been interpolated into the text. According to Luke, however, the risen Lord walked upon the earth with "flesh and bones", and ate with his disciples (Luke 24.39ff.; cf. John 20.27). Of course Luke and John are also aware of the mystery surrounding this event; for the Lord who appears so concretely with "flesh and bones" can still penetrate closed doors (John 20.19; cf. Luke 24.36).

But do all the Gospels not tell of the discovery of the empty tomb? Once again, questions arise as soon as we inquire into details. We notice first the striking fact that Paul does not mention the empty tomb; this is the more astonishing because he expressly mentions Jesus' burial (1 Cor. 15.4). This might be because he did not consider the witness of the women very important in comparison to the far more decisive witness of those to whom the risen Lord himself had appeared, and was therefore not worth mentioning. But what actually happened on the morning of Easter? According to Matthew, the women, Mary of Magdala, and another Mary see the angel come down and roll the stone away. Sitting on the stone outside the tomb he speaks to them. According to Mark, the women—Mary of Magdala, Mary the daugher of James, and Salome—enter the tomb, which is already open, where they see a youth in a white robe, who speaks to them. According to Luke, the women—Mary of Magdala, Mary the daughter of James, Joanna, and several others—come upon two men in dazzling garments, who also speak to them; but the men do not tell the disciples to go to Galilee, as in Matthew and Mark, but remind them of Jesus' words concerning the dying and rising of the Son of Man. According to John, Mary of Magdala alone discovers the empty tomb, then gets Peter and John, and finally, when the latter have left once more discovers two angels in the tomb who speak to her. Then, obviously outside the tomb, Jesus himself speaks to her.

If we ask what historical conclusions we can arrive at with reasonable assurance, the answer might be roughly as follows. On the morning of Easter, Mary of Magdala discovers the empty tomb. This is often questioned, but the very inconsistencies that we have listed argue very persuasively that this actually happened. The only name common to all the evangelists is that of Mary of Magdala, who, according to John, was alone at the tomb, at least at first. If the story of the empty tomb were a late invention to prove the realistic resurrection of the body, as many witnesses as possible would have been mentioned from the outset, but not a single woman.[40] It may even be correct to add that Jesus' resurrection could hardly have been proclaimed in Jerusalem if people knew of a tomb still containing Jesus' body. In addition, the early tradition concerning the burial of Jesus makes sense only if people were already familiar with the discovery of the empty tomb. But all of this does not amount to proof of Jesus' resurrection. How do we know that Mary was not at the wrong tomb? This is possible, because she had only observed the burial from a distance. It is also possible that Jesus' body had been removed on the grounds that an executed blasphemer should not have proper burial, or because the Friday evening burial, which had to be performed in great haste before the Sabbath began, was from the outset considered merely provisional.

The second certain fact is that Jesus appeared to the witnesses named by Paul; he probably appeared from heaven, as the exalted Lord. Again, however, this does not prove Jesus' resurrection. In this very fashion Jesus' appearance could be explained psychologically as a vision in which the wish-fulfillments or hopes or religious conceptions of the disciples were concretized and projected externally. Of course there are many arguments against this explanation. In all the traditions we can still see that the resurrected Lord appeared to all sorts of people who were by no means expecting such an encounter, who in fact resisted it and doubted it (Matt. 28.17; Luke 24.11, 23–24, 37; John 20.15, 25; Gal. 1.13–16, 23). Furthermore, it is hard to conceive a mere vision shared by more than five hundred people without something like an accompanying ecstasy, of which there is not the slightest suggestion anywhere.[41] Finally, there is almost nothing to

[40] Cf. Matthew 27.62–66; 28.4, 11–15, where we already find attempts to prove the resurrection of Jesus.

[41] It is admittedly not absolutely sure that the more than five hundred saw the risen Lord at the same time. The parallel with Pentecost is also worth considering. The only passage that speaks of Pentecost (Acts 2.1ff.), however, assumes only that the Spirit came upon the twelve apostles, although many were moved to faith by their words.

suggest that these people were predisposed to visions and susceptible to such experiences.[42] Nevertheless, proof cannot be given of Jesus' resurrection. Here, too, very much as in the crucifixion of Jesus, God exposes himself to scepticism, doubt, and disbelief, renouncing anything that would compel men to believe.

The immediate effect of this conclusion is extremely liberating. The earliest Christians obviously cared astonishingly little about all the details of the Easter event—the where and how of it. But this means that the Easter faith does not depend on our success in believing in the possibility and historicity of all kinds of remarkable happenings, like the ability of the risen Lord to eat. It means, furthermore, that our assurance of Jesus' resurrection does not wax or wane depending on how precisely we read these accounts and on what new sources are discovered. But if there are no guarantees for the Easter faith, on what is our assurance based?

Once more, we shall begin with simple historical inquiry. Of course we must argue backwards from the sources, which were written at least twenty to sixty years after the fact. Some things are nevertheless clear. All the accounts show unequivocally that the discovery of the empty tomb did not awaken anyone's faith; this was done by the risen Jesus himself, who encountered his disciples. But this means that the assurance is based only on Jesus himself, the risen Lord. This agrees with the observation that all the New Testament witnesses understood Easter primarily as a call to service (Matt. 28.19–20; Luke 24.47–49; Mark 16.15; John 20.22–23; 1 Cor.9.1; Gal.1.15–16). This call to service was anything but expected. All our texts preserve the memory that all whom the risen Lord encountered resisted and doubted. What took place then was anything but a guarantee of eternal life for them; it was much more likely to cost them their lives —which was in fact the outcome for almost all of them! What began with the appearance of the risen Lord ended as a rule in prison and at the place of execution. From this perspective, Marxsen is by no means wrong in saying that Easter stands for the continued life of Jesus' cause, or Bultmann in speaking of Jesus' resurrection into the words of his disciples.[43] In quite remarkable fashion, Jesus' resurrection

---

[42] This possibility might be suggested by Mark 9.2ff. and Acts 10.1ff. Whether this could also apply to James, who, according to Mark 3.21, was highly sceptical of Jesus, is very questionable. Of the others we know nothing.

[43] Willi Marxsen, "The Resurrection of Jesus as a Historical and Theological Problem" in C. F. D. Moule, ed., *The Significance of the Message of the Resurrection for*

repeats what had already taken place in his parables or in his call to discipleship. There, too, Jesus had made it as clear as possible that there are no guarantees for the reality of God, no easily assimilated propositions in which God's reality might be comprehended—only an assurance that grows as one lets oneself be carried along, sentence by sentence, in Jesus' parables, really giving one's heart to them; that grows as one lives with Jesus day by day, experiencing with him all the trivialities or, on occasion, important events of daily life, fully trusting in his word.

Even the first Christian community did not gain its assurance of the resurrection by learning of a demonstrable miracle that had taken place and repeating a proposition about it, but by living under the dominion of the risen Lord. Here, then, arose the assurance—once more in very different ways—that Jesus' resurrection also implies our resurrection, that he who proved himself alive in his resurrection will also prove himself alive in us, in our physical death and beyond.[44] For life under the dominion of the risen Lord demonstrated a hundred times that it was not merely recollection of Jesus' words or deeds but rather Jesus himself who became the Christians' power when they failed, their life when they came to their end. This reality of the dominion of the risen Lord, this presence of God's power in the service they performed for him were the assurance of the resurrection, and of their own resurrection. For how could this reality be interrupted by their death, how could it cease to be true in physical death and beyond? How could he who had come to be their master not be also the master of their death?

When such assurance grows out of life with the word of the risen Lord and in obedience to him, the historical details of what happened at Easter become incidental. For faith no longer needs the guarantees of proof. To faith, the empty tomb will be a sign of what has taken place. It will not, however, fight for the empty tomb as for an article of faith, because the truth of Easter does not in fact depend on the empty tomb. What is important is whether the believer has such faith in the risen Lord that he will live under his dominion, will hold fast

---

Faith in Jesus Christ (SBT II 8, 1968), pp. 37ff.; Rudolf Bultmann, "Das Verhältnis der urchristlichen Christusbotschaft zum historischen Jesus", in his *Exegetica* (Tübingen: Mohr, 1967), p. 469.

[44] Cf. below, pp. 52, 117f, 121f.; for a discussion of the entire topic, see Karl Lehmann, *Auferweckt am dritten Tag nach der Schrift* (Quaestiones disputatae 38, Freiburg: Herder, 1968).

o the lordship of Jesus even when it leads him to his death. Only then will he find out whether he really relies on him "who raises the dead" (2 Cor. 1.8–9). And so the disciples, too, had to learn to understand what really took place at Easter through years of service under the living Christ, by living under his dominion and letting him show them what his resurrection really meant.

Even in the Palestinian community, that is, in the first years after Easter in and around Jerusalem, we can see very diverse attempts to understand Easter. All these initial attempts were more or less emphasized, developed, elaborated, or discarded when the message of Easter penetrated first to the Greek-speaking Jews in Jerusalem itself, to Stephen and his circle (Acts 6.1—8.2); then crossed the boundaries of Palestine and reached the Greek-speaking Jews of the Diaspora, especially in Syrian Antioch (Acts 11.19ff.), and was passed on by them to the "God-fearers" (i.e., the uncircumcised pagans who had not converted to Judaism but nevertheless regularly attended Jewish worship); and finally to complete pagans. We must follow up these various beginnings in the coming pages. We shall do so by pursuing one particular motif at a time: first the expectation that Jesus would soon return as judge and consummator, an expectation that continued strong in the first community; then faith in the exalted Lord, which was especially powerful in the Jewish Diaspora; the understanding of the cross, which achieved its most profound statement in Paul; and then the reminiscence of Jesus' earthly ministry recorded in the Gospels. The beginnings of all these developments, however, are found already in the first post-Easter community; they go back, in fact, to Jesus himself.

III

JESUS, WHO WILL SOON RETURN

EASTER AS THE BEGINNING OF THE END

In the early history of the Christian community, about which we know very little, one fact is sure.[1] The disciples of Jesus move to Jerusalem with their families and settle there. Discipleship to Jesus continues; it is still Jesus himself who sets his stamp on the disciples' lives. Whether, as seems likely to me, the disciples fled back to their Galilean homeland on Good Friday and then decided to move to Jerusalem on the basis of their encounters with the risen Lord, or whether they summoned their families to Jerusalem after the appearances of the risen Lord does not make any real difference. In either case encounter with the risen Lord precipitated everything that happened to the disciples. If they and their families left Galilee, their houses and boats, their relatives and their jobs, their decision is conceivable only on the assumption that they expected God would shortly do something decisive at Jerusalem. What could this be other than the irruption of the kingdom of God itself, the end of the world, the last judgment, and the resurrection of all the dead? The extent to which contemporary Judaism expected the resurrection of the dead at the end of all things is still disputed. But when contrary to all

---

[1] Acts records the picture of the first community that was current towards the end of the first century; the actual course of events must be reconstructed through critical analysis. It is noteworthy, for instance, that according to Acts 2.45 all the Christians sold their property and held everything in common, whereas according to Acts 4.36–37 (and 5.4) this is considered a praiseworthy exception. According to Acts 8.1, the whole community was persecuted; but the leaders of the community are able to continue in Jerusalem unchallenged. According to Acts 6.1–6, exclusively Hellenists rather than a mixed group were chosen to guarantee an equitable distribution between Hebrews and Hellenists. Many more examples could be given.

xpectation a resurrection took place, it must have been taken as a
ign of the imminent end, as a beginning of the end of the world, of
he last judgment, and of the final establishment of God's kingdom.

First Thessalonians 4.15–18 shows us how Paul imagined the course
of these eschatological events at the beginning of the fifties: God's
ommand sets everything in motion; the archangel gives the command and the trumpet is sounded; while Christ descends from heaven
ll the dead arise and ascend into the air to meet Christ, together with
hose still alive, including Paul.[2] They would then live with him forever (on the new earth?). We can still see in this tradition signs of a
heory that looked upon the Easter events as the immediate beginning
of this eschatological process. Matthew 27.51–53 gives a remarkable
ccount concerning the dead who arose from their graves immediately
fter Jesus' death and wandered about Jerusalem; this story must go
ack to a community or faction that looked upon the death and
resurrection of Jesus as the beginning of the eschaton and obviously
expected that the general resurrection was about to take place.[3] It is
alutary to suffer the shock of these strange ideas. Perceiving the
"strangeness" of accustomed ideas is usually the beginning of real
attention to them. Three points illustrate the salutary effect of this
perspective, which seems to us so strange and alien in its conceptions:

(a) The community learned from the experiences of Easter that
alvation rests completely in God's actions. *Their* faith had failed completely. *Their* attitude toward what had happened had not prevailed.
Their accomplishments in the field of religion or ethics were negative.
But God had acted. It was a strange and mysterious act, which they
could share only as witnesses. Their contribution had been nil. What
took place came to them as a pure gift. God's battle cry, his archangel,
and his trumpet blast underline the point so that it cannot be missed:
the crucial event, the "end" that is the beginning of God's kingdom,
depends absolutely upon God.

(b) The events of Easter comprehend a world. What took place
then could not be calculated within the sphere of individual experience; it could only be described in terms of divine creation. What was
manifested here was nothing less than the abrogation of the entire

---

[2] This expectation probably goes back to the practice according to which the
population of a city would go out to meet an eminent visitor and accompany him
into the city.

[3] Matthew himself, of course, no longer interpreted the story in this way, seeing
in it only a sign of the power of Jesus' crucifixion, which overcomes death.

world of death, and God was restored to his proper place. This, too, is underlined by the expectations of the first community. Jesus' descent from heaven, the ascent of the faithful into the air, above all the idea of a new earth under a new heaven, which originates in the Old Testament (2 Peter 3.13)—these stress the universality and concreteness of Easter, show it as an act of God transcending all that takes place merely within the human heart.

(c) From the very beginning Easter was understood as an open door to the future. Certainly none of the disciples saw in it a historical event completed in the past, able at best to exercise its influence indirectly. Many of them brought their families to Jerusalem; this shows how strongly they felt Easter to be, as it were, a continuing event. Once again eschatological expectations emphasize the pregnancy of what God did at Easter for the future. Presumably the first disciples hardly distinguished Easter from the Parousia.[4] What took place in Jerusalem and Galilee at Easter was the beginning of God's mighty eschatological acts that destroy the old world. For them, Easter continued on, as it were, into the consummation of the kingdom of God, in which Jesus' disciples will live "with Christ" forever.

To think of Christianity as timeless is to deprive it of hope. In contrast to such a view, the first community speaks with a refreshing and perhaps terrifying simplicity of God's mighty act that comprehends a world and culminates in the consummation of God's kingdom. Here the important thing is not the conversion of individuals, powerful as that can be; what matters here is a transformed world, in which God is Lord not only of individual hearts, but of all power, of all life, of all history, so that nothing can oppose him, however much all his creatures stand apart from him and are not simply absorbed by him. But we must examine the meaning of this more closely.

THE SON OF MAN AS THE ONE TO COME

Whether the community introduced the title, whether Jesus expected someone else to come as the Son of Man; or looked upon himself as the Son of Man walking the earth, who would be exalted to God's presence and appear as witness at the Judgment; or described

[4] The Greek word *parousia* is usually translated as "return" (of Jesus), but it actually means "presence", "appearance". The latter expressions are more correct because the expectation that the Lord will be visible at the end of all the world does not always include the notion that he will then come down to earth.

is role as future judge in these terms[5]—after Easter the Son of Man in his eschatological role becomes increasingly the focus for the thought of the community. At the same time, he is equated unambiguously with Jesus. The judge who comes to confront the world will be none other than Jesus. Here we find the goal of Jesus' life, his death, and his resurrection.

First of all, Old Testament texts cast new light on the future. The only Bible the community has is the Old Testament. This is where it must look for information when bothered by questions. Whatever Jesus' own views may have been, the community in any case borrows from Daniel (7.13) the image of the Son of Man to whom kingdom, power, and glory will be given, and thus emphatically places Jesus' future role in the center of its eschatology. It is no accident that this crucial passage comes from the only unambiguously apocalyptic book of the Old Testament. Typically apocalyptic, too, are the images associated with the final coming of Jesus. The angels who appear with the Son of Man are regularly mentioned (Mark 8.38; 13.26–27; Matt. 13.41; 25.31; Luke 12.8–9; cf. John 1.51). He comes as judge (Matt. 25.31; 19.28) and as he who gathers his chosen (Mark 13.27) or his enemies (Matt. 13.41) for salvation or destruction. His appearance comes to an unsuspecting world like that of a thief or of lightning (Luke 12.39; 17.24–30).[6] For the community and its listeners, however, it is a matter of certain knowledge that he who comes is none other than Jesus. At the same time, the community states its belief that a man's future depends on the attitude he now takes toward Jesus. This is stated explicitly in such passages as Luke 12.8; Matthew 16.27–28; Mark 8.38. The preservation of this statement in two or three different forms shows that, whether or not it can be traced back to Jesus himself, it was a matter of concern to the community. It shows also that the community found here a statement of what had already taken place in Jesus' coming upon earth and what will take place at his eschatological appearance. We are here assured that the attitude of the man who confesses or denies the Jesus that has already come will constitute the basis on which he will be judged in the last judgment of the Son of Man.

This conception must be examined in more detail. Matthew 25.

[5] Cf. above, pp. 19–21.
[6] If the future tense was really in the original text, Luke 11.30 also belongs in this context; Matthew 10.23 shows how imminently the coming of the Son of Man was expected.

31b–46 is an account of the last judgment whose basic features prob
ably go back to Jesus himself. The later introduction (vs. 31a) refer
explicitly to the Son of Man: men have already encountered him i
beggars and the sick, in prisoners and those who hunger, and wha
they have done or failed to do for these needy they have done or faile
to do for the Son of Man who comes as judge. How closely the com
ing Son of Man was identified with him who already dominated th
life of the community is shown by many details. Acts 2.46 mention
the eschatological joy that marked the eucharistic celebration of th
first community. Even if we cannot accept uncritically all the state
ments of Acts as historically accurate accounts, this picture is sup
ported by a special tradition concerning the Last Supper found i
Luke 22.15–18, 28–30. Here the Last Supper is set totally in the con
text of the coming banquet in the kingdom of God, when the disciple
will not only celebrate at the table of their Lord, but will even "si
on thrones" sharing in his rule and judgment. Probably the acclama
tion "*Marana tha*—Come, O Lord!" (1 Cor. 16.22; Did. 10.6; Rev
22.20) was very early linked with the Eucharist.[7]

Baptism, too, especially at the beginning, probably concentrate
heavily on the imminent judgment and incipient kingdom of God.
Finally, the Revelation of John, which probably did not reach it
final form until the very end of the first century, still contains echoe
of these ideas, and especially the significance of the coming Son c
Man for the present life of the community. In the call vision Revela
tion 1.13,[9] it is the exalted Son of Man, given divine predicates, wh
seizes the attention of the seer. Here, of course, the title "Son of Man"
is no longer used, but only the Old Testament image from Danie
7.13.[10] It is clear, however, that the one like a son of man intervene

---

[7] In all three passages the acclamation follows a statement of sacral law (furthe
developed in Did. 10.6); see below, p. 61. It was therefore probably first pro
nounced by early Christian prophets, who thus called upon the judge to come t
his eschatological judgment (K. Wengst, *Christologische Formeln und Lieder des Ur
christentums*, Dissertation, Bonn, 1967, pp. 47–8). In Didache 10.6, i.e., in a churc
order of the Syrian (?) church dating from the eighties, it occurs in the eucharisti
liturgy. This was probably true as early as the time of Paul, as is suggested by th
kiss of peace and the expulsion of nonbelievers in 1 Corinthians 16.20–22. Since th
letter is to be read in the course of worship, Paul can use the passage as a transitio
to the Eucharist that follows. Cf. below, pp. 66f.

[8] Cf. below, p. 117.   [9] Cf. below, p. 59.

[10] The author of Revelation is familiar with the Christian titles of Jesus, bu
always uses them with great restraint. i.e., in such a way as might still be possib

directly in the life of the seer and calls him to his service, just as God calls the prophets in the Old Testament.

The community also gradually borrows from apocalyptic thought a programmatic schedule of the stages in which the final age will unfold, so that it becomes possible to determine how far the world-clock has advanced, how near the end is. Such a schedule, however, could be incorporated into the thought of the community only in opposition to the words of Jesus, and we therefore find only the beginnings of such a tendency. The Revelation of John, which, in addition to much else, now contains *also* a temporal sequence of events, is the most outstanding witness to this type of thought. On a smaller scale, however, it already occurs in Mark 13.[11] Beyond any doubt, fragments of quite diverse origin have here been combined to form a kind of programmatic schedule. The nucleus is probably the threefold omen of sword, famine, and plague, frequently mentioned in the Old Testament (Rev.6.3–8; Luke 21.9–11).[12] The Old Testament already mentions earthquake in association with sword and plague (Ezek.38.19) or with cosmic catastrophe (Amos 8.8–9; Joel 2.10) as an omen of the end. A period of war and persecution was likewise expected in the last days before the end (Mic.7.6; Jub.[13] 23.22–25; etc.). The result was a series of omens including war and international expansion, earthquake, famine (plague), persecution, and the collapse of all heavenly and earthly order (Mark 13.7–8, 12, 24–25); a similar series occurs in Revelation 6. It is far more instructive, however, to note how this traditional schema has been used. In particular, what is expected is not simply chaos and judgment, but the Son of Man, i.e., a figure already known to the community, who comes to gather in his own (Mark 13.27). This expectation probably explains the addition of a remarkable passage in verses 14–20, depicting circumstances in Judaea quite concretely. This shows that the

in Jewish thought (Traugott Holtz, *Die Christologie der Apokalypse des Johannes* [TU 85, 1962], esp. pp. 14–20).

[11] This chapter probably attained its final written form towards the end of the sixties (or perhaps after the fall of Jerusalem in AD 70; see Rudolf Pesch, *Naherwartungen* [Kommentare und Beiträge zum Alten und Neuen Testament, Düsseldorf: Patmos, 1968]).

[12] There is no mention of plague in Mark 13.5–8, perhaps merely because the Greek words for "famine" and "plague" are almost identical, so that "plague", for instance, has demonstrably been omitted from the Greek translation of Jeremiah 38.2.

[13] A Jewish document dating from the second century BC.

eschaton is not just something far removed from the life of the community, which will someday take place in a future that has no relationship with the present. Above all, this expectation explains the direct address to the community in verses 5–6 and 21–23, at the very beginning and again just before the conclusion, in which a warning is sounded against dissatisfaction with Jesus and apostate faith in others who promise salvation. The extended references to persecution in verses 9–11 and 13 serve the same purpose. The same thing can be seen in Revelation, where the seven letters in chapters 2—3 are without parallel in Jewish apocalyptic literature. Here, too, we see how immediately the apocalyptic movement spoke to the contemporary Christian community, depicting God's intervention in their concrete situation. At the same time, it is still Jesus Christ who remains the focus of all these expectations. The faith of the Christians has not lost its basic theme.

 'The dangers of such apocalyptic speculation are obvious. When a schema develops comprising a temporal sequence of events, there is an immediate danger of separating what is to come from the present. This would turn Jesus into an amazing miracle worker, whose deeds could be recalled the way any past history is recalled, and whose future deeds, even more wonderful, could be looked forward to the way any future events are looked forward to. Then—assuming belief in all this—a man could still consider what conclusions he should draw for the present. In fact, however, at the very beginning of this apocalyptic period the presence of the living Christ was the absolute focus: he encountered his disciples and impelled them to move to Jerusalem. This remains true in the period of the author of Revelation, whom the Son of Man encounters directly and calls to his service, and it is true once more for the redaction of the apocalyptic vision in Mark 13 carried out by the community and the evangelist. With all that remains to be said, apocalypticism helped prevent Jesus from being transformed into a principle or an ideal, so that he remained the same person—intervening, troubling, judging, comforting, strengthening—as when he first encountered his disciples on his journeys through Galilee. At the same time, at least in the early period, apocalypticism kept the community from small ideas, kept it from retreating into sectarianism. For what apocalyptic thought looked forward to was an event embracing the entire world, nay, the entire cosmos, because its author was the Lord of the universe, not merely the spiritual support of individual souls.

The Revelation of John provides ample material to illustrate the difference between the apocalypticism of the New Testament and that of contemporary Judaism.

1. The very presence of a call narrative, as in the Old Testament prophets (Rev. 1.9ff.; 10.8ff.; cf. 22.8ff.), shows the great difference: the living spirit is present. Jewish apocalypticists, by contrast, write under the pseudonymn of some great figure from the past (Daniel, Ezra, Enoch, Baruch). This assurance is based on the Easter experience. Comparison of 2.1 and 2.7 shows that the Spirit is none other than the living Christ, and that he speaks to all of them, to "the churches".

2. The summons to the community, which takes seriously the temptations that befall the community and the demands of the present, is an essential element (chapters 2—3). The time between Easter and the Parousia is thought of as a time of temptation and challenge, recalling Jesus' words in Matthew 11.12 (cf. the witnesses in Rev. 11.3ff. and the situation of the church in 7.14; 12.6ff.).

3. This view is possible only because it is grounded in the central significance of Jesus' death[14] (1.18; 2.8; 3.14; 5.6, 9, 12; cf. 13.3). "Lamb" has here become the most important title of Christ (it occurs twenty-eight times).

4. All that matters is God's triumph and power; there is no description of the triumph of the community and the destruction of the enemy (cf. the songs of victory in 7.10ff.; 11.15ff.; 12.10ff.; 14.1–2; also 4.2, 8 and 19.1ff.).

5. We note finally how much the totality of the church, represented in the fullness of the seven communities, is the focus of the author's thought and faith, not simply the small band of the individual faithful. The community, not the individual, has its angel standing in the presence of God (1.20); the community as a whole is extolled or rejected, and even a single individual who dies a martyr's death illustrates the unshakeable faith of the *community* (2.13).

6. Thus present and future are inextricably intertwined, much more than would otherwise be the case. In God's perspective, the end is already present (cf. 7.9ff.) for the temptations and trials that still afflict the community upon earth (7.1ff.). Thus the Revelation of John, with its radical concentration on God, on God's power and glory, in a certain sense transcends apocalypticism.

[14] Cf. below, pp. 77–80.

PENTECOST AS THE REALIZATION OF THE COMING END

From the very beginning, expectation of the coming Christ largely determined the present. The disciples left their houses and fields behind and moved to Jerusalem with their families. Thus was repeated in a new setting what had once taken place in the call to discipleship issued by the earthly Jesus. However one interprets the Easter appearances, the risen Christ still determines the path of his disciples, as he did before his death. And again it was not heroism or devotion that made the disciples decide to move, but Jesus' intervention and call. What happened to the disciples who went from Galilee to Jerusalem was repeated for a great multitude at Pentecost.

What took place at Pentecost can no longer be reconstructed with certainty.[15] It is probably safe to assume, however, that the early period of the community in Palestine and neighboring areas was particularly marked by religious enthusiasm. We have definite information concerning prophets in communities of Hellenistic Christians from the time of Paul[16] until the later period of Revelation.[17] The Didache attests to the same phenomenon to a great degree in Syria. As late as the second century, the letters of Ignatius show how vital and highly esteemed the enthusiastic working of the Spirit was in Asia Minor.[18] The experience of the Spirit did not take root first in the Hellenistic communities, however; it is probably associated directly with the Easter experiences in Galilee and Jerusalem. This is

[15] The account in Acts 2.1–41 is ambiguous in many respects. The Greek term "glossolalia" can mean speaking in various languages (foreign languages or the language of angels) or in tongues (incomprehensible language). According to 1 Corinthians 14.1–25, glossolalia is incomprehensible to others, and therefore presumably means speaking meaningless sounds that belong to no human language. This conclusion agrees with that reached by the onlookers, who assume that the apostles are drunk (Acts 2.13). Verse 4, however, clearly suggests that the disciples were speaking in foreign languages, while verses 8–11 presuppose that the miracle affected those who were listening, not those who were speaking. Acts 10.44 and 19.6 also are not thinking of foreign languages. According to John 20.22, the gift of the Spirit took place on Easter, and without external phenomena.

[16] This applies to Corinth (1 Cor. 12.10; 14.1–5, 24–25) and Thessalonika (1 Thess. 5.19–20), as well as to the Roman community (Rom. 12.6), which Paul did not found. It also holds true for the communities addressed in Ephesians, among whom "drunkenness" prompted by the Spirit appeared during worship (Eph. 5.18–19).

[17] Chapters 1.1–11 and 2—3 suggest that Revelation was composed in Asia Minor toward the end of the first century.

[18] Didache 11.3—13.1 (cf. above, p. 56, n. 7); Ignatius *Ad Philad.* 7.

supported by the observation that Luke, although assuming the presence of prophets everywhere, can name only those in Jerusalem and the border region of Syria (Acts 11.27–28; 15.32; 21.8–9; compare Acts 13.1 with 4.36). The crucial observation, however, is that statements of divine law occur, primarily in the Gospel of Matthew, but also in Paul. Enforcement of the law is left entirely to the imminent judgment of God; there is no provision for the administration of ecclesiastical law. These statements follow the pattern of 1 Corinthians 3.17: "Anyone who destroys God's temple will himself be destroyed by God"[19] (NEB). In other words, there were prophets who appeared in the name of God or the exalted Lord and proclaimed his norms. Law is proclaimed in these passages in such a way that God's retributive action in the Last Judgment (presumably imminent) is proclaimed. This is also the setting of the cry that summons the coming Lord, "Maranatha".[20] In this fashion the Son of Man, soon to return, is already present in his community and determines its law. This notion can go so far that Paul, united in spirit with the whole Christian community, can consign a man to judgment, clearly expecting that the man will die at once, as a proleptic sign of the judgment to come (1 Cor. 5.3–4; cf. 11.30). The Twelve, as the group to whom the risen Lord appeared (1 Cor. 15.5), played an extremely important role in the Jerusalem community; they were the future judges of Israel chosen by the Son of Man, who would sit on twelve thrones (Matt. 19.28). Therefore judicial authority was accorded them in the present (cf. Matt. 16.19; 18.18; John 20.23).[21]

[19] The translation imitates the chiastic structure of the Greek. On this whole question see E. Käsemann, "Sentences of Holy Law in the New Testament", in his *New Testament Questions of Today* (NTL, 1969), pp. 66–81; cf. also 1 Corinthians 14.38; 5.19; 6.14; 10.32–33; Mark 4.24–25. The form, it is true, also occurs in wisdom instruction (Schweizer, *Das Evangelium nach Markus* [NTD 1*, 1967], p. 61, n. 65.

[20] Cf. above, p. 56, n. 7, and below, pp. 66–7.

[21] It is not impossible that the term "apostle" derives from the designation of the Twelve by the Son of Man and Judge to be his "ambassadors", as is suggested by the content of Matthew 19.28 and the terminology of Revelation 21.14. The Greek translation first suggested a missionary function. This could explain why at first the Twelve were called "apostles" in Greek along with many other missionaries (Gal. 1.17, 19; 1 Cor. 15.7; Rom. 16.7). Since Paul claimed to have been specially called by the risen Lord to be an apostle and missionary to the Gentiles, and since others made similar claims without foundation, Luke later came to refer to the Twelve as the "apostles" in the exclusive sense, on whose preaching the church is founded. See below, pp. 147–8.

Acts of authority such as healings—and above all exorcisms—and probably also judgment miracles (Acts 5.1–11), occurred in the Palestinian community; even these, however, are signs of the presence of the coming Lord. In them we catch the first light of God's victory over all opposing powers and of the coming kingdom in which misery, suffering, and sin will not be found. In Matthew we still find the clearest evidence for the development of the Christian community in Palestine and neighboring Syria; he presupposes such eschatological wonders taking place in the community and views them with unqualified approval.[22] Of course if the coming Son of Man determines the community's way of life by means of his eschatological law, proclaimed through prophets, and by his judging, healing, and saving intervention, we are confronted once more with the problem of whether the Old Testament law still obtains, a problem that had already appeared during Jesus' earthly ministry. The evidence still available to us suggests that this problem had already led to disputes within the Palestinian community. According to Matthew 7.22–23, Jesus, acting as judge at the Last Judgment, will turn away prophets who perform miracles and exorcize demons, but refuse to uphold the law.[23] This probably also explains the division of the Jerusalem community into the group around the Twelve, who remained faithful to the law, and the group around Stephen,[24] which dissociated itself from the law and later turned to the Gentiles.

Enthusiasm of this sort is associated directly with exaggerated apocalyptic expectations; even the Old Testament prophets, not to mention the Qumran sect, expected an outpouring of the Spirit at the eschaton. [25] The attitude of Judaism at the time of Jesus is not absolutely clear. On the one hand, prophets kept appearing, often assert-

[22] See below, pp. 132–7.

[23] The bitter rejection of "lawlessness" probably establishes the origin of this passage in a legalistic community of Jewish Christians. The expression itself could conceivably go back to Matthew (cf. Matt. 13.41; 23.28; 24.12). Luke 13.26–27 substitutes the much more general word "injustice". The Lukan variant clearly refers to Palestinians who boast that Jesus taught among them; there is no reference to miracles, however. Luke probably made the threat refer more generally to the Jews and altered the wording towards that end. On the other hand, Matthew 23.8–11 opposes a hierarchy of teachers.

[24] Cf. below, p. 123.

[25] Isaiah 44.3; Ezekiel 11.19; 36.26; Joel 3.1ff.; Zechariah 12.10; cf. Isaiah 32.15; Haggai 2.5. The passages bearing on the endowment of the Messiah with the Spirit have been assembled by E. Sjöberg, "$\pi\nu\epsilon\hat{\upsilon}\mu\alpha$, $\pi\nu\epsilon\upsilon\mu\alpha\tau\iota\kappa\acute{o}\varsigma$", in *TDNT* VI, p. 384; cf. also *ibid.*, pp. 384–5, and, for Qumran, 1QS iv. 19–22.

ing that the eschaton had come; on special occasions some individuals claimed to give instructions in the name of God, inspired by his Spirit.[26] On the other hand, official rabbinic teaching maintained that the Spirit would be silent from the death of the last Old Testament prophet until the eschaton,[27] and the apocalypticists themselves without exception wrote under pseudonyms, not least because people believed that the Spirit spoke through the men of the sacred past, but not through their contemporaries.[28] Both sides, however, seem to assume that the speaking of the Spirit is a phenomenon of the eschaton —present, anticipated, or imminent. Thus the early Christian community must have considered the appearance of the Spirit a sign of the events signaling the eschaton.

God was no longer restricted to the sacred age of a distant past and an equally distant future, accessible only through the mediation of Scripture. God had become immediate. God was speaking once more, acting once more, here, now, affecting the concrete circumstances of today. This was the irruption of the eschaton.

Of course the borrowing of current popular apocalyptic thought-forms and conceptions involved dangers. In Jesus' preaching, the nearness of the kingdom was in part temporal, but primarily "spatial", because Jesus spoke of the God who comes to meet man here and now. This could easily be misunderstood as mere temporal proximity. Original sayings of Jesus or even newly created sayings were understood as emphasizing the shortness of the time remaining: the parable of the unjust steward, for example, who is called to account and has only a few hours at his disposal before the catastrophe (Luke 16.1ff.); or the parable of the legal adversary with whom one should settle one's differences while still on the way to court (Luke 12.58–59). As time went on, more emphasis came to be placed on the relative nearness of the eschaton—some of the first generation will live to see Christ's coming (Mark 9.1; John 21.22). At the same time, however, there came a call to keep alert watch during a period of waiting whose duration is unknown—the doorkeeper does not know what time

[26] The primary source for their activity is the Jewish writer Josephus, writing at the end of the first century, who himself appeared as a prophet (*Jewish War* iii, 351ff.). For other passages, see R. Meyer, "προφήτης", in *TDNT* VI, p. 823.

[27] Psalm 74.9; Syr. Baruch 85.1–3 (*ca.* AD 100?): ". . . the prophets have gone to sleep"; Strack-Billerbeck, *op. cit.*, I, p. 127: "When Haggai, Zechariah, and Malachi, the last prophets, had died, the Holy Spirit vanished out of Israel"; other similar passages are cited.

[28] Cf. above, p. 59.

the master of the house will return, the master of the house does not know when the burglar will break in, and prudent girls keep a supply of oil in reserve (Luke 12.35–40; Matt. 25.1ff.). Finally, increasing emphasis was placed on the responsibilities of God's servants in the interim period (Luke 12.42–46; 19.11ff.; cf. Mark 13.34), for a thousand years are like a single day in the sight of God (2 Peter 3.8). But one must not forget that the delayed arrival of the end never became a serious problem, because the presence of the Spirit and the irruption of God into the here and now of life were understood from the very beginning as signs of the coming end.

We must also not overlook the immense benefits that apocalyptic thought conferred on the early community. It helped the community continue its discipleship in a totally new situation. When the first disciples were travelling with Jesus, the future kingdom of God filled and dominated every moment of their wanderings; after Easter, the effectual presence of the Spirit of God also implied the presence of the kingdom. Because God is a God who comes and not simply a timeless and eternal deity, he invaded the realm of everyday life. At the same time, though, the strong future hope of the disciples prevented them from substituting for God and his kingdom the irruption of the Spirit or of faith in their own hearts, and taking it as the theme for their lives and preaching. They were not what mattered. Neither their faith nor their failures, neither their obedience nor their doubt were important in themselves. What was important was God, who had suddenly ceased to be a revered relic of the past and had become reality. And God's victory was important, the coming of his kingdom. Therefore the world was also important—the world that God was now reclaiming for himself, the world already standing in the light of God's coming and yet not obedient to him. And so to the best of our knowledge the Spirit impelled the disciples from the very outset not to retreat into themselves, into an inner life where faith can be cultivated, but to leave their secure homeland for the crowds of Jerusalem (Acts 2.14ff.), for the "Hellenists" (Acts 6.1), the Greek-speaking and generally progressive Jews in Jerusalem, for the Jewish groups in Arabia (Gal. 1.17; cf. Acts 9.1ff.), for the Samaritans (Acts 8.5ff.), and finally for the pagans (Acts 11.20).[29]

[29] On the question of the Christian mission, see below, pp. 77–80.

IV

THE HEAVENLY JESUS

We have already spoken of the disciples' belief that the risen Christ would soon appear as judge and consummator of the world. This perspective was probably most dominant during the initial period of the Palestinian community. But it continued to live in the community, at times coming to the fore, as in Thessalonians and especially in Revelation; at times retreating into the background, as in the Gospel of John. Our discussion has already shown, however, that expectation of the coming Jesus had another aspect as well. Soon to return, he was already setting his stamp on the present life of the community. He was the risen Lord, and for the first disciples this meant that he was divinely exalted, as the one who would come to consummate and judge the world. At first this motif was merely implicit in the faith of the Palestinian community, and was not consciously expressed. It nevertheless undoubtedly influenced their lives until, probably among Greek-speaking Jewish Christians, it received increasing theological emphasis. We shall now examine this line of development.

It is conceivable that the discipleship practised by Jesus' followers during his earthly life, which they were now called to continue in a new form, might have become the basic theme of Christianity. In other words, the major emphasis of the life of the community and of its proclamation to the outside world might have been on the ethical realization of what the disciples had learned while with Jesus. That this is not what happened is due, humanly speaking, first of all to the movement of apocalyptic enthusiasm that began with Easter. But Jesus' own actions had laid the groundwork. The disciples had not come forward as willing followers; he had called them, and with an authority that prevailed over their own wills. Thus the call to discipleship was the Lord's act from the very outset, and discipleship itself was a gift. It remained so because it was always Jesus who chose the way, filled the days, and put the stamp of his words and deeds on his followers' discipleship. All this applies to Easter to an incomparably greater degree. The new beginning of discipleship was here once again established by Jesus himself. The risen Lord gathered the fugitives and, with his appearance, opened to them the way to post-Easter discipleship. Therefore if the disciples wanted to discuss what had happened in appropriate terms, they had to speak of Jesus, not of their discipleship.

It was he, Jesus, who distinguished the Christian community in Jerusalem from the Jewish apocalypticists. In what Jesus said and did, the presence of the coming kingdom of God had been proclaimed in a completely new way, so that a witness to Jesus' deeds, a hearer of his preaching, could no longer take refuge in an attitude of patient neutrality. How much more were the disciples confronted with the irruption of the eschaton in their encounters with the risen Lord! Here one could no longer take refuge in a future still unfulfilled, however great the expectations one might have of the future. The situation was plain: the present was already so numinous; so completely filled with Jesus, who encountered his disciples day by day; so determined by the living operation of the Spirit, that it was impossible to distinguish an empty present from a fulfilled future. The future had already come upon the community and taken possession of it.

But if Jesus appeared to the disciples from heaven at Easter,[1] then he was also from the very beginning the exalted heavenly Lord of his community. The prophets of the Palestinian community summon the coming judge, calling him *marana* (our Lord). Even here it is difficult to distinguish him who will come for judgment (certainly the original meaning) from him who already judges the community in the sacral law proclaimed by the prophet. This is all the more true when the cry *maranatha* becomes incorporated into the Eucharistic liturgy.[2] But miracles, healings, and exorcisms also bore witness to the presence of him who would one day come. Even the miracle-workers in Matthew 7.22 address him as "Lord, Lord".

There is in fact much evidence that the proclamation of the coming Lord was very soon associated with the proclamation of the exalted Lord of heaven.[3] The Aramaic cry *maranatha*, "Our Lord, come", became a part of the Eucharistic liturgy; and the Greek title

[1] Cf. above, pp. 45–7. [2] Cf. above, p. 56.
[3] Cf. E. Schweizer, *Erniedrigung und Erhöhung*, §7c, especially A. pp. 325–6; an

kyrios, "Lord", appears to be particularly associated with the Eucharist.[4] It is therefore hard to escape the conclusion that the *mare* of Judgment Day had become the present *mare* of the Aramaic-speaking community, and the "Lord" of the Greek-speaking community celebrating the Eucharist. Additional evidence also supports this conclusion. Above all, there is not a single passage in Jewish literature that speaks of the coming of the Son of Man (or the Messiah or the Son of God) from heaven to earth. All the Jewish expectations concerning the Son of Man speak of his exaltation to heavenly majesty.[5] Whether they are earlier or later than the New Testament, they show what was possible in the world of this period among Jewish apocalypticists of the synagogue or the Christian community, since the two can hardly be distinguished prior to AD 70. The Easter proclamation of the Lord, addressing his disciples from heaven (Matt. 28.18–20), refers explicitly to Daniel 7.13, the apocalyptic text concerning the Son of Man to whom "the power and the kingdom" are given. Here, however, it has been put in the mouth of the heavenly Lord. In Mark 14.62, the same text is already linked with Psalm 110.1, which bears witness to the exaltation of the "Lord" to sit at the right hand of God. On the other hand, both 1 Corinthians 15.25–27 and Ephesians 1.20–22 independently link this verse with Psalm 8.7, which speaks of the "Son of Man". Finally, Mark 12.36 cites Psalm 110.1 in a form whose conclusion has been altered through the influence of Psalm 8.7.[6]

This is not surprising. Markedly apocalyptic Jewish groups like the members of the Qumran community by the Dead Sea expect that at the eschaton God will do battle against the demons and Belial, their prince, and finally subjugate them. The word used here is also used

---

important recent discussion is that of W. Thüsing, "Erhöhungsvorstellung und Parusieerwartung in der ältesten nachösterlichen Christologie", *BZ* XI (1967), pp. 95–108, 205–22; XII (1968), pp. 54–80.

[4] The Eucharist is referred to as the "Lord's Supper" in 1 Corinthians 11.20; the liturgy itself begins "The Lord Jesus . . ." (vs. 23; cf. the conclusion in vs. 26). Especially interesting is the statement concerning the death of the "Lord" and his body and blood (vss. 26–27), since the usual title in these contexts is "Christ". In 1 Corinthians 10.21, too, we read of the table and cup of the "Lord", contrasted, interestingly, with the table and cup of demons.

[5] Cf. above, pp. 18–20.

[6] Note also the juxtaposition of the two psalm verses in Hebrews 1.13 and 2.6–8. Polycarp (*Ad Phil.* ii. 1) also bears witness to the close association between Jesus' exaltation and the Parousia.

in the New Testament for Jesus' exorcisms.[7] When these exorcisms
continue within the community under the lordship of the risen
Christ, who has appeared from heaven to his disciples, the community cannot help seeing therein the fulfillment of Psalm 8.7 (all things
have been laid at the feet of the Son of Man) or the realization of
what Psalm 110.1 says about him who is exalted to sit at God's right
hand (all his enemies have been made a stool for his feet). Thus there
is already taking place within the community that which will soon
involve the entire world and will culminate in the appearance of him
who comes to judgment. This apocalyptic perspective still dominates
in the time of Paul (1 Cor. 15.22–28). This is a model apocalyptic
passage, which, like 1 Thessalonians 4.13–18,[8] depicts the eschatological drama: each of the powers hostile to God is subjected to the
exalted Lord, until death itself, the last enemy, is slain. This will take
place on the "day of the Lord", when the eschatological kingdom of
God is inaugurated with the coming of the exalted Christ (the Last
Judgment), and the resurrection of all the dead to eternal life. The
same holds true for Philippians 2.9–11, at least as interpreted by Paul.
As Romans 14.11 and 1 Corinthians 15.24–27 show, Paul associates the
final subjugation of all hostile powers with the time of the Parousia.[9]

This explains the view that Easter marks the beginning of the
eschatological drama. Jesus' exaltation is still basically understood as
the beginning of the eschatological appearance of the Son of Man;
this makes it clear how central God, God's kingdom, God's victory,
and God's glory are in these passages.[10] Of course this view goes
beyond a mere statement that the Son of Man will come at the end
of time; it also expresses his significance for the interim period between Easter and the final inauguration of God's kingdom. Even in
respect to the present significance of the Son of Man, however, various
motifs are brought together in the fact of the Easter appearances.

[7] H. C. Kee, "The Terminology of Mark's Exorcism Stories", *NTS* XIV
(1967/68), 232ff.

[8] Cf. above, pp. 52f.

[9] Whether this holds true also for the hymn Paul is citing remains unsettled. Cf.
below, pp. 73f.

[10] The concluding words of Philippians 2.11 (". . . to the glory of God the
Father") may have been added by Paul himself to maintain the gravity of the
metaphorical statement. This is suggested by Romans 14.11, where the same quotation refers to the subjugation of all powers to God. The hymn itself, however,
definitely associates all the actions of the Son with God; cf. the emphasis on obedience in Philippians 2.8.

First, Jesus appears to his disciples as the man who became their master, controlled and guided their lives, required their obedience, and provided hope and assistance. At the same time, however, Jesus appears as a man acknowledged, accepted, and perfected by God, so that exaltation is a predication of majesty in purely christological terms, anticipating Jesus' future position as Son of Man and judge of all the world, with its dominions and powers. The Lord before whom all dominions and powers of a whole world will bow was also the Lord of his disciples, who had already put his stamp on their lives. This was self-evident, because the imminent inauguration of God's eschatological kingdom already determined the life of the community, or, to put the same thing in the language of modern theology, the cosmological understanding of Jesus' exaltation still coincided completely with the existential.

In the following period, however, the two points of view began to diverge. We can observe this divergence already in the way Paul uses Isaiah 45.23. In the context of Romans 14.7–10, the lordship of Christ is seen unambiguously as determining the life of each member of the community. The expectation that all will finally be subject therefore comprehends not only the cosmic powers, but "all of us" (vs. 10), that is, the people summoned to God's judgment (or perhaps only Christians); furthermore, the expectation refers to God, not to Christ. In the context of Philippians 2.9–11, however, the cosmic lordship of Christ himself is clearly the focus of interest. Of course the two cannot be torn asunder. In Romans 14.7–9, Jesus is Lord of his community only because he has already overcome death; and in Philippians 2.9–11, the Christian community is included in the company of those who extol the Lord. In fact, the community practises such worship and lives in obedience to its Lord by singing this hymn, thus incorporating itself into the company of those who glorify the Lord. Thus Paul can use the hymn as a basis for his ethical requirement that members of the community learn proper conduct toward their brethren through obedience to Jesus (vs. 5). We could make similar statements concerning 1 Corinthians 15.26–27. The emphasis, however, differs greatly. We must now consider this observation at more length.

THE CHANGING CONCEPT OF "LORDSHIP"

It is interesting that this twofold perspective began just at the point where apocalyptic expectation began to fade, as was probably the

case even in the Jewish Diaspora, and finally disappeared completely
—as in the primarily Gentile communities—to the extent that they
were no longer under the influence of Paul or other teachers strongly
influenced by Jewish hopes. Naturally the various movements run
intersecting and parallel courses. But one can say that by and large in
the Jewish Diaspora the notion of the people of God going forward
under the leadership of its Lord continued to play a significant role,
while in primarily Gentile communities an individualistic hope for
eternal life probably dominated.

The former notion can be seen clearly in Romans 1.3–4. Here Paul
cites a formula that he found ready to hand and was probably
familiar to the Roman community:[11] ["Jesus Christ], on the human
level . . . born of David's stock, but on the level of the spirit—the
Holy Spirit— . . . declared Son of God by a mighty act in that he
rose from the dead." This summary of the faith obviously came into
being in a community for which Jesus' Davidic descent was crucial.
This means a community for which the history of God's relationship
with Israel was crucial. In this history, the prophecy of Nathan (2
Sam. 7.12–13) plays an important role: Nathan had promised David
that God would be father to David's successor, that this successor
would be God's son, and that his throne would endure forever. This
was at first interpreted to mean that the chain of successors to David's
throne would not be broken but would endure forever under God's
special protection. Soon, however, the promise was interpreted as
referring to the son of David who would come at the end of time, since
the chain of successors to David and indeed the very kingship over
Israel had been ended by the destruction of Jerusalem and the Babylonian exile. The important role played by this expectation can be
observed in Jewish documents of the period just before Jesus. The
community that formulated Romans 1.3–4 knows that the history of

---

[11] Nowhere else does Paul speak of Jesus' being born as a descendant of David;
on the other hand, he would not fail to mention Jesus' death in such a context if
he were formulating the material himself. Wherever he links "on the human level"
with a verb or contrasts it to "on the level of the spirit", it always has a negative
implication (*pace* Wengst, *op. cit.*, pp. 105–6). Furthermore, the Greek expression
"Spirit of Holiness" used in verse 4 is a Jewish phrase; elsewhere Paul refers directly
to the "Holy Spirit". The word "declared" derives from the confessional language
of the community (cf. Acts 10.42; 17.31, where the same Greek root is used), not
from Paul's language. This does not mean, of course, that Paul disagreed with the
essential content; cf. P. Stuhlmacher, "Theologische Probleme des Römerbrief-
präskripts", *Ev Th* XXVII (1967), esp. pp. 381ff.

God's relationship with Israel has found its fulfillment in Jesus. He is the promised son of David.

But where was his eternal kingdom as Son of God? The community replied that it was to be found in the rule of the exalted Lord over his people. At Easter he was appointed to his new position as Son of God. All the emphasis is on this point. There is no mention of the eternal nature of Jesus Christ as true man and true God nor even of his divine sonship for all eternity. As in the Old Testament, "Son of God" is merely a term that designates his functions as Lord (Ps. 2.7). Apocalyptic conceptions are not discarded: the discussion still concerns the acts of God, not the eternal nature of Jesus—and these acts are associated with the Easter event. But there is no longer any reference to a future act of God that will inaugurate the eschaton. Of course we cannot be sure that such a statement was not originally present.[12] However that may be, the quotation shows how the major emphasis can be placed on the present lordship of the exalted Christ precisely where one would expect it as the fulfillment of God's relationship with David, that is, within the schema of the Jewish concept of the Messiah and Jewish eschatology.

Even here, however, the influence of Jewish apocalyptic thought makes itself felt. It is possible to make the lordship of the exalted Christ the focus of attention; but the glorification of Jesus as "Son of God" refers to his present acts, not to his eternal immutable nature, and furthermore his complete lordship over all dominions and powers is conceived, explicitly or implicitly, as lying in the future. Where apocalyptic notions were explicitly retained, as in 1 Corinthians 15.24–27, this future reference could be emphasized by citing Psalms 110.1b ("till I make your enemies your footstool"). It could also remain implicit, with the focus only on Psalm 110.1a ("The LORD says to my lord: 'Sit at my right hand'"), as Romans 8.34, for example, presupposes. It could also be linked with expectation of the Davidic Messiah and his eternal kingdom, as happened in Romans 1.3–4. In this case, the basic emphasis rests on Jesus' lordship over the people of God, his community; but the Lord of the disciples is naturally Lord also of all dominions and powers, against which he protects

---

[12] It is possible to read 1 Thessalonians 1.10 as suggesting a connection between the events of Easter and Judgment Day in the thought of the Christian community. Paul may have omitted any reference to Judgment Day in our passage because he does not address himself to this theme until Romans 8.17ff. and 11.11ff. (cf. the advance references in 2.5–6 and 5.10).

his band of followers. The members of this community share a faith
whose structure does not differ much from the structure of the faith
shared by those who followed Jesus during his earthly life: day by day
he acts towards them as Lord. Herein the kingdom of God becomes
present reality, although it is not forgotten that the kingdom still
suffers attack and persecution, and that the hostile powers will not be
subject to God until the consummation of the world.

The term for "Lord" was no longer *mare*, as in the Aramaic-
speaking community, but *kyrios*.[13] In the Greek Bible, this word was
no longer distinct from *adonai*, the term used for God in the Old
Testament and in Jewish worship. In other words, unlike *mare*, it was
also a title for God,[14] with the result that Old Testament passages that
mentioned God could be applied directly to Jesus by the Greek-
speaking community. It was likewise an important influence that the
Greek mystery cults worshipped their various *kyrioi*, such as Osiris and
Attis, who, as "lords" of the universe, would deliver and protect their
adherents from the snares of every conceivable dominion and power.
Both influences set their stamp on the image of the exalted "Lord"
Jesus. The Old Testament passages affected primarily the Christian
communities that had been gathered from former Jews and "God
fearers" of the Diaspora; the pagan cults affected primarily those who
came from their milieu. What was the result of these changes?

The adoption of Old Testament passages that mentioned the Lord
of heaven and earth, not to mention the competition of pagan "lords"
who had subjected all the dominions and powers of the cosmos, led
the Christian community increasingly to look upon Jesus as Lord of
the universe. Thus his exaltation came to signify more than a pre-
requisite for his future position as judge or his present requirement of
obedience; it became the focal point of faith. Jesus was no longer
quite so plainly the person in whom God spoke to the disciples, became reality in their midst, and day by day required and gave them
their obedience. He became "cosmocrator", Lord of the universe,

---

[13] Contrary to what has been said above (pp. 66f.), many scholars think that
the appellation "Lord" for Jesus was adopted directly from the Greek *kyrios*-cults,
and was only later associated with the notion of the *mare*. Our discussion presupposes tne reverse course of events.

[14] Whether the word *kyrios* was already used in the Greek Old Testament at this
date is still unsettled. But even if the text in fact contained the four Hebrew letters
of the Old Testament name of God, which was never pronounced, the reader would
have to say *kyrios*, just as the reader of the Hebrew text said *adonai*.

sitting "at the right hand of God" and sharing in God's rule over the world. Thus faith discovered a completely new dimension. The question is not whether this confession of Jesus as Lord of the universe is correct—which it certainly is—but how it is applied and how it is reconciled with the sober fact that other powers than God rule the real world and necessitate the efforts of Jesus' disciples.

THE LORD OF THE UNIVERSE

The statements concerning the exalted Lord who rules the universe occur primarily in the hymns sung by the Greek-speaking community. We have already mentioned Philippians 2.9–11. Here an Old Testament statement concerning God is transferred to Christ the "Lord" to whom every knee bows—of those in heaven, on earth, and in the depths: and whom every tongue confesses. Paul understood the hymn as a confession of Jesus' future victory, telling how he would one day appear on earth at the eschaton. Primarily through his argument in Philippians 2.1–5, he has made the whole hymn serve his summons to the community, in which he calls on every member to be subject to his brother and look after his interests. He therefore attached central importance to the description of the obedience of Christ, who humbled himself to death on the cross, and still interpreted the exaltation of Christ as glorifying God, as the last words show.

We cannot be certain how the community that sang the hymn even before Paul understood it. Perhaps it expressly interpreted the cosmic worship of Christ on the part of all the powers as something already taking place. In any case, it would not have been difficult to sing away all the counter-arguments, enthusiastically experiencing in advance what will one day come to pass. This is certainly the case in 1 Peter 3.22, which may also be based on a hymn of some kind. According to this passage, the exaltation of Jesus to the right hand of God means the subjection of the angels, dominions, and powers. The same holds true for Colossians 2.14–15, with its image of the triumphant heavenward procession of the victorious Christ leading his enemies captive. The hymn in 1 Timothy 3.16[15] also sings of the victory procession of the risen Christ; and the third line, "seen by angels", probably describes the same event as Colossians 2.14–15, i.e., the appearance of the ascending conqueror to all the powers, who may or must now worship him. The second stanza of the hymn in Colossians 1.15–20

[15] Cf. below, pp. 79f.

is also noteworthy,[16] although it contains material added by the author of the Letter and has been reinterpreted by the remarks that follow. Here, too, the original theme was simply the resurrection of Jesus, the purpose of which was "to reconcile the whole universe to him". The qualifying phrase "to him" still retains the eschatological perspective, but the theme is a reconciliation that embraces the entire cosmos, not just mankind. In this form, the idea is unique in the New Testament, but it is comprehensible against the background of the passages that speak of the Lord of the universe.

But what do all these passages really mean? As long as it is the singing community that formulates these statements, they constitute a confession focusing on Jesus himself. The praises sung in a hymn can easily anticipate what faith alone can see. When the singer confesses Christ, he can tell him that faith acknowledges him to be Lord of all the universe. For Jesus in fact desires the universe, and includes the whole world in what he does; God's love embraces the whole world, and therefore Jesus' life and death and resurrection have effected a fundamental change in the world and all it contains. But this truth is falsified as soon as it is turned into a general proposition that would still obtain apart from the act of praise, of such a nature that it could simply be accepted and transmitted to others. We must discuss this point now in more detail.

We find an extreme hellenization of this attitude among the Corinthians. Of course we can reconstruct their position only from Paul's

[16] What belongs to the original hymn and what to the author's interpretation is still a matter of dispute. It is clear that the hymn pictured Christ as the head with the universe as the body, while the author interprets the body of Christ as the church, following Romans 12.3ff.; 1 Corinthians 12.12, 27; Ephesians 1.23; 4.12–16. In the second strophe, the reference to the cross is probably the major interpolation by the author. The original form of the hymn was most likely something along these lines:

He is the image of the invisible God, born before all created things;
    for in him everything in heaven and on earth was created;
    the whole universe has been created through and for him.
And he exists before everything,
    and all things are held together in him,
    and it is he who is head of the body.
He is the origin, the first to return from the dead;
    for in him the fullness chose to dwell,
    through him to reconcile the whole universe to himself.

For a more detailed discussion, see E. Schweizer, "Kol 1.15–20", in *Vorarbeiten zum Evangelisch-Katholischen Kommentar*, I (1969), pp. 7ff.; = *idem, Beiträge*, pp. 113ff.

reply to their questions and from his argument with his opponents. Some points, however, are clear. In particular, the Corinthians no longer have any real future expectation in the sense of a resurrected life to come that is fundamentally distinct from the present (1 Cor. 15.12). Paul probably misunderstood them when he suggested that they no longer thought in terms of eternal life (1 Cor. 15.32).[17] In their case, the line of development observed in the New Testament hymns has, as it were, come full circle: the anticipation of the eschatological consummation in the hymn of faith has become for them a present reality, sacramentally mediated, albeit restricted to the reborn soul. Decades later, in like manner, the false teachers against whom the Second Epistle to Timothy is directed preach that the resurrection has already taken place (2 Tim. 2.18). This is in complete accord with Greek thought, which has no place for any end of time. For the Corinthians, therefore, the Kyrios Jesus was very similar to the lords of the pagan cults. He had already overcome all powers and dominions. Through baptism and the Lord's Supper the believer is sacramentally united with Jesus (1 Cor. 10.1–13; 15.29), entering thereby upon a new and eternal life that lives in the reborn soul of man, while the body is considered nothing more than a prison. The corporeality of apocalyptic Jewish thought was incomprehensible to them. For this very reason, forsaking all the corporeal realities of the present world, they could retreat into their reborn, divine, and immortal souls.

This can be observed, first of all, in the restriction of their interest to the gifts of the Spirit that manifested miraculous, supernatural, heavenly powers—above all, glossolalia[18]—coupled with complete indifference to such things as care for the physical welfare of the poor and sick or the necessary task of administration.[19] In writing to them, therefore, Paul has to stress the fact that the Corinthians knew such "miraculous" phenomena even in their pagan past (1 Cor. 12.2), and that the only criterion of the true gift of the Spirit is whether it leads to acknowledgment of Jesus as Lord and the edification of the community (12.3, 7; 14.4ff.). In the second place, retreat into the reborn soul leads to disdain for everything corporeal. This can be put into practice in two ways: one can deliberately subdue the body by means

---

[17] Cf. verse 29; for a different view see J. H. Schütz, "Apostolic Authority and the Control of Tradition: I Cor. XV", *NTS* XV (1968/69), pp. 447–8.

[18] Cf. p. 60, n. 15.

[19] Paul mentions these in 1 Corinthians 12.28, whereas he naturally omits them in 12.29–30, where he recounts the gifts desired by the Corinthians.

of asceticism, by refusing to have sexual intercourse within marriage for example (1 Cor. 7.1ff.); on the other hand, one can be indifferent to everything pertaining to the body, declaring, for example, that intercourse with a prostitute is permitted (1 Cor. 6.12ff.). Finally, such an attitude implies indifference towards one's neighbor with his questions and needs.

Paul illustrates this attitude of the Corinthians, for example, by citing the question of food offered to idols: theologically, there is nothing wrong with eating such food with a clear conscience; in certain cases however, one must refrain out of consideration for the conscience of another (1 Cor. 8.1ff.; 10.23ff.). The contrast is clearest, however, with respect to the Eucharist (1 Cor. 11.17–34). The Corinthians have been anticipating the meal associated with the sacrament precisely because, in their opinion, only the sacrament itself was important. Paul has to remind them that a sacrament which refuses to take seriously table fellowship with the very weakest and poorest is no longer the Supper of the Lord. He therefore recalls emphatically the example of Israel, which had enjoyed a kind of baptism and spiritual banquet in the desert, but was still rejected by God (1 Cor. 10.1–10). Writing to the Corinthians, he can, like them, refer to the Lord's Supper as communion with the body and blood of the Lord, but only in the sense that the body and blood of the Lord, i.e., his death on our behalf, unites the community so completely that no one can neglect or despise his neighbor (1 Cor. 10.16–17).[20]

By interpreting a hymn that sings of the heavenly worship of Christ by all the angels and dominions so that it refers to humble service of one's brethren in the community, by recalling ascetic enthusiasm or indifference to everything earthly from the heights of heaven to the difficulties of the weak brother, and by seeking to transform sacramental assurance into a life under the blessing and authority of the Lord of the sacrament, Paul reasserted the basic meaning of discipleship against the enthusiasts in Corinth and elsewhere. To follow Jesus as a disciple is to be moving towards a goal, not the state of having arrived there. The lordship of Jesus is therefore a power that lays claim to the corporeal nature of his disciples; it is not a guarantee of eternal bliss, but an assurance that evokes obedience. To share the road taken by this Lord is therefore to be newly placed in the service of men in need; it is not sacramental security. Paul's reference to the Old Testament at this point (1 Cor. 10.1ff.) is absolutely justified.

[20] Cf. below, pp. 115–22.

THE LORD OF THE UNIVERSE IN THE UNIVERSAL MESSAGE OF HIS COMMUNITY

The author of Colossians also undertakes a similar correction in the hymn he borrowed.[21] He, too, transforms the original image of Christ as head of the cosmos, making him instead head of the community, adding the reference to the cross of Jesus, and speaking plainly of the reconciliation of the community, not of the universe, as well as of the community's faith, which must continually be strengthened (Col. 1.18a, 20b, 21–23). In like fashion, he speaks of battle with the powers of the world and their subjugation, not of their reconciliation (2.15). Above all, the life of faith is for him still hidden in temptation, not a matter of visible salvation; only at the Parousia will it be revealed as what it already is in essence (3.1–4). In Colossians, however, we find a completely different understanding of the "Lord of the Universe". He is now the Lord who fills the world through the missionary work of the disciples. This appears most strikingly in 1.23, where, following the enthusiastic cosmic language of the hymn, there appears the sonorous reference to "the whole creation under heaven"; now, however, we read that the Lord fills this creation not as a mysterious force of nature inherent in all the forces of the cosmos, but rather in the preaching of his disciples.

This passage draws on an understanding of the exalted Jesus that played an important role in many portions of the Hellenistic community. Even Jesus himself did not look on the boundaries of Israel as insurmountable barriers to his message. His freedom with regard to the Mosaic Law implied a similar freedom for those that did not follow this Law. Signs of this attitude include such figures as the centurion of Capernaum (Matt. 8.5–15) and the Syrophoenician woman (Mark 7.24–30), but above all such sayings as Matthew 8.11–12 (cf. Luke 13.28–29): "I tell you, many will come from east and west and sit at table with Abraham, Isaac, and Jacob in the kingdom of heaven, while the sons of the kingdom will be thrown into the outer darkness." Even the Palestinian community would hardly have been closed to a universalism seeking to embrace the entire world, such as had been a living force in Israel since Deutero-Isaiah (Isa. 40ff.).[22]

---

[21] Cf. above, p. 73f. The author in question may not be Paul himself, but one of his disciples (cf. below, p. 172f.).

[22] Cf. above, pp. 42f.

But Jesus, like this earliest community, pictured the expected influx of the Gentiles in the imagery of Isaiah 2.2ff.; 66.19ff.; that is, they were expected to pour into Zion and join themselves to Israel. This accounts for the struggle, recorded in Galatians 2.1ff.; Acts 10.1ff.; 11.1ff.; 15.1ff., over whether the pagans entering the community must first become Israelites through circumcision and acceptance of all the commandments, or whether their faith in Jesus had already made them incorporate in the people of God. We shall later examine the theological importance of this question.[23] Here we need only note that Paul's defence of the latter position, which later, at the so-called Apostolic Council in Jerusalem, was successful and led to the recognition of his missionary work on the part of the Jerusalem community (Gal. 2.1–10; Acts 15), opened the doors to worldwide proclamation of the Gospel. One must of course free oneself from the picture given by Acts and the Epistles of Timothy and Titus, which present Paul as a solitary genius with new and progressive insights not yet seen by anyone else, who effected the breakthrough. In fact, of course, the Christian community at Rome had been founded by unknown missionaries long before Paul came in contact with it. The communities in Galilee, Samaria, and Syria were founded before Paul was summoned thither by Barnabas; and even in Ephesus there seems to have been a Christian community before Paul began his extensive ministry there (Acts 18.24ff.). But none of this alters the fact that Paul made the decisive theological breakthrough. What, historically speaking, was already taking place before him and around him and could no longer be held back, Paul grasped as a theological problem and pressed to its correct conclusion.

In Paul we can still sense strongly the theological importance of this decision. He describes his call in the words of the call of Jeremiah (Jer. 1.5; Gal. 1.15), understands his mission as a parallel to the mission of the prophets (Rom. 1.2, 5), and interprets the passages from Deutero-Isaiah (except for the section dealing with the Suffering Servant in chapter 53) as referring to his own missionary work among the Gentiles.[24] Thus he sees in the fact of the worldwide proclamation of the Gospel a fulfillment of Old Testament prophecies concerning the eschaton.[25] But there is still life in the Old Testament images of

[23] Cf. below, pp. 102–6.

[24] T. Holtz, "Zum Selbstverständnis des Apostels Paulus", *TLZ* XCI (1966), pp. 321–30.

[25] Cf. below, pp. 98f.

those chosen by God, whom he sends to the nations, that they may "declare [his] glory among the nations and bring all your brethren from all the nations as an offering to Yahweh" (Isa. 66.19–20), which we find in Romans 15.16.[26] For Paul, therefore, the Gospel preached to the Gentiles is in all essentials identical with what had already been proclaimed to Israel (Rom. 1.2).

In the period that followed, as the novelty of the Gospel preached to all nations became clearer, a different thought-pattern came to the fore. It, too, is an outgrowth of Jewish apocalypticism, but derives from circles more interested in eschatological knowledge of the hidden God than in the course of events at the end. Like the Qumran community by the Dead Sea, they are convinced that the mystery of God, hidden for centuries, has now been revealed to them, and that they are therefore living in the eschatological age. The closest approach to this notion in the New Testament is probably Mark 4.10–12, a peculiar interpolation that Mark presumably borrowed from tradition.[27] According to this passage, the secret of the kingdom of God is given to the disciples, but remains hidden from everyone else. A different note is struck, however, by all the passages in which the schema (called the "revelation schema") is fully developed: there the revelation of this secret, hidden for ages but now revealed, is linked explicitly with the preaching to the nations, which obliterates all distinctions between "believers" and "pagans".

We find this schema especially well developed in an appendix to Paul's Letter to the Romans, whose style differs markedly from that of Paul: ". . . the revelation of the mystery which was kept secret for long ages but is now disclosed, and through the prophetic writings is made known to all nations, according to the command of the eternal God, to bring about obedience to the faith" (Rom. 16.25–26). Similar statements occur, however, in Colossians 1.25ff. and Ephesians 3.3ff. But the noblest monument to this line of thought is the short hymn in 1 Timothy 3.16.[28] This passage, a single rhythmical unit, is introduced expressly as a universally accepted confession of the church. Six parallel lines, each containing a passive verb in the same

[26] The "offering of the Gentiles" can hardly refer to the money being collected from them by Paul (cf. Isa. 56.7; 60.11); it refers to the Gentiles themselves, who, having come to faith, represent a thank-offering presented to God.

[27] For a discussion of the passage, cf. E. Schweizer, *Good News according to Mark*, pp. 91ff.

[28] Cf. below, pp. 171–6; also above, p. 73f.

tense and a phrase indicating place, describe the victory procession of the risen Christ:

> [29][Who] was manifested in the flesh,
>   vindicated in the Spirit,
>   seen by angels,
> preached among the nations,
>   believed on in the world,
>   taken up in glory.

The structure is essentially that of an enthusiastic hymn which merely exults in Jesus' exaltation over all the powers of the universe. Only the first line, which can be easily misconstrued,[30] refers to Jesus' incarnation; lines 2–6 go on at once to Jesus' Easter victory, his "vindication" before the heavenly forum, and his triumphal procession up to heaven.[31] But between the line that speaks of Christ's appearance to the angels and the last line, which tells of his entrance into heaven, two lines are inserted that describe the victory procession of the exalted Lord through the nations of the earth. The hymn, therefore, no longer merely depicts an event that takes place in heaven, which need only be acknowledged as a matter of information. This victory procession involves the community, through the "proclamation" of the gospel and the response of "belief". Of course the hymn does not go on to explain how the life and death of the earthly Jesus, which these texts either omit entirely or touch on only in passing, are connected with this universal proclamation of the gospel. The inner unity of Jesus' cross and resurrection, which was to become so central to Paul's thought,[32] has not yet been perceived, much less elucidated theologically. We have therefore still not escaped the danger that an exalted Lord might suddenly spring from the concrete Jesus, with his particular characteristics, gradually become more and more nebulous, and finally end up as a mere symbol for the universality of the Christian faith, or, at best, for a timeless divine grace.

---

[29] A single tiny stroke can change the Greek *OC* (= "who") into *ΘC*, the abbreviation for "God", the actual reading of later manuscripts which were followed by the translators of the Authorized Version. This erroneous reading, which refers to Jesus expressly as "God", could even have come about purely mechanically, as the result of a defect in the paper or a smudge of ink.

[30] Cf. below, pp. 88f.   [31] Cf. Colossians 2.15, discussed above, p. 77.

[32] Cf. below, pp. 121f.

THE HEAVENLY SON OF GOD

The hymn cited by Paul in Philippians 2.6–11, which we shall discuss at the end of this chapter, already links the ascent of the Lord with his descent, that is, associates Jesus' exaltation at Easter with the condescension of him who lived with God before his life on earth. This conception probably also lies in the background of the first two lines of the hymn in 1 Timothy 3.16. There was no mention of this idea in the description of Jesus' exaltation in Romans 1.3–4. In fact, the strong emphasis on Jesus' Davidic descent makes such a conception impossible. Palestinian Judaism could conceive of a righteous man like Enoch or a prophet like Elijah being transported to the presence of God and dwelling in heavenly glory, only to return to earth shortly before the end to recall the people to their God. Here, however, we read of one who was equal to God (Phil. 2.6), and other passages (1 Cor. 8.6 etc.) presuppose that he already dwelt with God at the time of creation. Such statements are first found in the community that developed among Greek-speaking Jews.

What is the background of these statements? With several variants, we read in Galatians 4.4–5; Romans 8.3–4; John 3.16, 17; and 1 John 4.9, "[God] sent his only Son [to save the world]". The verb "sent" can be expressed in various ways; the formulation of God's purpose, the salvation of the world, is also variable. Always, however, "God" is the subject, not, say, the "Father" or "the Lord"; the object always "his Son", not "our Lord", "The Messiah", "the Lord Jesus", or "Jesus".[33] This shows that even before Paul this statement had received a fixed form in the usage of the community, because it was obviously used often in the liturgy or in catechesis.

But what does this expression mean? The Old Testament speaks of the sending of prophets and angels; the New Testament can speak in the same terms and have a parallel notion of the sending of Jesus. But never does the term "son" occur in the context of such a sending. This is only to be expected, because according to the Old Testament way of thinking, which is shared by the confession in Romans 1.3–4,[34] "Son of God" is a functional concept, i.e., it refers to one who carries out the function of God's Son, by exercising sovereignty over God's people. He who is sent by God is therefore not God's Son until he

[33] In John 3.16–17 (not in the Nestle edition), many manuscripts read "his Son" instead of simply "the Son"; the former reading is presumably correct.
[34] Cf. above, pp. 7of.

carries out the purpose for which he is sent; his sending is an appoin‑
ment to sonship. Greek-speaking Judaism, especially in Alexandri
spoke quite differently of the Son of God. There the concept of Gc
was so exalted that he tended to vanish more and more into the di
tance. If one wanted to speak of God's action here on earth, one dare
speak only of God's wisdom, his word, or his power. These attribut
tended to lead increasingly separate existences as independent divir
entities. Thus God's wisdom, through which he had created the worl
and continued to rule it, was referred to as God's daughter. But tl
"logos", God's "word" (or, better, his "spiritual power"), could als
be called God's Son. Of course this logos has been God's Son for a
eternity, or at least since the creation of the world. Thus wisdom ca
be expressly said to "sit beside" God on his throne—the same idea ;
that expressed by the New Testament notion of "sitting at the rigl
hand of God". Here, in contemporary Judaism, we find talk of th
"sending" of the preexistent Son of God (preexistent in the sens
that he lived with God as God's Son even before he was sent).[35] B
we also find a similar schema in the contemporary Greek worl
presumably also due to Egyptian influence: the Logos, the Son of th
gods, is sent to deliver mankind.[36]

These are the roots of the affirmation made by the pre-Paulin
community, "[God] sent his Son [to save the world]". Only amon
Greek-speaking Jews outside Palestine do we find parallels to th
formula. There we also find parallels to the view that only the So
can make the faithful into (adopted) sons of God, as Paul also state
in Galatians 4.4–6 and Romans 8.14–17 (read in conjunction wit
8.3–4). Conversely, this statement is found only in Paul and Joh
among the New Testament writers, that is, in the two writers wh
mention Christ's existence in heaven before his birth.[37] But it is eve

---

[35] Cf. Philo, *De agricultura*, li; also E. Schweizer, "Gottessohn", in C. Wester
mann, ed., *Theologie*, pp. 67–77. For the citations from Philo and the other writing
discussed see *idem*, "Zum religionsgeschichtlichen Hintergrund der 'Sendung
formel' Gal. 4,4f; Röm. 8,3f; Joh 3,16f; 1 Joh 4,9", *ZNW* LVII (1966), 199f
(= his *Beiträge*, pp. 83ff.).

[36] This notion is found in a North African contemporary of Paul, albeit as
rationalistic explanation of the ancient myths telling how Hermes, the messenge
of the gods, was born to Zeus and Maia; the myth refers, he says, to the Logos, i.e.
the spiritual and intellectual power of man, which grows out of theory and investiga
tion. Plutarch, writing around the end of the first century of our era, reports
similar belief among the Egyptians.

[37] Elsewhere in the New Testament, the preexistence of Christ is mentioned onl
in Hebrews.

ssible to show that almost all the passages in which Paul speaks of
e preexistent Son, who dwells with God from all eternity, have
rallels among the Greek-speaking Jews of the Egyptian diaspora;
ese parallels speak of the Wisdom or Logos of God. In 1 Corinthi-
s 8.6, we read that all things were created "through" the "Lord"
sus, an exact parallel to similar statements concerning Wisdom.[38]
1 Corinthians 10.4, Paul explains that the rock from which Israel
ank in the desert was the preexistent Christ, while Philo, a Greek-
eaking contemporary of Jesus who lived in Alexandria, had said
e same thing about God's Wisdom. Romans 10.6–7 speaks of him
10 went down to the abyss and up to heaven, but is nevertheless
ar in the word (Greek: *logos*); the same Old Testament affirmation
as made concerning Wisdom in Baruch 3.29–30. Finally, the crucial
itement that God sent his Son and his Spirit (Gal.4.4–6) has a
rallel in a saying concerning Wisdom (Wisd.9.10, 17).[39] John
1–18 makes it quite clear that the coming of Jesus is described in the
ords applied to the Logos by diaspora Judaism, and most likely
so by heretical groups whose thought bore a more markedly mytho-
gical stamp. It is therefore an indisputable fact that statements of
aspora Judaism concerning Wisdom or the Logos of God furnished
e intellectual schema used by Greek-speaking Jewish Christians to
rmulate their confession of Jesus, the Son of God. Here, therefore,
is no longer Palestinian apocalyptic thought that moulds the com-
unity's affirmations concerning Christ, but the Wisdom thought of
Judaism that is more involved in the Hellenistic world.

When the community was forced to find words to express the sig-
ficance of Jesus for the world, it was naturally compelled to use the
rms and images that were meaningful and comprehensible in their
ontemporary environment. In Palestine, therefore, they had to draw
oon the expectation of the eschatological Son of David, whose father
ould be God himself. What took place at Easter was the official
auguration of God's long-promised Son as regent over God's
ople.[40] It was equally natural that Greek-speaking Jews of the

---

[38] Cf. Proverbs 3.19; 8.22–31; Wisdom 9.1–2, 9. For other quotations, including
rallels to the affirmations discussed below, see E. Schweizer, "Zur Herkunft der
äezistenzvorstellung bei Paulus", in his *Neotestamentica* (Zürich: Zwingli, 1963),
. 105–9.

[39] The verb used for "send", which Paul uses only in Galatians 4.4–6, is the
me, and the parallelism between the sending of the Son and the sending of the
irit or Logos is the same in both passages.

[40] Cf. above, pp. 71f.

Diaspora outside Palestine should have to draw on the concepts th
were familiar to them. If they wanted to say that in Jesus God real
encountered the world, they had to speak of the Logos, the Son of Go
who became flesh in Jesus on behalf of the world. They thus affirm
that God's presence in the world was to be found only in Jesus.

The crucial point, however, is what the community did with t.
traditional concepts. The community reflected in Romans 1.3–4 ha
to relearn its old ideas completely, because the kingdom of Jesus, t.
Son of David, was not a nationalistic kingdom on earth, restricted
Israel, and because Jesus led his followers not to honor and glory b
to obedience and suffering. A similar relearning had to take pla
within the community rooted in diaspora Judaism. Even before Pa
and John, this community had applied to Jesus the notion that G
had sent his Son, the Logos, for the salvation of men. In doing th
however, it had used the old form to state something completely ne
The words no longer refer to something that happened ages ago a
is therefore timelessly true, so that one might equally well say that
takes place afresh in everyone who believes. The words now refer
what took place in the precisely defined years of Jesus' life, death, ar
resurrection, at a very specific place on earth, namely in Palestin
Another observation is even more striking. In all four passages th
speak of God's sending his Son, both in Paul and in John, the stat
ment focuses not on Jesus' incarnation, but on his crucifixion.[41] It
even more striking to note that the sending of the son in the parab
of the vineyard (Mark 12.6), where there is no idea of any pr
existence in heaven, refers clearly to Jesus' death on the cross.[42] Th
means that the affirmation concerning the sending of the Son, wl
had lived with God from all eternity, was not intended to make a
claims about the time between creation and the birth of Jesus or t
time before creation, nor even about his coming from the Father
his birth; it was intended to outline the "dimension" in which o

[41] Galatians 4.4–5 merely takes up the theme of 3.13 and expands on it.
Romans 8.3–4, the judgment against sin "in the flesh of Jesus" takes place at t
crucifixion, as the parallel to Galatians 4.4–5 shows, as well as the phrase "as
sacrifice for sin" (cf. below, p.95, n.13). John 3.16–17 is explained by vss. 14–
whose structure is parallel. 1 John 4.9 is interpreted by verses 10–11 (cf. 3.16 ar
also 1.7; 5.6–7).

[42] The parable can hardly go back to Jesus; it is a product of the Christi
community, in which the allegorical equation of the vineyard owner with God, t
servants with the prophets, and the son with Jesus is already influential. The ima
was probably suggested by such passages as Galatians 4.4–5; John 3.16–17.

ust perceive what took place on the cross. In other words, the com-
unity is seeking to explain that what took place in the death of Jesus
is an event involving God, and that God shared in the Passion of
e Son in a way that had never taken place before on earth.

This circumstance makes it clear how little point there would be
simply juxtaposing all the christological statements of the New
estament: preexistence, incarnation, virgin birth, miracles, pas-
on, death, resurrection, ascension, parousia. One can use the image
an ascension into heaven, for example, to proclaim the beginning
Christ's lordship over all the world; but one cannot turn around
d proclaim an ascension in the spatial sense and at the same time
pend an affirmation concerning Christ's lordship over the world.
is likewise possible, according to the New Testament, to describe
e profound meaning of what took place in Jesus' death by saying
at it is the Son sent by God who died here.[43] It is fitting, therefore,
at what took place in Jesus should have attracted the most diverse
nages and conceptions from the environment of the community.
it this took place in such a way that, while many images were
lopted, others—like those of the mystic absorbed in the deity or the
ity embodied in the sacrament—were rejected. At the same time,
also took place in such a way that the cross and resurrection con-
ituted the real focus, while new images, though they might remind
e community of other events, basically provided a deeper know-
dge of what took place in the cross and resurrection.[44]

THE INCARNATION OF THE PREEXISTENT CHRIST

Without any mention of the Son of God or his being sent, John
1–18 draws on the statements of Hellenistic Judaism concerning the
ogos, and perhaps even in more markedly mythological form, to
escribe Jesus' coming into the world. Here, too, we must distinguish
pre-Johannine Christian hymn[45] from what John used it to express.

[43] The opposite affirmation, namely that death on the cross only marked the
timate depth of the incarnation of the preexistent Christ occurs only in the hymn
ted by Paul in Philippians 2.6–8; cf. below, pp. 87f.

[44] Cf. E. Schweizer, "Ecumenism in the New Testament: The Belief in the Son
God", *Perspective*, IX (1968), pp. 39–59.

[45] This hymn comprised roughly vss. 1–5, 9–12a, 14a, 14d, 16; cf. the biblio-
aphy cited by E. Schweizer, "Aufnahme und Korrektur jüdischer Sophiatheo-
gie im Neuen Testament", in his *Neotestamentica*, pp. 113–14; also C. Demke,
Der sogenannte Logoshymnus im johanneischen Prolog", *ZNW* LVIII (1967),

The interest of the hymn clearly focused on the work of the Logos
the creation of the world and the presence of the Logos in the wor
before the coming of Jesus. In the hymn, Jesus' coming (vs. 14) w
the climax that revealed to all what had always been true, though n
acknowledged by men. Even externally little was said about tl
latter event in comparison to what was said about the Logos befo
his incarnation. What took place in Jesus was, strictly speaking, n
something truly new and different from the presence of the divi
Logos in the world. God's grace was manifested in Jesus in that the
was now revealed what men had previously failed to see. The evang
list borrows the hymn, but following verse 5 inserts at once a restri
tion with respect to the Baptist: he was only a witness of the Light, n
the Light itself. This shows that the evangelist, unlike the hymn that I
borrowed, refers verse 5 to the incarnate Logos, to Jesus.

Here, too, we find the same tendency at work. An affirmation th
had been concerned primarily with the Logos and his work in tl
world is reinterpreted. What had originally been said of the time b
fore Jesus' birth concerning the Logos, who became flesh in Jesus,
now focused entirely on the earthly life of Jesus "in the flesh". On
the first three verses, which speak of the creation, can hardly ref
to the earthly Jesus. What the passage says, therefore, about the li
of Jesus before his earthly ministry, about his "preexistence",
meant only to tell who it is we encounter in Jesus, namely, he who w;
present as the "Word" of God even at creation. This means that i
Jesus it is really God himself who encounters the world. Most impor
ant, however, is the fact that the evangelist borrowed this hymn on
as the prologue to his Gospel. All the emphasis lies on that whic
follows, on what is told of the incarnate Jesus.

In this context we should also mention the first strophe of the hym
cited in Colossians 1.15–20, which had probably long been familiar 1
the community.[46] Its primary point is to maintain the significance (
Jesus for the whole cosmos. In Greek thought, the Logos was tl
divine force permeating all things—men, animals, plants, even tl
stones—in varying degree. Jesus was now understood similarly as God
creative force, maintaining, embracing, and permeating the cosmo;
"All things are held together in him." There is, of course, a difference

---

pp. 45–68. Demke finds the original hymn in verses 1, 3–5, 10–12b, 14, 16; I
assumes, however, that even the original hymn refers to the incarnate Word i
verse 5 (p. 56).

[46] See above, p. 73.

e act of creation is mentioned explicitly. Thus the community
ce again transformed an eternally valid affirmation into a con-
sion of God's creative act, maintaining, albeit in a form open to
any misunderstandings, that even the creation can only be under-
od as God's gracious gift to man, that is, only from the standpoint
Jesus Christ. If it was revealed in Jesus that God is really a God on
e side of man, then Jesus is *ipso facto* Lord of creation, because God
oved himself a God on the side of man by the very fact of his desire
t to remain alone, but to create a world.

The congregation that sings this hymn can follow the first strophe,
ich describes creation as taking place through or in Christ, with
e second, which tells of the reconciliation of the universe accom-
ished through Jesus' resurrection, because in this hymn of praise to
sus they glorify him as Lord of the universe. He is "firstborn of all
eation" by virtue of his participation in the creation, "firstborn of
e dead" by virtue of his resurrection. Both are juxtaposed because
e hymn glorifies Jesus' present position of honor, which is of course
e to the two acts of creation and resurrection, not the temporal
quence of the two acts. For this reason also the original hymn does
t mention the fall of man nor the atonement that took place on the
oss. When the hymn was incorporated into the Letter, however, when
was no longer addressed to Christ but was used for the instruction
the readers, its language had to be interpreted to prevent Christ
m becoming a purely mythical heavenly being, divinely pre-
istent and resurrected in God's glory. Just as the sending of the
n of God was embedded in the message of the cross, and as the
mn to the Logos was made by John (or perhaps by the community
fore him) to refer to the incarnate Jesus, so here the author of Colos-
ans made sure that the hymn he cited would refer to the man Jesus
Nazareth and in particular to his crucifixion.[47]

In the hymn cited by Paul in Philippians 2.6-11, the image influ-
ces the content more markedly. Here the first section (vss. 6-8)
tually speaks of the incarnation of the preexistent Christ, dwelling
God's glory, while the second section goes on to describe his
altation in the resurrection and the worship offered him by all the
wers of the cosmos.[48] This is the only New Testament text to link
e descent and ascent of Christ in this fashion.[49] It is still a matter of

---

[47] Cf. above, pp. 84-6.   [48] Cf. above, pp. 73f.

[49] In 1 Timothy 3.16 (see below, pp. 88f.), there is at most an intimation of the
scent. In Romans 10.6-7, the order is reversed. The situation is similar in John

debate whether this form was influenced by a non-Christian myth o
savior who descends to earth and then ascends once more. There a
no certain pre-Christian parallels. One passage (Eth. Enoch 42.2
states that the Wisdom of God, rejected by men, returns disappoint
to heaven and takes her place among the angels. However the ca
may be, the pre-Pauline hymn gives evidence of a theology in whi
the incarnation as such is even more emphasized than in the p
Johannine Logos hymn. Of course even the pre-Pauline hymn und
stands the incarnation as self-humiliation, including the entire life
Jesus and culminating in his death. Here, too, the statements co
cerning what took place in "heaven" before Jesus' birth and after
resurrection are meant to describe the dimension of depth in whi
the life and death and resurrection of Jesus took place.

Whatever the prototype may have been on which the communi
modeled its statement concerning the descent of him who is equal
God, the actual content of the statement is stamped by the lowline
of the earthly Jesus, by such sayings as that concerning the Son
Man who has nowhere to lay his head (Matt. 8.20), and above all
the fact of his obedient approach to the cross. As soon as the commu
nity took Jesus' coming from God seriously, it was forced to consid
not only the details of his lowly life but the totality of his coming as
expression of such humiliation.

Paul focuses the passage even more narrowly by the interpolati
of "death, even death on a cross", making the whole first half of t
hymn center on the crucifixion of Jesus. Nevertheless, there is stil
perceptible tension between this passage and the rest of Pau
thought. Paul only uses statements about the sending of Jesus fro
heaven to describe what took place on the cross;[51] in the theology
this hymn, however, the incarnation itself is the crucial event, a
even Paul's added reference to the cross of Jesus can only serve in t
context to throw the depth of Jesus' humiliation into sharper reli
Here, then, pre-Pauline thought has not been reinterpreted by Pa
as thoroughly as was the case in Galatians 4.4–5 and Romans 8.3–

Finally, we must discuss the short first line of the hymn in 1 Tim
thy 3.16.[52] It is admittedly so tersely formulated that it can give litt
insight into the theological views of the community that sang t

3.13, although here both are closely related; nowhere else in the Gospel of Joh
however, is the incarnation of the preexistent Christ (1.1–18) linked directly wi
his exaltation (which is here associated intimately with the crucifixion).

[50] Cf. above, p. 18.   [51] Cf. above, pp. 84f.   [52] Cf. above, pp. 79f.

hymn: "He who was manifested in the flesh." This phrase obviously presupposes existence in heaven; the first thing acknowledged as a miracle of God is his appearance in the body. Even though this probably refers to a true incarnation, not merely to the appearance of a divine being in human form, concealing his divinity, as was told of many Greek gods, it is easy to see how the image could easily free itself, as it were, from the Jesus-event and take on independent life, becoming nothing more than a description of the descent and ascent of a heavenly being, finally being reduced to a mere symbol for the eternally valid, ever repeated event of God's sympathy, his grace, his revelation.

That is what happened in Gnosticism. In a certain sense, this reduced the affirmation to the status it had before it was adopted by the community of Jesus. The image served the community to express the dimension of what had taken place in the life and death of Jesus; when it became separated from his life and death, it became once more a mere description of an eternally valid truth. This was the danger of a view of Christ that focused on his exaltation or on the incarnation of him who was already exalted before his earthly ministry, a danger that was already visible at Corinth in the time of Paul, but was not completely clear until, decades later, Gnosticism followed this train of thought to its radical conclusion.

When we review these texts, we see that when the community spoke of the exaltation of Jesus to lordship at the right hand of God, its primary purpose was to maintain what the disciples had learned while following Jesus: life under a Lord who completely determined their path; life that was both God's gift and God's requirement; life in hope of the coming kingdom of God. The tone could vary greatly: there might be a strong expectation of coming fulfillment, so that the lordship of the exalted Christ was understood as an interim pointing forward to the end, as in the thought of apocalyptic groups; or faith could be concentrated entirely on the now of Christ's lordship. This concentration could lead to marked emphasis on the community's obedience, without ignoring the fact that this obedience marked the life of the eschatological people of God and was therefore salvation, God's gracious gift. It could also, however, lead to enthusiastic ignoring of earthly reality when people forgot that, although God's final kingdom determined the present life of the community through hope, it was not yet actually present. This enthusiasm went hand in hand with a misunderstanding of the lordship of Christ, which increasingly ignored the obedience of the community and came more and more to look upon Jesus merely as Lord over all powers, who guarantees eternal life to all who believe in him. The strong impression made on the community by the Gentile mission, especially that of Paul, made it possible to understand the Lord of the universe primarily as one who claims all the nations as his own, advancing through the world in the figure of his messengers. Where salvation was seen primarily as the progress of this world-wide proclamation of the gospel, one could sing the glories of Jesus' kingdom; what was celebrated was in fact visible to all. But one could not do so without being reminded of one's obligation to further this proclamation. When Jesus' exaltation was linked with the incarnation of the heavenly Son of God, or when the incarnation alone stood at the center of the community's confession, the primary purpose was definition of the "dimension" in which the Christ-event took place: it was really God himself who was the "heaven" that came to earth in Jesus. This was the experience of the first disciples when Jesus called them to discipleship and they realized it was the summons of God himself breaking into their lives. Here, too, there was an imminent danger that all interest would be concentrated on the divine Logos who was already working as a creative force and was to be found throughout the earth even before the incarnation.

Essential as the affirmation was that was contained in this form of Christological confession, it could not suffice by itself. None of the confessional formulas or hymns typical of this section originally contained any reference to the cross of Jesus; in them, in fact, the earthly Jesus plays at most a peripheral role. Of course the community repeatedly added this reference to the cross of Jesus,[53] but this very fact shows that the crucifixion did not really fit into this type of thought. The significance of the cross will be our next topic.

[53] Cf. above, pp. 87f.

V

JESUS, CRUCIFIED FOR THE WORLD

When the risen Christ appeared to his disciples, they took it as a sign that God had been with Jesus, even and especially in his failure. It was indeed God's chosen one whom they had followed, and whom they would now follow once more in his resurrection. If so, however, the cross must have been according to God's plan and will. Of course it is most unlikely that the Jerusalem community reflected consciously on this point at the very outset. Everything we hear concerning the expectation of Jesus' return, the exultation of table fellowship, the experience of the power of the risen Christ in exorcisms and miracles suggests that at first Easter overshadowed everything else, and that the cross was understood basically as a passage to Jesus' exaltation at Easter.[1] Of course the community believed that it was also according to God's will (Acts 2.23, etc.) that the Messiah should suffer according to the Scriptures (Mark 8.31; Luke 24.26; John 3.14; etc.). At first, however, the bare statement sufficed without detailed mention of the Scriptural passages that spoke of the Messiah's suffering, and also without any theological explanation why this suffering must take place. Initially, therefore, the "Scriptures" are mentioned, but no specific passages (1 Cor. 15.3–4). From the very beginning, however, the image of the righteous sufferer, at least in general outline, stood in the background. It had probably played an important role in Jesus' own thought,[2] and it gradually impressed itself more and more on the mind of the community.

[1] This state of affairs may still be implied in Matthew 27.52–53, where eschatological events, including the resurrection of the dead, begin at the time of Jesus' death. Cf. above, p. 53.

[2] Cf. above, p. 21.

Since the time of the Babylonian exile (587–38 BC), the idea of the suffering of Israel was never allowed to rest. It was always considered characteristic of the life of the righteous man. It is the very men called by God, the prophets and those who obey him, who are led into suffering. The Psalms in particular tell of this suffering. According to Isaiah 53, finally, the service offered by the Servant of God reaches its fulfillment in innocent suffering. The Passion narrative, which must have been produced quite early by the community, is full of reminiscences of the Psalms depicting suffering, though these Psalms are not explicitly mentioned in the earliest stage of the narrative. This shows that the community was not trying to explain away the scandal of Jesus' suffering or prove Jesus' divine majesty when they cited the Old Testament prophecies. The community as a matter of course looked on Jesus as the consummator of the way of Israel in the light of all the suffering undergone by the righteous of Israel. Isaiah 53 was not yet incorporated into the Passion narrative;[3] in other words, the uniqueness of this suffering in contrast to all suffering that has gone before is not really emphasized. Its uniqueness lies instead in its being "eschatological", a suffering that fulfills all previous suffering. This is understandable, if Jesus himself did not concentrate on the figure of the Servant of God, messianically interpreted, but on the suffering of the righteous man, which is linked with the exaltation of the Son of Man. Just as Enoch[4] and Elijah (Mark 9.12–13), the typical righteous men of the Old Testament, had to suffer and were then exalted to the presence of God, so too is the fate of the Son of Man. In this sense, Jesus' suffering was probably looked upon as necessary in the earliest community: this was the path to his exaltation, ordained by God.

Of course, even at this early stage the suffering was on behalf of the "many". Jesus held unwaveringly to his faith in God and could not be forced to change his course; this tenacity led to his death. But his tenacity was on behalf of his disciples and all those who would follow after him. This realization led to the adoption of Isaiah 53 in various formulations, undoubtedly still in the Palestinian community. According to Mark 14.24, Jesus at the Last Supper says of the

[3] Luke 22.37 is a late discovery, and refers to a peripheral point; furthermore, Isaiah 53 was frequently interpreted collectively as referring to all the righteous of Israel. Wisdom 2—5 may even have come into being as parenetic elaboration of Isaiah 53.

[4] Cf. above, p. 21.

cup: "This is my blood of the covenant, which is poured out for many." Of course Jesus himself can hardly have made this statement, since Paul records a different tradition concerning the words about fifteen years earlier: "This cup is the new covenant in my blood."[5] In any case, the form in Mark, which has noticeable traces of Aramaic usage, goes back to an early period in the history of the Christian community. In it Jesus' death is clearly looked upon as something suffered for and on behalf of others. Isaiah 53 probably furnished the model for this formulation. The same applies to Romans 4.25, a formulaic phrase that Paul probably borrowed from the language of the community: ". . . who was put to death for our trespasses and raised for our justification." The same, finally, is probably also true of Mark 10.45, another saying that can hardly go back to Jesus himself.[6] In all these cases, Jesus' suffering is understood as being vicarious, borne on behalf of "many".[7] Mark 10.45 describes it more precisely as a "ransom" that makes others free. The conception that the suffering of an innocent man benefits others was widespread;[8] even today members of other cultures take it as a natural assumption in their thought.

How central this idea of vicarious suffering was is shown by the confession cited by Paul in 1 Corinthians 15.3–5. Since Paul himself "borrowed" it, it certainly goes back to the community at Antioch,

---

[5] Since this form is not parallel to the words concerning the bread and avoids the notion of drinking blood, which would have been unthinkable to a Jew, it is probably much closer to what Jesus actually said. It is a frequently observed principle that phrases used together repeatedly in the liturgy are assimilated to each other. Cf. E. Schweizer, "Abendmahl", in *Theologie für Nichttheologen* (Stuttgart: Kreuz, 1966), pp. 17ff., reprinted in C. Westermann, ed., *Theologie*, pp. 123ff.

[6] Luke 22.24–27 contains another version of Mark 10.43–45, in which there is no reference to any "ransom". Since Jesus nowhere else refers to the saving significance of his death in this sense, the statement was probably added by the community to interpret Jesus' death. The expression "ransom" is of Greek origin, but could be a free rendering of the original text of Isaiah 53. It is therefore no longer possible to determine whether the saying came into being in the Aramaic or the Greek-speaking community.

[7] In Hebrew and Aramaic, this word simply refers to a total collection of individuals, so that it could almost be translated "all".

[8] Cf. 2 Maccabees 7.37–38; 4 Maccabees 1.11; 17.20ff. Of course these passages already point to Greek-speaking Judaism, so that it remains uncertain how early we should date such formulations as "on behalf of many". For a further discussion, see E. Schweizer, *Erniedrigung und Erhöhung*, pp. 2–3.

and probably, at least in substance, to the Jerusalem community.[9]

It reads:

> Christ died for our sins, in accordance with the scriptures;
> he was buried
> he was raised on the third day, in accordance with the scriptures;
> he appeared to Cephas, then to the twelve.

Like the formula quoted in Romans 1.3–4,[10] this confession suggests a community that sees Jesus completely within the context of God's history with Israel; for the twofold repetition of "according to the scriptures" in such a terse formula shows how essential this context was to the community. The two longer lines mention two saving events, which are confirmed by two historical facts in the two shorter lines. Jesus' burial proves his death to be real, and his appearance to his disciples gives assurance of his resurrection. If anything, the emphasis is on the former; only Jesus' death is explicitly given saving significance, "for our sins".[11] This confession also reveals a community that explicitly sees in Jesus' death and resurrection a fulfillment of God's dealings with Israel as contained in Scripture, which looks forward at the same time to the coming judgment of God. This can be seen in the central position accorded the question of the forgiveness of sins, which Jewish thought naturally associates with the Last Judgment. On this basis we can understand how an apocalyptically oriented community could adopt statements concerning the suffering of the righteous Son of Man and the forgiveness of the community in the coming judgment by virtue of this suffering.

In the period that followed, however, the two motifs began to diverge. Even before Paul, presumably for the most part in the Hellenistic Jewish community, emphasis was placed on Jesus' death for the salvation of the community, which was described in a wide array of expressions. This can be seen in the fact that Paul can borrow them without expanding on them and without using them to support his own theologizing. If we collect only the images drawn upon by

[9] Joachim Jeremias, "Artikelloses 'Christos'", *ZNW* LVII (1966), pp. 211ff.; B. Klappert, "Zur Frage des semitischen oder griechischen Urtextes von 1 Kor XV, 3–5," *NTS* XIII (1966/67), pp. 168–73; Lehmann, *op. cit.*, pp. 111–12, 147ff.; for a contrary view, see Wengst, *op. cit.*, pp. 91–3; cf. also Peter Stuhlmacher, *Das paulinische Evangelium I (FRLANT* 95, 1968), pp. 266ff.

[10] Cf. above, pp. 70f.

[11] In the present context, Paul is emphasizing the resurrection of Jesus, but this has nothing to do with the significance of the original formula.

Paul in the Letter to the Romans, we still have a great variety: Jesus' death is expiation (3.25), sacrifice (8.3),[12] reconciliation (5.10–11), vicarious action (4.25; 5.6–11; 14.15), an act of liberation (3.24; 7.4 probably; 8.3 with the parallel in Gal.4.4–5), justification of the sinner (3.24–26 and *passim*), example (15.3–5), and prototype experienced by the believer (6.4–6).

In addition, we find the special notion of the "blood of Christ" (3.25; 5.9), a widespread theme naturally linked with the Old Testament sacrificial idea (cf. Mark 14.24; John 6.53–56; Acts 20.28; Col. 1.20; Eph. 1.7; 2.13; Heb. 9.12 and *passim*; 1 Pet. 1.2, 19; 1 John 1.7; 5.6ff.; Rev. 1.5; etc.). If we go beyond Romans, we also find the image of the slaughtered Passover lamb[13] (1 Cor. 5.7; the same idea is probably present in John 1.29, 36; 19.36). The very wealth of these images shows that the community was not restricted to a single explanation beyond the fact that Jesus' death is for the benefit of all. The central affirmation, however, is already firmly established. In the various formulations it is always "Christ", not the "Lord" or the "Son of God" or some other term that is the subject; "died" always occurs in the same Greek form; even "for [us]" is almost always expressed by the same Greek word. We can therefore legitimately call the statement a formula.[14]

But what is the community actually saying? In 1 Corinthians 15.3–5, the affirmation concerning Christ's death, as we have seen, stands beside another concerning his resurrection. This is also true in Romans 4.24–25, where both affirmations are expressly referred to as the "faith" of the community. We find a similar juxtaposition in 1 Thessalonians 4.14a, while Romans 10.9 mentions only the resurrection. This shows that the Easter event appears as the primary content of the "faith"; but what took place in the Easter event was soon interpreted on the basis of Jesus' death for sinners. Even during Jesus' lifetime the "faith" of the men who encountered him played an important role; but in this case "faith" was understood as unconditional trust in him, above all in his power to make men whole. This

[12] In Romans 3.25, the Greek word *hilastērion* most likely refers to the place of God's presence, and could therefore be translated "place of expiation"; it is easily understood as "means of expiation", however. The expression "for sins" is frequently employed in Leviticus as a technical term for the sin offering. The Letter to the Hebrews later takes up the sacrificial notion in detail (9.11–14).

[13] Although originally the Passover lamb was not a means of expiation, it was later so understood.

[14] Werner Kramer, *Christ, Lord, Son of God* (SBT I 50, 1966), § 4d.

changes after Easter; in contrast to Greek usage and that of the Old Testament, there appears a completely new formulation of "faith in" Jesus, his resurrection, and his expiatory death. Even the verbal form "[I] believe . . . that God raised [Jesus] from the dead" (Rom. 10.9) is a linguistic innovation; its use is in full accord with that of the substantive.

What is being expressed here? Clearly this: the only ground of our salvation is what God did in the death and resurrection of Jesus; everything depends on God, not on us. This was already the experience of Israel, which understood the election of Abraham or the deliverance from Egypt as the only possible basis of its life.[15] This was the Easter experience of the disciples, in the midst of whose utter failure God had intervened unexpectedly and powerfully. This was the experience that proved true again and again in the life of the community. Men who lived completely from what God had done for them learned to say: "I *believe in* what God did in Jesus' death and resurrection" and "I *believe that* Jesus died and rose again".

This very statement of the resurrection, but above all the statement of Jesus' death for our sins, underscored the fact that the basis of our salvation lies outside the human sphere. Within Palestinian Judaism, as well as in Hellenistic Judaism, this notion was in direct opposition to the attitude that expected salvation to come through fulfillment of all the commandments, i.e., through the "works of the law". How early and how completely this notion had been thought through to its radical conclusion, how much men thought instead of Jesus' expiation as making up for the perfection they had not attained despite faithful observance of the law is hard to tell. In actual fact, a community that could express its faith through these affirmations no longer really lived by observance of the law, even if it did in fact continue to observe the law. The attitude that expected salvation to come through the righteousness of the individual had been fundamentally denied ever since Jesus claimed complete freedom with respect to the law, and above all since the risen Lord had encountered those very men who had failed him completely. Where this fact became the real focus of attention, the questions that brought one face to face with the event of Jesus became further and further removed

[15] In this connection, it would also be appropriate to mention the fact, unique in the history of religions, that only in the Old Testament are the sayings of the prophets dated, just as later Jesus' crucifixion is dated "under Pontius Pilate" (von Rad, *op. cit.*, II, pp. 363–4).

from preaching whose orientation was purely apocalyptic or which placed special emphasis on the exaltation and incarnation of Jesus.

When Jesus called his disciples to follow him, he gave new meaning to their lives by filling them with great hope and by making God and his acts real to them once more; this fact was maintained by apocalypticism. Day by day he determined their lives and set his stamp on them; this fact was emphasized by the affirmation of Jesus' exaltation as Lord of the community. It was God himself whom the disciples encountered in this way; this fact was incorporated in references to the incarnation of him who dwelt with God. But when Jesus called his followers to discipleship, he also brought them from a more or less conscious distance (Mark 2.14!) into the immediate presence of God. This is even more true of the new call extended by the risen Christ. This side of the matter is made central by the statements that we are now examining. The community that speaks in these statements is oppressed by its alienation from God and is asking for reconciliation. It found the answer to its questions in the initially incomprehensible event of the crucifixion. This, too, must be told. It would be impossible to live continually by Easter, whether one is thinking more of the kingdom and glory to come or of that which is already present, without coming to terms with what took place in the crucifixion of Jesus.

Of course it is not yet really clear how the cross of Jesus is linked with his resurrection, his appointment to lordship at the right hand of God, or even with the consummation of the kingdom of God. But in the long run it is not enough simply to juxtapose the various affirmations, so that, say, the cross effects the forgiveness of sins, the resurrection establishes Jesus' lordship over the community, and the world will finally be saved at the consummation. The problem that therefore confronted Paul, who was theologically sophisticated, was the need for a perspective that would bring together the various aspects of the Jesus event that the community had rightly observed and emphasized.

THE RIGHTEOUSNESS OF GOD

In Philippians 2.8, Paul added to the original text, "even death on a cross". The statement in Galatians 4.4–5 concerning the sending of the Son, which actually describes the incarnation, he reinterpreted so as to refer to Jesus' death on the cross.[16]

He can say that he has nothing to proclaim but Christ crucified

[16] Cf. above, pp. 84f.

(1 Cor. 2.2), and can draw upon the most diverse images from the language of the community to express his meaning to the community.[17] In similar fashion, he can represent the resurrection of Jesus as the central tenet of the faith, basing on it the justification of sins (Rom. 4.24–25; 1 Cor. 15.17). In Paul's thought there is no conflict between an understanding of Christ that focuses on his vicarious death and one that looks upon him primarily as the exalted Lord or the coming judge; he welds them together in a new unity, thanks primarily to his reflection on the righteousness of God. Here theology found its true theme, because Paul—following Jesus, whose preaching he never heard directly—bases his thought radically on God, not on man.

Now the phrase "righteousness of God" has been the subject of lengthy debate; is it to be understood as an attribute or act of God (God's being righteous or acting righteously), or as an attribute or gift conferred on man (righteousness given by God or like God's or valid before God)? There has also been discussion over whether it is a present value, as most of the passages seem to suggest, or something yet to come, as described, for example, in Galatians 5.5. At this point we must clearly try to find new categories to express what Paul means. Now in the Old Testament "the righteousness of God" refers to his saving acts on behalf of Israel, his judgment upon the nations, in which he remains faithful to himself and to his covenant with Israel. It is a conceit, in other words, that refers to God's "righteous" (i.e., faithful to the promises of the covenant) conduct toward Israel.[18] In the face of a world of complaints against God, even the Psalms maintain that God's righteousness will show itself in glory at the eschaton, that all the world will recognize that God is not dead but alive, not unrighteous but righteous. The point in question, therefore, is God himself, his righteous actions, the realization of his purpose on earth.

Paul uses the concept of God's righteousness to describe what Jesus himself means by the kingdom of God.[19] Even in the Old Testament the notion of God's righteousness is closely related to that of the kingdom of God. Take the famous "superscription" of the Letter to the Romans, which was the crucial passage for Luther's Reformation: "For I am not ashamed of the Gospel: it is the power of God for

[17] Cf. above, pp. 94f.   [18] Cf. especially von Rad, *op. cit.*, I, pp. 368ff.

[19] On this point, see especially E. Jüngel, *Paulus und Jesus* (Hermeneutische Untersuchungen 2, Tübingen: Mohr, 1962), pp. 263ff.

salvation to every one who has faith, to the Jew first, and also to the Greek. For in it the righteousness of God is revealed through faith for faith; as it is written, 'He who through faith is righteous shall live'" (Rom. 1.16–17) This actually restates what Ps. 98.2 had already promised for the eschaton: "The Lord has made known his victory; he has revealed his vindication in the sight of the nations." This becomes even clearer when one realizes that verse 17 merely furnishes the basis for 16b, 16b for 16a, and 16a for 14–15, where Paul maintains that, as missionary to the Gentiles, he is under obligation to preach the gospel to all nations. What is said here concerning God's righteousness supports the thesis that Paul has been developing ever since verse 1: God has entrusted the Gentile mission to him, and the gospel, which has already a long history in Israel, is now advancing through the world under the lordship of the exalted Christ in order to confirm God's victory in the sight of all nations. What concerns Paul is not so much the question that was on Luther's mind, that is, the problem of the man who knows his sin and seeks God's grace. Unlike Luther, Paul never went through a period of despair because of his sins. On the contrary, he declares that, by the standard of the righteousness that stems from the law, he has been faultless. (Phil. 3.6; cf. Gal. 1.14).

The question that concerns Paul is the question of God's righteousness, whether and how it is true that the world belongs to God and that he proves himself to be God. God is in the right, not those who accuse him; God's victory stands out clearly; the nations are in the grip of God's power: this is what Paul proclaims, this is what fills his life and carries him through all the lands of the Roman Empire, to Rome, the capital city, and finally to the ends of the known world (Rom. 15.16ff.).

Of course the coming of God's righteousness surpasses and transcends all promises. It places all men under judgment, even Israel, i.e., the man who would look down upon others in his righteousness according to the law (Rom. 1.18—3.20). Only thus is it revealed—again in fulfillment of Old Testament prophecies—that God alone is righteous (Rom. 3.4). The miracle that took place in Jesus was this: God's judgment befell him who for our sakes became "accursed", became "sin" (Gal. 3.13; 2 Cor. 5.21). Thus God established his righteousness as a "power" (cf. Rom. 1.16) that creates and sets its stamp upon a new world. Thus God's righteousness is also given to men. The living power of God that stands over a man's life is what he

lives from. Just as a small child lives from being born into a good
environment in which he is met with love, so the man who has been
justified lives from the "Yes" God says to him, which is the power that
stands over his life.

These considerations make comprehensible the unity of Paul's
statements, which at first appear antithetical. Paul's meaning is like
that of Jesus in his talk of the kingdom of God: the righteousness of
God is both a present event and at the same time a future. When a
ruler exercises his power, he does so here and now; but this exercise
of power is always open towards its goal, the time when all enemies will
be subjugated and all will obey him. In the exercise of political
power, the attainment of this goal is of course always relative; only
with respect to God can faith hope that the kingdom of his righteousness will one day comprehend heaven and earth.

In the second place, the righteousness of God is something established completely by God himself, long before man even hears of it;
at the same time, however, it is something that engrosses man totally.
When a ruler exercises power, it is a fact that cannot be altered by
recognition or lack of recognition on the part of his people; there can
nevertheless be no rule without a people, whose conduct is therefore
characterized from the very outset as obedience or disobedience,
cooperation or indifference. The position of the allied armies, for instance, which recaptured France on a specific date, did not depend on
individual French citizens. The life of each individual citizen, however, was determined thereby. This was true even before he heard of
the victory—the partisan suddenly found no more German troops
fighting against him. It was also true for the man who refused to
recognize this power—he became thereby a member of the resistance.
But it was particularly true for the man who welcomed this power
and thus was given an active and constructive role to play.

In the third place, the righteousness of God is an event that takes
place constantly outside of man, yet puts its stamp on man's heart.
When a ruler exercises his power, it is he himself who does so; but he
does so in such a way as to look after his people. When such power is
the power of love, it is the inmost heart that it engrosses (Rom. 5.5).
Here again the event of God's righteousness naturally transcends all
analogies of the exercise of political power, which can never command
more than loyalty.

In the fourth place, it is now understandable how the expression
"righteousness of God" (which refers primarily to conduct on the part

of God that is acknowledged by man) comes to refer to the gift that, through God's action, invades human life and lives on there (cf. "the righteousness that comes from God" in Phil. 3.9).

The crucial point, however, is that for Paul, all these assertions stand under the rubric of Jesus' cross. God's kingdom therefore cannot come in the form of a triumphal church, but only through a summons to discipleship that often enough can outwardly resemble Jesus' way of the cross. And God's righteousness as a gift to man can therefore never be merely accepted on the intellectual level; it can only be lived in such discipleship. Thus the lordship of the exalted Christ is always realized as the lordship of the crucified.

For this reason, Paul's suffering plays such an important role in the thought of the apostle. When he speaks (Gal. 6.17) of the "marks of Jesus" that no one is to dispute, he is most likely thinking of the welts on his body caused by scourging. In any case, he can state that, as an Apostle, he is "regarded as [a] sheep to be slaughtered" and "killed all the day long" for the sake of Jesus (Rom. 8.36), that he "dies every day" (1 Cor. 15.31). On his apostolic journeys he is exposed to robbery and shipwreck, hunger and cold, imprisonment and scourging, more than once to threatened execution. Once, goaded by his opponents, he produces an impressive catalog of the dangers he has withstood (2 Cor. 11.23–27). In this very realistic fashion he bears the "death of Jesus" in his body, so that the "life of Jesus" may be revealed, that is, in all the communities for which the message of the apostle has been made credible through its power revealed in the totality of his life and its awakening of men to faith (2 Cor. 4.10–12). Paul can develop this in detail by the example of his experience in Ephesus, where—we do not know whether as a consequence of sickness or persecution—he was in extreme peril. On this occasion his suffering bore fruit because, in the first place, he himself stood so in need of God's consolation that he learned to transmit such consolation to others; because, in the second place, the bond uniting him with his community came to life in intercession and thanksgiving; and because, in the third place, when he himself stood face to face with death, he learned what it really meant to have faith in him who was also raised from the dead (2 Cor. 1.3–11). And so Paul experiences what everyone who believes must experience; but he, the apostle, must go through it as an example on behalf of all his congregations. In weakness he must learn to live by the strength that comes from God, unknown but known to all, dying yet living, disciplined by

suffering but not done to death, rejoicing in sorrow, poor but bringing wealth to many, penniless but owning the world (2 Cor. 6.9–10).
He learns that this must be so, in order that all power may really belong to God, not to the religious individual (2 Cor. 4.7; 12.9; 13.4).

CHRIST, THE END OF THE LAW

Paul sets this "righteousness of God" or "righteousness based on
faith" in contrast to the "righteousness based on law" (Rom. 10.5–6;
Phil. 3.6, 9). This concept shows clearly who Christ is, but at the
same time it shows clearly who God really is. Even in the Old Testament the law was understood as a sign of the God who opens himself
to man, who comes near to man. It is the great gift by means of
which God allows Israel to share his way; Paul himself attaches great
importance to maintaining the "holiness" of the law, asserting that
its commandment is "holy and just, and good" (Rom. 7.12). This
gift of the law distinguishes Israel, God's own people, from all other
peoples (Rom. 9.4). But what, to speak concretely, is the uniqueness
of this people and its life under the law? Paul can use the name of
Abraham to describe the uniqueness of Israel, and speaks of the special
promise that has been given to Israel, which finds its goal in Jesus
Christ (Rom. 4.1ff.; Gal. 3.6ff.). He can also use the name of Moses to
describe it; then he speaks of the special burden imposed on Israel,
which finds its goal in Jesus Christ (Rom. 10.4). But we must examine
this notion in more detail.

The law is undoubtedly God's good gift to Israel. It tells Israel
what God's will is, and enables Israel to live according to God's will.
On this point no feelings of inferiority afflict Paul. Of himself he can
say that so far as a man can be righteous by obeying the commands of
the Law, he is without fault (Phil. 3.6). He can insist that there are
enormous differences, and that he himself is among those who live
according to the law and are not "Gentile sinners" (Gal. 2.15). But
the crucial question remains; does this make a man righteous in the
sight of God (Gal. 2.16)?

It is a striking fact that, except where Paul draws upon extant
tradition (as in 1 Cor. 15.3), he speaks only of sin, never of sins.
Naturally Paul is also familiar with "particular sins", but for these
he always uses other expressions, such as "transgressions", "offences",
and the like. This shows clearly that, for him, *sin* does not consist in
ethically defined transgressions of the law; conversely, an ethically

blameless life, without transgression of any commandment, does not of itself mean righteousness in the sight of God. He can therefore also declare that he is aware of nothing on his conscience, but this does not make him righteous in the sight of God (1 Cor. 4.4). For Paul, sin is clearly the attitude of the man who, in his moral depravity or perfection, seeks himself and not God, thus ultimately transgressing the first commandment, on which all the others depend. This can express itself in a life of greedy acquisitiveness or sexual excess, but also in a search for ultimate wisdom (1 Cor. 1.18ff.) or for absolute righteousness in the fulfillment of all the commandments (Phil. 3.3ff.). When the question is put this way, breaking through all the limitations of mere morality, and plumbing instead the depths of the human soul, we find that for Paul the special position and vocation of Israel is understood most profoundly in the realization that God has revealed to no other nation such a clear picture of the human situation.

With a brevity that is shocking and almost impenetrable Paul states in Romans 5.20 that the law came "to increase the trespass", but "where sin increased, grace abounded all the more". Here, too, Paul does not deny that the law has produced ethically exemplary, even "faultless" men. But the cross of Jesus reveals that this very man, faultless and exemplary, this ethically correct individual, has displaced God and substituted himself as a kind of proxy or replacement for God (Phil. 3.3ff.).[20] Only in Israel, therefore, has the human situation been truly revealed. Only in Israel has the ethically correct man been unmasked in such a way that we still feel the effects of the unmasking. In essence the wise man of the Greeks, who seeks to get through life by means of his wisdom, is no different from the righteous man of the Israelites, as we can see from the parallel between 1 Cor. 1.18ff. and Phil. 3.3ff., the Letter to the Galatians, or the Letter to the Romans. But the Greeks never undertook their search for God so radically, with such personal investment, as did the Pharisees. Therefore their disillusionment was not as extreme as that of Paul, who discovered that in his ultimate effort to serve God with all his heart, as one who in the practice of his national religion outstripped many of his Jewish contemporaries in his boundless devotion to the traditions of his ancestors, he had become a savage persecutor and destroyer of the church of God (Gal. 1.13–14). Paul had in fact done the very thing he hated, the very thing he did not want to do (Rom. 7.15).[21]

[20] Cf. above, p. 99.
[21] This statement cannot be understood in the primitive psychological sense

Thus Paul learned clearly what sin is: not ethical imperfection, which depends in large measure on our natural tendencies, but basic concentration on one's self, one's own righteousness, based on strict observance of the law, one's own wisdom, gained by strenuous efforts, or one's own pleasure, attained by all possible means, good or ill. And he suddenly realized what righteousness is: complete concentration on God, a concentration that can recognize the good in one's own actions, because this recognition exalts God's power, not one's own (1 Cor. 15.10–11!). True righteousness also entrusts to God everything that is dark and perverse in one's life.

It is a remarkable fact that Paul, who hardly ever cites any of Jesus' sayings, who says nothing of Jesus' earthly life except for his birth and crucifixion, understood better than all the others who speak to us in the New Testament the meaning of Jesus' life in association with tax collectors and prostitutes. This is connected with the fact that Paul, like Jesus, lives in the Old Testament, or, more precisely, in certain parts of the Old Testament.[22] Like Jesus, Paul is concerned to unmask self-righteousness, that is, the self-confidence with which man would press his claim before God. Both, however, are also concerned for that ultimate and unshakable liberty of heart that Jesus describes with the image of a childlike character, Paul as justification through faith. The message that man cannot stand before God even if he is ethically correct is also the message that he no longer *has* to stand by virtue of his own righteousness, but may learn to live completely from what is given him. He is thus set free from daily—or even yearly—self-examination, in which it does not much matter whether, like a Pharisee, he lists all his plusses, all his obedient fulfillment of the law, or, like a well-trained Protestant, lists his minuses, all his sins and failings. In either case the man's life revolves about himself rather than about God, from whose continual gifts alone he can live.

In what sense, then, is Jesus "the end of the law" (Rom. 10.4)? Paul is the first to place maximum emphasis on the cross of Jesus. Of course the community spoke of Jesus' death, even of his vicarious or

---

that he was continually subject to ethical temptations. Philippians 3.6 contradicts such an interpretation. With his faultless legal righteousness Paul wanted to give God glory and serve him; in fact, however, he lived only for his own glory and multiplied his own righteousness.

[22] Cf. passages such as Deuteronomy 7.7; Isaiah 1.2ff.; 43.27; Hosea 12.3–4; Amos 2.4ff.; 9.7.

atoning death, even before Paul did. But to Paul the fact that Jesus was crucified was especially important. Why? Galatians 3.13 cites the Old Testament curse on "everyone who hangs on a tree". In other words, the curse of the law took effect against him in order that those who stood under the law might be set free. Romans 8.3–4 makes a similar claim. What is important to Paul is not that Jesus died, nor even that he died a painful death, but that he met his end on the cross, under the curse of the law. How is this to be understood? In the first place, Jesus' death on the cross revealed in full clarity the human situation—above all, the situation of the man who is righteous according to the law: the very man who sought to fulfill the last detail of God's law brought about the crucifixion of the man in whom God sought to encounter him. But Paul does not expressly mention this aspect of the cross. His point is even more profound. It is the law itself that brought the curse upon Jesus, thereby losing its power. This refers, of course, to the law as men understood it and used it to gain righteousness in the sight of God. Jesus—who broke the Sabbath, ate and drank with unclean tax collectors—was brought to the cross by this law, and thus put under God's curse. But this spelled the end of the law; for now it was revealed for all time that this law, as an instrument in human hands, could not determine who lived according to God's will and who did not. It therefore lost its final claim on man; it was robbed of its power, and man could once more stand face to face with God without the necessity of seeing God only through the law and its demands. Thus Jesus was, for Paul, "the end of the law".

But what does the life of faith mean? If the law determines precisely what must be done and what must not be done in every individual case, a man can follow it to the very letter without really seeking him who gave the law to win men's hearts: God. Through legal interpretation or creation of a customary law, he can even determine what must be done and what must not be done in all cases not envisioned by the law. He can go to the limit and cultivate an obedience to the law that is heroic and immensely impressive. But even the most precise observance of all these regulations cannot keep him from being self-satisfied and unloving, that is, from being a sinner, in the Pauline sense, in the eyes of God. But when the law loses its power because faith sees through it, because faith understands that Jesus freed men from the letter by revealing in the Sermon on the Mount the meaning of the law that God intended, then the righteousness of God can come upon a man and win his heart for God. This is far from

implying faultless conduct in every single instance. But it sets a man
free really to seek God with his entire life, and it sets him free to see his
neighbor and his neighbor's needs. Here discernment of the will of
God (Rom. 12.2) becomes the decisive gift of God. The law can help
man in this discernment, but it cannot deprive him of it. For the important thing is now to live in each particular case from the gift of
God's righteousness, so that one can see his neighbor and give him
what he needs. No formulized law removes the burden and responsibility of freedom. Indeed, obedience to the law can blind a man to
God's will and the real need of his neighbor, letting him content himself with precise observance of what is prescribed. Just as the preaching of Jesus did away with all casuistry, i.e., with a legalism that
prescribes precisely the conduct appropriate in every conceivable
case, so it was also with Paul's preaching of the righteousness of
God.

For this very reason there are no areas in which the righteousness
of God should not operate and reign. Freedom is absolute. According
to Paul, a man is free every moment to discover what is right, and no
law can ultimately bind him. Every moment, however, he also stands
under the will of God, which confronts him with his neighbor. Luther
once summarized life under the righteousness of God in two sentences:
"A Christian man is a free lord over all things, and subject to no one.
A Christian man is a willing servant of all things, and subject to
everyone."[23] Paul's term for this duality of ultimate freedom and
ultimate subjection is life "in Christ". To this term we shall now turn.

LIFE "IN CHRIST"

This formula, which occurs frequently in Paul, is quite remarkable.
How can a man be said to live (Rom. 6.11; 8.2) or die (1 Cor. 15.18),
speak (Rom. 9.1) or think (Phil. 2.5) "in Christ"? How can one toil
(Rom. 16.12) or marry (1 Cor. 7.39), welcome a brother (Phil. 2.29)
or stand firm (1 Thess. 3.8), hope, be confident, rejoice (Phil. 2.19,
24; 3.1) "in the Lord"? How can one be or become "united in Christ"
or "in the Lord" (Rom. 8.1; 16.7; 1 Cor. 1.30; 9.2; 2 Cor. 5.17;
Gal. 3.28)?

These phrases were long understood to mean that Paul conceived
Christ as some sort of fine airy substance permeating the world, in

---

[23] Weimar edition vii, 21.

which one could literally live.[24] I would then live in him and from him the way a consumptive lives in and from the mountain air that sustains and heals him, without always being consciously aware of the fact. The consumptive would have to be reminded to return to the mountains when he goes to the lowlands and takes sick once more; this is analogous to the Pauline juxtaposition of summons and statement. Others have maintained the opposite interpretation, that by "in Christ" Paul means simply that a man lives in a historical situation, namely in the history that bears the stamp of Jesus' ministry, death, and resurrection.[25] In this case, the "in" would be like the "in" that we use when we say that a man lives in the American republic, i.e., in a political economy determined by the history that begins with the signing of the Constitution; the summons that accompanies Paul's statement would be like the summons to take politics seriously and be a responsible participant.

What Paul is trying to express by saying "in Christ" probably lies somewhere between these two extremes. If what we have said about the righteousness of God is correct, then life "in Christ" is a life that can be understood spatially as being lived within a certain sphere. But this sphere is not a fluid substance; or, if Paul ever did imagine it in this way, as would be relatively likely for a Hellenist of that period, the conception was at least not constitutive for what he was trying to say. On the other hand, the concept of a history bearing the stamp of a specific event will also not suffice, because Paul conceived the presence of the historically past life, death, and resurrection of Jesus much more realistically than the model of historical after-effects suggests. Once again, the category of power is probably most appropriate. The exercise of power is based on an event in the past, but it surrounds a man and determines his life as a present force; so it is with the lordship of Jesus. Of course Jesus' power can only be understood as the power of love. Life "in Christ", then, corresponds to the life in an atmosphere informed by love in which my parents or my spouse have said "yes" to me, and constantly continue to say "yes" to me.

If we think in these forms, it becomes clear that there can be no question of a "being in Christ" observable to the naked eye. Whoever lives above three thousand feet lives in the mountain air. This is

[24] Gustav Adolf Deissmann, *Die neutestamentliche Formel "in Christo Jesu" untersucht* (Marburg: Elwert, 1892).

[25] Fritz Neugebauer, *In Christus* (Göttingen: Vandenhoeck & Ruprecht, 1961).

no different from the way a fish is "in" the water. Even if we think historically, every American can be said to live in the American republic, although of course the question remains whether he does so in the proper sense. The situation is different when we speak of the power of love. Love lives only where it is received. A person who is loved by another but does not realize it does not live "in the love" of the other. He certainly lives in this love before he responds to it, even when he responds negatively to it; but in any case he really lives in this love only when he receives and experiences the love as a participant in some sense. Love calls for love in response. Therefore Paul always understands life "in Christ" as a blessing and as a claim to sovereignty. The rather common phrase "chosen in the Lord" indicates that man is brought to salvation by God *and* that he is called to live in this salvation by living the will of God.

This also explains the juxtaposition of statement and summons (indicative and imperative) in Paul. They are often intimately associated: "If we live by the Spirit, let us also walk by the Spirit" (Gal. 5.25); "Only let us hold true to what we have attained" (Phil. 3.16); "If then you have been raised with Christ, seek the things that are above" (Col. 3.1). Such statements maintain the duality of life in Christ. On the one hand, it is wholly a gift; on the other, what is given is real only when it is lived. Another comparison will help make the point clear. When a child is given something beyond his wildest dreams, say a bicycle, he must obviously reach out his arms and set his whole body in motion to take possession of the bicycle. But it would be absurd for the child to say anything to his friends except that, quite fantastically, he has been given a bicycle. If he tried to describe his exertions, how he stretched out his arms and grabbed the handlebars, he would be mentally ill. On the other hand, a shy child must be given an imperative: "Take the bicycle, it's really for you!" Thus Paul can say that he ventures to speak of those things alone in which he has been Christ's instrument (Rom. 15.18), and at the same time that he exerted himself like a runner in a race and like a boxer who masters his own body (1 Cor. 9.24–27). In other words, all he invests is by virtue of the power of the love of Christ which surrounds him; but this love can develop its power only through this personal investment. For this reason, too, when the community asks Paul about proper conduct in certain cases, he cannot simply respond with authoritative instructions to be accepted by the community. Paul is not content until he can show the community why their faith in the crucified and risen Lord implies a certain course of action.[26] Only in this way can the obedience of the community become life "in Christ".

For Paul it is also essential that life in Christ is also life in the "body", that is, in the world, not, say, a retreat into heaven, as the Corinthians imagined it.[27] At the crucial point in the Letter to the Romans, where Paul turns from statements concerning Christ and salvation to practical questions of conduct, he begins: "Therefore I call upon you, because God in his mercy has said 'yes' to you, to take your bodies as a holy, living sacrifice, pleasing to God, as your worship, which can be understood."[28] In other words, worship takes place when we are in the midst of "bodily" life, that is, the externals of everyday life; it takes place through our surrender of our selves and our willingness to live for our neighbors. For this reason "being in Christ" does not lead the individual into the stillness and solitude of his reborn soul, where he might soar high above the rest of mankind, but into society. This holds true in two ways. First, a man always lives in the society of those for whose service he must be open; but he also lives in the society of those who, together with him, live "in Christ". While the decision to discern the will of God remains essentially open at all times (Rom. 12.2), Paul nevertheless conceives that, as a rule, the community as a whole will face the question of what its true and rational worship should be (Rom. 12.3ff.). When it is no longer two individuals who encounter each other, but rather the question of responsibility for the welfare of a larger group, such as the state (Rom. 13.1–7), a whole series of problems enters in, the consequences of which are beyond the grasp of the individual at a given moment.[29] Both aspects, being open to all who stand in need of service and personal involvement, and being open to the brother who lends counsel and assistance, are expressed by Paul in the phrase "body of Christ".

[26] See, for example, 1 Corinthians 6.1–11 or 12–20; also Romans 14.1—15.6; etc.

[27] Cf. above, pp.75f. [28] Romans 12.1, freely translated.

[29] Karl Barth provides the illuminating image of the law as a "railing", which is not necessary for those who are practised and mature, but should not be scorned by those who are unpractised or still weak. Social ethics lends new weight to this image. The increasing interdependence of all realms of life makes it necessary to climb "stairs" that no one can now climb "without a railing", because no one today can see all the consequences of a decision. Such railings are not law in the sense that they anticipate the solution, but they are often an indispensable aid in the task of perceiving anew the will of God.

THE CHRISTIAN COMMUNITY AS THE BODY OF CHRIST

Paul uses the phrase "body of Christ" to refer to the sphere in which Christ exercises his lordship and in which men live from this power, and, in turn, respond through their faith and their obedience. How does he arrive at this expression and what does he mean by it? The Old Testament, and above all the Judaism of Jesus' period—which bears the stamp of the Old Testament—thinks in terms of spheres.[30] There are places, like the temple, where God dwells, where one can sense something of his presence or his power and glory, his blessing or his judgment; and there are other places, like the underworld, where God does not dwell. It is true that the author of Psalm 139 already recognized that there was nowhere he could escape from God: "Whither shall I go from thy spirit? Or whither shall I flee from thy presence? . . . if I make my bed in Sheol, thou art there!" (vss. 7–8). But however much truth there is in the omnipresence of God, it also remains true that there are places where God's beneficent lordship is experienced more directly and less ambiguously than it is in other places. Israel is the object of God's gifts and of God's demand in a special way, even though it knows, from the time of Deutero-Isaiah during the Babylonian exile, that it has been set apart by God not for its own benefit, but for all the nations of the earth. God's particular presence therefore cannot simply be associated with a place definable in geographical terms, such as the temple. God is also present for his exiled people in Babylon or in Egypt. Neither can God's presence be understood as occupying one place unchallenged while another place is under the equally unchallenged dominion of darkness, or however one might wish to express it. The spheres merge into one another, just as man dwells in both the sphere of death and of life. To use modern terminology, we can speak in similar fashion of a certain atmosphere that fills a house or a family, setting its stamp on all who dwell in the house and at the same time radiating from the house to other people or groups.

It is therefore easy to understand how Jewish thought could consider such a sphere of life to bear the stamp of a man like Abraham or Jacob, called by God, and to be dominated by this figure through many generations. Jacob is a typical example. In a Jewish document of the first century BC, we read: "I know that the Lord will choose him

[30] See especially Heinz-Wolfgang Kuhn, *Enderwartung und gegenwärtiges Heil* (SUNT 4, 1966), pp. 183ff.

[viz., Jacob, the individual] for his own people" (Jub. 19.18); "He will establish the heavens and make fast the earth and renew all the lights that are in the firmament" (Jub. 9.25), which means that in choosing Jacob, a particular individual, God also chooses the people who spring from him, who mediate God's blessing and dominion not only to all nations, but to the entire cosmos, because heaven and earth are to be made new when God's dominion is extended. It is therefore possible to say already "that God's blessings will remain on the head of his tribe" (Jub. 22.13), an image in which an individual man and his head are extended spatially to encompass an entire people and temporally to extend over many centuries.[31] When one considers that according to the Old Testament God himself gave Jacob the name Israel, making him representative of the people yet to come, it is not surprising to find a Jewish story, based on the Bible, using a common Old Testament image to describe the people of Israel as a vine that reaches from the underworld to heaven and therefore fills the entire cosmos. The point of this image is to describe the sphere in which God, through Israel, seeks to establish on earth his dominion that encompasses the underworld and the heavens. Of course the question is already raised whether the failure and defeat of Israel does not mean that God must destroy this vine and plant a new one.[32] Against this background we can begin to understand the statement that the Gospel of John (15.1ff.) places in Jesus' mouth on his last evening with his disciples: "I am the true vine, . . . you are the branches." This statement maintains the truth that the disciples can find life only "in him", and that Jesus, although he and he alone is the real vine, is this vine only in company with his branches. Jesus must not be misunderstood as being an outstanding religious personality; he can be looked upon only as Lord of his church. What Paul meant by his references to the body of Christ, what later writers—the author of Colossians and Ephesians—expressed through the image of Christ as the head of his body, the church, is here already expressed in language strongly colored by that of the Old Testament.

If one asks how Paul came to use this language, one must take as his point of departure the fact that for Paul, unlike general Greek usage, the "body" refers primarily to a means for encountering others

<hr>

[31] For a further discussion, see E. Schweizer, "Die Kirche als Leib Christi in den paulinischen Homologumena", in his *Neotestamentica*, pp. 280–3.

[32] Pseudo-Philo, *Antiquitates biblicae*, xii. 8–9; E. Schweizer, "Die Kirche als Leib Christi", pp. 272–3.

and serving them. This development was aided on the one hand by the Eucharistic liturgy, in which two directly juxtaposed statements gradually took shape: "This is my body, which is [given] for you . . . This cup is the new covenant, in my blood" (1 Cor. 11.24–25), and on the other by Paul's opposition to the Corinthians and to their retreat into mere spirituality, of which we have already spoken.[33] In both cases, the body is looked upon as the place of service for others and therefore emphasized. Many other relationships have made specific contributions. First of all, the body of Christ is of course the body of Jesus, sacrificed on the cross (Rom. 7.4). The community lives from Jesus' sacrifice of himself for others. Using the language of Judaism and the Old Testament, Paul could therefore say that this act of self-sacrifice is the "place" where God made real his love for man. From this point, then, there radiates the "sphere" in which alone there can be true life, that is, life under the "yes" of God. Just as Paul can use the traditional language of the community before him, saying that the community lives "from the blood of Christ" or finds its life "in the blood of Christ",[34] he can also state that it lives "in the body of Christ [given for it]", that is, in the "sphere" created by the death of Jesus.[35]

A second source for our understanding of the expression is the equation of Christ with the new Adam. In the Old Testament, "Adam" refers to the first man created by God, but also to mankind as a whole. When Paul describes Christ as the new Adam (Rom. 5.12ff.; 1 Cor. 15.20ff.), he means that Christ bears and in fact incorporates a totally new humanity. Just as Judaism spoke of Jacob, so now Paul speaks of Christ, not restricting his discourse to Jacob, Israel but talking in universal terms of Adam and all mankind. Christ, Paul says, is the new Adam, who incorporates in himself the new people of God, made up out of all nations. Greek, furthermore, in contrast to the ideas just discussed, consciously used the language of the body and its members as a pure metaphor, having applied it for centuries to social groups such as the state or the body politic

[33] Cf. below, p. 117, and above, p. 109.

[34] Romans 3.25 and 5.9 (freely translated) say "in the blood of Christ", as does 1 Corinthians 11.25 in the Eucharistic formula; cf. Ephesians 2.13–14; Hebrews 10.19; Revelation 1.5; 5.9; 7.14; 1 John 5.6.

[35] The formulation with "in" occurs in this sense in Colossians 1.22, (probably written by a disciple of Paul) and perhaps also in Ephesians 2.16, read in the light of verse 13.

Finally, Greek, like English, can use the word "body" as a collective term for a group of associated persons.[36]

Much more important than the elucidation of these background ideas, however, is the question of what the "body of Christ" meant to Paul. When one traces the origin of this expression, it becomes clear how "body of Christ" refers at the outset to the sphere created by Jesus' sacrifice of himself for men. This means that the Christian community is the "space" in which the believer is placed, in which he may find God's salvation and blessing, God's "yes" to man. At the same time, however, the "body of Christ" is the sphere in which God intends to establish his dominion upon earth, in which he seeks man's obedience, and through which above all he intends to serve the world.

Life in the body of Christ is therefore identical with life "in Christ". But Paul uses the expression "body of Christ" when he wants to describe certain aspects of this life in Christ, above all the solidarity of those who live in Christ. Of course "body of Christ" does not designate a self-contained entity, more or less removed from this earth and describable only in mysterious mystic images. It refers rather to God's personnel, his crew of workers, in which he seeks to encounter the world and enter into it. Just as God reaches into the world in Christ and serves it, so he reaches into the world of the "body of Christ",— the community of those who allow themselves to be set afire by Christ, brought to life, and made his companions. Therefore although "body of Christ" refers to an entity that is always a fixed datum for the individual and his life in faith and service to the world, Paul never speaks of it in the "theological" sections of his letters, where he discusses salvation, but in the "ethical" sections, where he speaks of what must be done to follow the will of God (Rom. 12.3ff.; 1 Cor. 12.12ff.). What the expression probably means is that this service cannot be performed by the individual acting alone, but must be performed by the community of which he is a participating "member". Paul can speak purely metaphorically here, as a Greek of that period might do, using the image of the body in which each member depends on the rest. Therefore there can be no sense of inferiority in the Christian community, because the ear, say, is not the

---

[36] One can speak, for example, of bringing the divided Peloponnesus together in a body, or say that a speech or melody must form a body, or call a nation or an army a "body" that must have a "head", etc. See the usages cited by E. Schweizer in G. Kittel, ed., *TWNT* VII, p. 1039.

eye.[37] Neither can there be any sense of superiority, because the head, say, is higher than the feet[38] (1 Cor. 12.15–25). But such metaphorical usage is possible only because it is based on reality, namely, Christ himself.[39]

What does this mean? Paul speaks of the reality of the Spirit, in which the resurrected Lord works today in his community and, through his community, in the world. The variety of members in the body corresponds to the variety of gifts given by the Spirit (1 Cor. 12.11). Here Paul distinguishes his position from that of the Corinthians, who restricted their attention to the outward manifestations of the Spirit's operation, and therefore took seriously only those gifts that manifested themselves in unnatural and miraculous form. Paul, on the contrary, emphasizes subordination to the Lord and the edification of the community (1 Cor. 12.3, 7; 14.1ff.).[40] Here, too, however, the community is not an end in itself; it is understood as God's host, reaching out into the world. According to 1 Corinthians 14.24–25, the unbelievers or "visitors" are the criterion by which the community must judge its worship. If it is true even within the community that one cannot simply say "Amen" on the basis of spiritual authority, but only when one has really understood and been persuaded (14.16), it is doubly important for those who come from outside the community. The speech to be used in the body of Christ is not "miraculous utterance"; the speaker must speak so that each member of the community and above all, the visiting outsider, can understand and be helped. In similar fashion, the exhortations in Romans 12.3ff., which address themselves first to the solidarity of the worshipping community, change imperceptibly but clearly into admonitions to serve the world outside the assembly.

Therefore freedom and order reign in the body of Christ. Freedom reigns for Christ, who works in his community as it pleases him. Therefore whoever is speaking must be silent when the Lord of the

[37] No one looks his beloved in the ear, but in the eye! Often covered by hair, the ear must stand to the side, while the eye takes the foremost place!

[38] The Greeks attached great importance to the superior position of the head (cf. E. Schweizer, '$\sigma\hat{\omega}\mu\alpha$', *TWNT* VII, p. 1029, n. 53; pp. 1032 line 17; 1035.23–24; 1040.1–2).

[39] 1 Corinthians 12.12 begins metaphorically ("As the body is one and has many members . . .") but ends with a grammatically unexpected twist: ". . . so, too, is Christ." The diverse abundance of Christ is more than a metaphor; it is based on his own nature.

[40] Cf. above, pp. 75f.

community commissions someone else to speak (1 Cor. 14.30). But order also reigns, because the Lord of the community wishes to reach all, and in such a way that they can understand him. Therefore only two or three may speak in tongues, and that only if someone can translate their message for the others. Similarly only two or three may prophesy. Furthermore, all are to speak in turn, not simultaneously (1 Cor. 14.26—29).

Thus for Paul the term "body of Christ" as the name of the Christian community stands as a corrective to the traditional notion of the people of God, borrowed from the Old Testament (cf. 1 Cor. 10.1ff.). While "people of God" emphasizes the movement of the people called by God toward their goal, and therefore historical continuity or discontinuity from the beginning down to the present, "body of Christ" underscores the unity between God's workers and their exalted Lord, his direct working in them and, through them, in the world. Both concepts belong together. If one were to place one-sided emphasis on the notion of the people of God, the historical development of the church would become the decisive factor, together with reference to the tradition of its beginning, the interpretations of the fathers, and the question of continuity guaranteed by canon of Scripture and ecclesiastical office. If one were to place one-sided emphasis on the notion of the body of Christ, contemporary spiritual experience would become the decisive factor, a human religiosity detached from history, detached from its beginnings in the life, death, and resurrection of Jesus.[41] Therefore Paul must use both concepts. He proclaims the crucified Jesus: the one who, as a real human person condemned to ignominious death, constituted the beginning of the community. At the same time, he is concerned to proclaim the crucified Jesus as the risen Lord who lives today in the Christian community. We shall illustrate this point once more by examining the meaning of baptism and the Eucharist for Paul, before we summarize our conclusions.

BAPTISM AND EUCHARIST

The origin of baptism is shrouded in obscurity. The only certain fact is that Jesus himself did not baptize anyone—only John 3.22 suggests that he did, and even this statement is corrected in 4.2.

---

[41] Cf. below, pp. 171ff.

But, on the other hand, the whole New Testament tradition takes baptism as a self-evident datum. To begin with, "baptize" means nothing more than "immerse", "wash". In this sense, the frequent ablutions performed by various groups in the vicinity of the Jordan (daily, for example, at Qumran) already constituted "baptism". As far as we can tell from the evidence, John was the first to introduce a different practice: here baptism became a single baptism of repentance in preparation for the imminent end. In addition, the penitent did not wash himself, but was baptized by John, so that John acquired the epithet "the Baptist".[42] He probably borrowed his practice from the ritual ablutions of these groups,[43] but allowed the change to a single baptism of repentance in light of the imminence of the Last Judgment. John baptized with water; the coming judge will baptize with fire (Matt. 3.11). Thus if a man really repents and allows himself to be baptized with water as a sign of this repentance, he has anticipated the judgment and he will escape the "baptism of fire".

Shortly after Easter, sizable groups of John's disciples probably joined the community of Jesus, bringing their baptism with them. Baptism was therefore probably first understood as an eschatological sacrament of repentance, which delivers from the coming judgment. One thing, of course, was different from the very outset. The community of Jesus knew the risen Lord. Men were baptized in his name (Acts 2.38; 10.48; 1 Cor. 6.11). They thus became attached to him. At first this probably meant primarily that he would intercede for them at the judgment and deliver them into the kingdom of God (Luke 12.8; Mark 10.15; John 3.5; cf. 1 Cor. 6.9–11). The idea of discipleship, however, was probably never completely absent. In the community that spoke Greek and thought in Greek categories, the Hellenistic divine "lords" into whose communities one was initiated through sacramental rites and who guaranteed their votaries eternal life were probably influential. In any case, we see in Corinth a piety that misunderstood the original eschatological perspective of baptism, with its reference to the Last Judgment and resurrection to life, maintaining instead that this resurrection has already taken place, that the

---

[42] This epithet for John is also attested outside the Bible.

[43] Later, and probably not until after the destruction of Jerusalem in AD 70 pagans desirous of becoming Jews were baptized in order to become ritually clean. It is unlikely, however, if only for chronological reasons, that John extended this so-called proselyte baptism to all Israel. Furthermore, there is no suggestion that all Israel had become (ritually!) unclean.

ul of the baptized Christian has already entered into heavenly
ernal life.[44]

The interpretation of baptism as resurrection "with Christ" may
e rooted in the primitive thought of the community, with its marked
pocalyptic stamp. The formula "with Christ" appears first as a
escription of the events of the eschaton, when God will bring those
ho have fallen asleep in company with Jesus, that they may "always
e with the Lord" (1 Thess.4.14, 17). This usage parallels the Old
estament image of God appearing "with his angels" or "with his
ints",[45] as well as the Jewish vision of the future, when the righteous
ill "eat, lie at table, and rise up with the Son of Man" (Eth. Enoch
2.14). The Corinthians at least understood baptism as bestowing the
schatological life "with Christ" in the present,[46] removing the believer
om this world, with its difficulties and limitations, and setting him in
lory. The short baptismal hymn preserved in Ephesians 5.14 betrays
ie same notion: "Awake, O sleeper, and arise from the dead, and
hrist shall give you light." This is almost surely a reference to bap-
sm, but the baptism is not death with Christ; the believer was dead
efore his baptism,[47] and experiences his resurrection when baptized.

In opposition to such views, Paul cites the example of Israel, which
xperienced a baptism but was nonetheless rejected by God because
became disobedient (1 Cor. 10.1ff.). Above all, Paul refers to
aptism as burial, even as crucifixion, with Christ, presumably draw-
ig on primitive Christian usage that spoke of baptism as "submerg-
ig" in death (Mark 10.38; Luke 12.50). But resurrection with Christ
akes place in the total transformation of the baptized Christian. There
fe with Christ and under Christ's dominion must be realized until
he resurrection from the dead at the end of the Christian's life finally
nites him with Christ (Rom.6.3ff.).[48] In other words, Paul recalls

---

[44] Cf. above, p.75.

[45] Deuteronomy 33.2 (Greek text); Zechariah 14.5; a similar image is found in
th. Enoch 1.9 (about second century BC).

[46] But John 3.5 still mentions the apocalyptic concept of the "kingdom of God",
hich does not occur elsewhere in John. Here the evangelist has borrowed a
raditional statement like that we have already noted in Matthew 18.3. Verse 3,
owever, shows how he understands the image: it refers to a kind of "seeing" that
possible in the present. The reference to (baptismal) water, too, occurs only in the
raditional statement in verse 5.

[47] This is also presupposed by Colossians 2.13, although verse 12 speaks of
eing buried with Christ in baptism.

[48] Not until Colossians 2.12, probably written by a disciple of Paul, do we come

the apocalyptic perspective of baptism, looking forward to the com
ing resurrection, judgment, and the kingdom of God. But he doe
this by way of warning against an enthusiastic religion that would pa
over concrete situations of this life and this earth, living already i
heaven. Therefore he declares with a frankness that is almost offen
sive that fornicators, idolators, adulterers, homosexuals, child
molesters, thieves, grabbers, drunkards, slanderers, and swindler
cannot inherit the kingdom of God, even though baptized (1 Cor
6.9–10). But this is not merely an ethical appeal such as any teache
of the law might issue; Paul continues: "Such were some of you
But you were washed, you were sanctified, you were justified in th
name of the Lord Jesus and in the Spirit of our God."

What we found in the case of God's righteousness and life i
Christ also holds true here: baptism places man within the sphere c
blessing and under the dominion of Jesus; therefore life uninfluence
by Christ is no longer possible except in the case of complete apostasy
When a man is baptized, he comes so completely under the blessin
and the dominion of the crucified and risen Lord that it is no longe
possible for him to want to sin (Rom.6.1ff.). It is indisputable tha
Paul thinks sacramentally in the sense that baptism actually incor
porates the baptized Christian into the body of Christ (1 Cor.12.13
setting him, by virtue of the Spirit, under the power of the "name" c
Christ (1 Cor.6.11). But since the "sphere" into which the baptize
Christian is brought, the "power" under which he is placed, is th
gracious lordship of the risen Christ, baptism can be called "efficac
ous" only when he continually acknowledges the lordship of Christ an
lets it work in him. The power of his Lord is not a force of nature
moving dead objects; it is the power of love, which becomes a forc
only when it is accepted.

The Eucharist, or, as Paul calls it, the Lord's Supper, is rooted i
the Last Supper of Jesus. Whether it was held on the evening of Pass
over, as the first three evangelists suppose, or on the eve of Passove
as John describes it, is hard to tell. In any case, Passover with it
associated ideas stands in the background; but these ideas are neve

---

to a different interpretation. Even there, however, burial with Christ takes plac
"in baptism", while resurrection takes place "through faith". This interpretatio
is secured by 3.1–4, according to which the new life is still hidden and will not b
manifest until the Parousia. Paul's sharp distinction between present and futu
can also be seen in his terminology: "reconciliation" is in the present; "salvation
is reserved for the future (cf. Rom.5.9–10).

stressed, and there is no mention of the Passover lamb (except in Luke 22.15). The words spoken by Jesus have been preserved in two forms: one is found in Paul (1 Cor. 11.23–25) and, in expanded form, in Luke; the other occurs in Mark (14.22–25) and in Matthew, who depends on the Marcan passage. The Pauline words are: "This is my body for you. This cup is the new covenant in my blood." The Marcan words are: "This is my body. This is my blood of the covenant, shed for many." In all probability, neither form is identical with what Jesus actually said, but the words as given by Paul are probably closer. They were written down about fifteen years earlier than the Marcan passage; above all, they are not formulated in exact parallelism. According to Jewish practice, both at Passover and at every meal eaten with friends, the entire dinner came between the blessing of the bread and the blessing of the cup (1 Cor. 11.25a); the lack of parallelism is therefore not surprising. But it is easy to see how the two formulas came to be assimilated when they were directly juxtaposed in the liturgy of the community; it would be difficult, however, to explain how originally parallel formulations could diverge.[49] Furthermore, the choice of the word "body" in Greek would be inconceivable if from the very beginning the formula had been parallel to the formula concerning "blood", because the opposite of "blood" is always "flesh", not "body".

In using the Aramaic word "body", Jesus was presumably referring simply to his own person, saying that he himself would be with his disciples whenever they ate his Supper. At the end of the meal, before their departure and Jesus' arrest, the words over the cup indicated that Jesus' death would furnish the basis for his presence among them as exalted Lord. All the accounts,[50] however, add to these two formulas a third that points forward to the imminent new banquet in the kingdom of God.

The various motifs present in this meal have been more or less strongly emphasized. The Palestinian community probably looked

[49] This assimilation continues beyond the New Testament. In Justin, the two formulas read: "This is my body. This is my blood." Modern liturgies often contain a cento of New Testament texts set in complete parallelism: "This is my body, broken (given) for you. This is my blood, shed for you (for the forgiveness of sins)"; such a formulation does not occur anywhere in the New Testament.

[50] Paul, it is true, preserves only an echo of this formula: "until he comes", a phrase added to the framework in 1 Corinthians 11.26. This expression probably has final meaning, as in Isaiah 62.1, 6–7 (O. Hofius, "Bis dass er kommt", *NTS* XIV [1967/68], pp. 439ff.).

forward primarily to the imminent kingdom of God with its festal banquet;[51] this community is probably the source of the ancient account still preserved in Luke 22.15–18, 24–30, into which Luke has interpolated the Marcan and Pauline account. The motif of the new covenant, within which the disciples enjoy table fellowship with their exalted Lord and which anticipates in a sense the eschatological banquet in the kingdom of God,[52] was probably central in the words as spoken by Jesus himself. This is true, at least, for the earliest determinable form of the Eucharistic words. As the assimilation of Mark 14.24 to Aramaic usage shows, the special emphasis on Jesus' sacrificial death "for many" was probably also common in the Aramaic-speaking community. All three motifs appear in all of our accounts, but with varying emphasis. The apocalyptic perspective is central to Luke's special account, but occurs also in Mark 14.25 and Luke 22.15. Recollection of the benefits for many brought about by Jesus' death on the cross is central to the Marcan tradition, but also occurs in 1 Corinthians 11.23 and Luke 22.27.

We see once more how the Corinthians were interpreting the Lord's Supper one-sidedly as a sacrament that already brought them into complete fellowship with God and eternal life. For this reason they attached importance only to the sacramental act itself. The rest of the meal could lend expression to this plenitude of bliss—the remark about drunkenness in 1 Corinthians 11.21 may go back to this idea—but it was not the crucial factor and could therefore take place before the arrival of the late-comers, as a rule probably the slaves, who could not take time off whenever they wanted. Now Paul in fact agrees with the Corinthians that bread and wine do represent a sharing in the body and the blood of Christ (1 Cor. 10.16). In his typical fashion, however, he transposes the two sentences, because he is only concerned with the statement concerning the bread, to which he appends his own interpretation: sharing in the eating of bread guarantees sharing in the body of Christ in the sense that it unites the participants in the one body of Christ (1 Cor. 10.17).

This is a most unexpected interpretation; but it is crucial for Paul because it protects against the kind of sacramental isolation in which everyone tastes the bliss of fellowship with God or Christ withou*

[51] Cf. above, pp. 66f.
[52] Cf. the juxtaposition of the same three motifs (deliverance through sacrificia* blood, table fellowship with God, and anticipation of eschatological glory) i* Exodus 24.8–11.

taking note of his brother. Paul has just warned the Corinthians against sacramentalizing either baptism or the Lord's Supper, using as an example what happened to Israel (1 Cor. 10.1–13). Above all, however, he declares that the Corinthians have completely subverted the Eucharist by refusing to take table fellowship with their brothers seriously and thus "humiliating those who have nothing" (1 Cor. 11.22). The same is true of the "unworthy" way in which they celebrate the Eucharist, which has brought sickness and death upon the community as the judgment of God (vss. 27, 30). Both before (vss. 20–22) and after (vss. 33–34) this warning, Paul accuses them of this one thing only: they have not waited for the poorest members, but have consumed the meal in advance, leaving only the sacrament till later. They are therefore guilty of the body and blood of Christ, because (according to 8.11–12) everyone who sins against his brother, for whom Christ died, sins against Christ himself.

Thus the very thing that happened to baptism has happened to the Eucharist. Paul rescues the Eucharist from an enthusiastic religiosity that would take by force today what will be given by God in the future. For Paul, this earth with its poor and needy is important enough that he cannot simply retreat from it in sacramental experience and flee to "heaven". The Lord's Supper itself incorporates the Christian into the body of Christ, placing him under the blessing and the lordship of him who unites each man with his brothers.

Here, then, we see the unity in Paul's view of Christ. The lordship of the risen Christ and all that it implies by way of hope and promise for the individual are important to him; but the risen Christ is always also Christ crucified. This renders impossible any enthusiastic theology of majesty. To live in Christ, to be a member of his body, means to belong to the host of those who are Christ's, through whom Christ seeks to serve the world. Thus for Paul the cross of Jesus is the real criterion of theological truth. This is not to be taken as meaning that the cross, properly understood, is opposed to the resurrection, properly understood. In the notion of the righteousness of God, of life in Christ, of the body of Christ, of baptism and the Eucharist, it always remains true that the crucified Christ bestows his blessing and exercises his lordship as the risen Christ. Recollection of the consummation to come in the kingdom of God—promised in the resurrection—recalls us from a false resurrection faith that would already dwell in heaven to life on this earth. Danger hardly threatens from the side of exaggerated discipleship to the crucified Jesus, with its implicit requirement of service to the world—by no means easy to perform. Danger threatens rather from a theology of majesty, which would have the glory of heaven guaranteed in the present, which would forget and leave behind this world and its needs. Paul writes in 1 Corinthians 15.12–19 that a gospel and a faith without assurance of the resurrection would be null and void; but he can also say that, as a preacher of the gospel, he had resolved "to know nothing among you except Jesus Christ and him crucified" (1 Cor. 2.2).

VI

THE EARTHLY JESUS: THE GOSPEL

THE TRADITION BEFORE THE WRITING OF
OUR GOSPELS

EASTER AS GOD'S ''YES'' TO JESUS' EARTHLY MINISTRY:
Q AND THE MIRACLE STORIES

When Jesus appeared to his disciples, they knew that God had said "yes" to their master, to his teachings and his entire conduct, although they had all supposed that everything had come to an end with his death on the cross and that it had been made clear that God had not been with him. His words and actions thus acquired new significance. God had expressly endorsed them by raising Jesus. That this was so from the beginning is clear; had it not been so, Jesus' words and deeds would not have been handed on from mouth to mouth. As far as we can tell, of course, the earliest community in Jerusalem naturally continued to live as a part of the Jewish cultic community, visiting the temple and following the law. This is shown not only by explicit references such as Acts 2.26 and 10.14, but above all by the account of Stephen and his circle. Although Acts seeks to soften the differences and postulates the unity of the primitive community, 8.1ff. reveals that only the "Hellenists" (i.e., the circle about Stephen) were persecuted by the Jewish population, obviously because these Hellenists had already impugned the validity of the temple cult and the law (Acts 6.11, 13–14).[1] Acts 8.14 reports that the Apostles—and naturally the community that adhered to them—were

---

[1] Here again Acts sees the work of false witnesses. It may be true that they maliciously aggravated the expressions in question, as seems also to have been the case in the trial of Jesus. They were probably right, however, in their estimation of the trend of Hellenistic preaching in Jerusalem.

still dwelling in Jerusalem unopposed. But the very naturalness with which the earliest community continues to live within the Jewish framework shows that they are not primarily concerned with Jesus' new, highly critical teaching concerning the law, but with expectation of the coming Lord.[2] At most, then, only small groups looked upon Jesus merely as a teacher of the law. Nevertheless, there can be no doubt that sayings of Jesus, especially those of an ethical character, were preserved and handed on, just as sayings of Jewish teachers of the law were repeated and memorized. They were gradually assembled in minor collections such as the related parables in Matthew 13. 31–33, and 44–48, or in various rules of conduct for the community of God, which were combined according to the catchword principle for ease in memorization (Mark 9.37–50).[3]

Finally, individual sayings and traditional groups of sayings were collected in the so-called Sayings Source (Q). We no longer possess this source, but can reconstruct it in part, although many questions of detail are sharply disputed. Apart from the material whose words and, for the most part, sequence Matthew and Luke have borrowed from Mark,[4] there is an additional series of sections not in Mark that both Matthew and Luke share. It turns out that those passages agreeing almost word for word usually appear in the same order in both Gospels, although the two evangelists often assign them to very different occasions.[5] In addition, there are other sections that agree in con-

---

[2] Cf. above, p. 52.   [3] Cf. E. Schweizer, *Good News according to Mark*, pp. 193ff.

[4] Luke follows Mark almost everywhere, incorporating all other traditions in the so-called "travel account" (Luke 9.51—18.14); Matthew composes his Gospel independently, concentrating the miracle stories of Mark, for example, mostly in chapters 8—9. On the question of Q and the Gospels, see Siegfried Schulz, *Die Stunde der Botschaft* (Hamburg: Furche, 1967).

[5] We list here only those sections with almost identical wording. Other sections, such as the "Sermon on the Plain" (Luke 6.20–49), appear in Matthew in almost the same sequence, but differ extensively in wording. These probably go back to a special tradition.

Luke		Matthew	
3.7–9	=	3.7–10	The Baptist's call to repentance
(16), 17	=	(11), 12	Announcement of the Judge
4.2–12	=	4.2–12	Temptations of Jesus
7.6–9	=	8.8–10	Centurion at Capernaum
18–35	=	11.2–19	Sayings to and about the Baptist
9.57–62	=	(8.19–22)	Sayings concerning dicipleship
10.13–15	=	11.21–23	Woes over Chorazin and Bethsaida
21–22	=	25–27	Jesus' exultation

tent but often differ considerably in wording; the two evangelists also cite them in different sequence. However one interprets this second observation, the first proves that there must have been a written source used by Matthew and Luke, because identical sequence and almost identical Greek wording cannot be explained on the basis of purely oral tradition.[6]

The message of this source is peculiar. On the one hand, it comprises only sayings of Jesus, provided with short introductions, situations, or similar material.[7] Primarily, then, Jesus was understood as

---

23–24	=	(13.16–17)	Beatitude
11.9–13	=	(7.7–11)	Parable on prayer
14–23	=	12.22–30	Discussion concerning Beelzebub
24–26	=	43–45	Parable on apostasy
29–32	=	38–42	Sign of Jonah; Judgment
39–51	=	23.23–36	Attack on Pharisees and scribes
13.34–35	=	37–39	Appeal to Jerusalem
12.22–31	=	(6.25–33)	Sayings concerning cares and riches
12.39–46	=	24.43–51	Parables on the Parousia

It is certain that Matthew shifted 8.19–22 (cf. below, p. 135, n. 22) and 6.25–33 because he assembles Jesus' ethical sayings from all sources in the Sermon on the Mount. In addition, he moved 13.16–17 up to its present position. He did this because he had so emphasized 13.13 (which he borrowed from Mark 4.12) with its curse on unbelievers by the addition of the Isaiah quotation in verses 14–15 that he had to introduce the contrasting beatitude concerning believers at this point. The Sermon on the Mount was a good setting for 7.7–11. Conversely, Matthew 23.34–39 still shows that the two sayings in which Wisdom was originally the speaker (Luke 11.49!) once stood next to each other. Luke moved 13.34–35 to the end because he wanted to link it with 13.31–33, Jesus' departure from Galilee and the saying concerning the death of the prophets at Jerusalem.

[6] For a different view, see the summary by H. T. Wrege in his *Überlieferungsgeschichte der Bergpredigt* (Wissenschaftliche Untersuchungen zum Neuen Testament 9, Tübingen: Mohr, 1968), pp. 1–4. Comparison between Mark and Luke shows that, when there is a written source, even though the wording may be greatly changed the sequence is preserved; when wording and sequence both remain the same, and we are dealing with as large a corpus as that represented by Q, an explanation on the basis of oral tradition is impossible. It is not completely out of the question for this source originally to have contained some Marcan material, and for Matthew and Luke to have borrowed from Q only what they had not already got from Mark. It is also conceivable that Luke was acquainted with a tradition of Mark already expanded by the addition of Q.

[7] In Matthew 8.8–10 (=Luke 7.6–9), only the conversation between Jesus and the centurion (or his friends) is identical, while the story itself is told in different ways; of course there must have been a brief statement of the situation.

a teacher. It is clear, however, that this does not exhaust his significance. The actual sayings brought together in Q point back to his miracles, so that an understanding of Jesus as a divine miracle-worker seems to be presupposed. This view has been corrected in a crucial way, however, through the express interpretation of the miracles as the fufillment of Old Testament promises. There is no reference to Jesus' cross or resurrection, but probably to the eschatological coming of Jesus, the Son of Man, as judge and savior. We may ask what this signifies.

It is probably certain that Jesus himself never spoke expressly of his death and resurrection. It is therefore to be expected that the cross and resurrection would not appear in a collection of Jesus' sayings. The situation is different with the sayings concerning the Son of Man, which probably go back to Jesus, even though in Q they have already been elaborated, expanded, and enriched by the community.[8] In 1 Corinthians 11.23 we find a reference in the Eucharistic liturgy to the events surrounding Jesus' arrest and execution ("on the night when he was betrayed"); this shows that at the Eucharist the community recalled at least parts of the passion narrative. Of course this does not prove anything for the Palestinian community, from which Q derives. Since, however, compilations of ethical sayings and collections of Biblical stories circulated independently side by side in the Jewish community, it is quite likely that the community that used Q as a collection of Jesus' sayings was also acquainted with the passion and Easter narrative in written or oral form and retold or recited this narrative during, say, the worship of the Easter season.

Therefore even if we cannot tell precisely what role the passion and Easter narrative played in the life of this community, we can still see that Jesus' ministry of authority, which fulfilled all the Old Testament promises, and his future role at the coming of God's kingdom were of crucial importance. Yet there had been no attempt to link the significance of Jesus' humility, his cross, or even his resurrection from the dead with what was known through the tradition of the community of Jesus' message. On the other hand, there is strong emphasis on faith (Luke 7.6–9), and Jesus is ranked high above the Baptist (7.18–35), so that those who see him see what the prophets longed to see (10.23–24), and those who reject him despite his acts of

[8] It is therefore not proper to conclude that Jesus' cross and resurrection were unimportant to this community. With respect to the Easter event, at least, such a conclusion is in any case almost inconceivable.

authority will fare worse at the judgment than Sodom and Gomorrha (10.13–15). With Jesus the kingdom of God has already come among men (11.20); in Jesus there speaks the Wisdom of God, which longs to gather God's people under her wings (11.49–51; 13.34–35). In him, indeed, the Son of God has come, for whom all miracles are possible (4.2–12).

This collection of the Lord's sayings is probably rooted in the Palestinian community, but it has undergone several decades of development and has also adopted motifs from Diaspora Judaism, with its more marked Hellenism. There may also have been Jewish Christians who merely considered Jesus a teacher of the law, like a Jewish rabbi, and were not inclined to go beyond this view. There is some evidence for such a theory,[9] but this interpretation of Jesus, which considered him in essence merely a divine teacher and a new interpreter of the law, probably was always limited to isolated circles bearing a strong Jewish stamp.

Probably, however, there was also a very different way of looking on the ministry of the earthly Jesus as the real focal point of faith. One could see in Jesus a divine miracle-worker like those venerated in the vicinity of Palestine, for example in Syria. Did he not heal the sick? Was not his resurrection the miracle of miracles, the ultimate revelation of the same divine authority that had been revealed during his earthly life in healings, in raising the dead, in stilling storms, so that the resurrection was the logical culmination of his miraculous ministry? Of course the Jewish Messiah was hardly expected to perform miracles apart from crushing God's enemies with superhuman force. In the world of Hellenism,[10] however, there were more or less strange miracle-workers, who performed prodigies and were venerated as possessors of extraordinary divine powers. It is possible that the picture of Jesus as a divine miracle-worker already played an important role among those opposed by Paul in 2 Corinthians. In any event, it placed its stamp increasingly on many of the stories told about

[9] Cf. the discussion of Matthew, p. 134 below.

[10] The connection between these figures and the Greek "divine man" is a matter of dispute. The divine man was originally only a philosopher, poet, or statesman inspired by God, while the figure of the miracle-worker does not appear in written sources until the second half of the second century. It seems more likely, therefore, that the picture of Jesus was shaped by the miracles performed by Old Testament men of God, as depicted by Hellenistic Judaism following the Old Testament, and by all sorts of magical figures in Egypt and Syria. Cf. W. von Martiz and E. Schweizer in G. Kittel, ed., *TWNT* VIII, pp. 337ff., 378–9.

Jesus that Mark found extant in the tradition when he set about writing his Gospel.[11] The community that told these miracle stories and developed them is therefore most likely to be sought in the vicinity of Palestine, say in Syria. Its influence, of course, penetrated beyond the borders of its homeland.

But was this understanding of Jesus correct? We noted as a striking feature of Q that it had no place for the cross of Jesus. Even if the community that produced Q was also familiar with the Passion narrative and took it seriously, no explicit connection was made between Jesus' death on the cross and the beginning of his ministry in Galilee. This holds true especially for the picture of the miracle-worker. The question cannot be evaded: why did his miraculous power, which overcame disease and tempest, even death itself, fail at Gethsemane and Golgotha? Q, like the miracle stories, had a true vision. Jesus' earthly ministry, especially his preaching, was the fulfillment of Old Testament hopes, was the presence of God's approaching kingdom. But it was by no means the whole Jesus that lived on in this tradition. At best, his cross was one element alongside his sayings and his miracles. But there was also as yet no understanding of Easter, apart from the assurance that God had ratified what had already been asserted by the message and ministry of the earthly Jesus. And so the question remains: how are we to understand Jesus' message and ministry on earth, which culminated on the cross and in the resurrection on the morning of Easter?

MARK

GOD'S REVELATION IN THE PASSION OF JESUS AND IN THE CALL TO DISCIPLESHIP

This is the situation in which Mark writes his Gospel. The writing of a Gospel is in itself a theological accomplishment of the first order. There was no model to follow. There were descriptions of the lives of great men, but this is not what Mark offers us. There is no mention of Jesus' birth and childhood. Jesus simply appears in Mark 1.9. Nothing is said of his inward or outward development; we are given not the slightest information about his age or his appearance or his family

---

[11] Dieter Georgi, *Die Gegner des Paulus im 2. Korintherbrief* (WMANT 11, 1964); for a contrary view, see W. Schmithals in *TLZ* XCII (1967), cols. 668ff.

status;[12] his mother and brothers are only mentioned in passing (3.21, 31; 6.3). On the other hand, his passion and death, which in a normal biographical account would be mentioned in a few sentences, are described in such detail that they constitute a major portion of the entire document, appearing again and again from 3.6 on. There were also collections of the sayings of wise men, which occasionally contained brief data concerning situation or circumstances. Once again, however, this is not what Mark offers us. There are very few sayings, not to mention discourses, of Jesus; the bulk of the material is narrative. But what is actually narrated? The mighty acts of God in and upon the man Jesus. For this there is only a remote precedent: parts of the historical books of the Old Testament or perhaps the book of Jonah. Thus the very form of the Gospel makes it clear that the focus is not on wise sayings that can be recalled from the lips of a teacher and handed down, or on exemplary actions that one must imitate so as to make them one's own; the focus is on the great act of God that stretches from the beginning of Jesus' ministry to his last breath, or rather to God's raising him from the dead.

Even more important is the way the Gospel is shaped in detail. Jesus probably does not appear until his baptism by John because Mark is still unacquainted with any stories about Jesus' birth or childhood. What we hear first, in fact, are two quotations from the Old Testament (1.2–3). Precisely because Mark draws very little on the Old Testament, this introduction makes it clear that in Jesus he is present who finally fulfills what God has done in Israel. This is underlined by the reference to the Baptist as the beginning of the proclamation.[13] He, too, points forward to him who is yet to come (1.4–8). Above all, Jesus' entire ministry is preceded by a kind of "Prologue in Heaven". According to Mark, when Jesus is baptized he alone sees the heavens open and he alone hears the voice of God, calling him to be God's Son (1.9–11). The temptation, too, involves only Jesus, Satan, and God's angels (1.12–13). Thus from the very outset the reader is shown clearly the dimension in which everything takes place. Therefore

[12] We should in fact be told that he was single, since normally every adult Jew married.

[13] While Mark speaks of Jesus' "teaching" about twenty times (and only once, using another Greek form, of the teaching of the disciples), the word "proclaim" is used (as well as the words "repentance" and "good news", which designate the content of the proclamation) when Mark speaks of the Baptist, as well as when he speaks of Jesus, the disciples, or the worldwide church.

only he will understand correctly who will hear that in Jesus God himself seeks to speak and act on earth.

Jesus' ministry is clearly divided by the event of Caesarea Philippi (8.27ff.). The first half begins with a thrice-repeated general description of Jesus' activity, followed by the call or sending of his disciples (1.14–15, 16–20; 3.7–12, 13–19; 6.6b, 7–13). Each section concludes with a rejection of Jesus, first by the Pharisees, who plot his death already (3.6), then by his fellow citizens in Nazareth (6.1–6), and finally by his own disciples (8.14–21). In the first of the three sections, Jesus' authority over the very demons is demonstrated by word and deed (1.21–45); but 2.1—3.5 goes on at once to show that this authority is properly understood only when it is recognized as authority over sin and the law.[14] In the second section it is shown that Jesus can speak of God only in parables because men cannot understand direct speech concerning God (3.20—4.34).[15] This section concludes (4.35—5.43) with several miracle stories that were associated with this material even before Mark; the stilling of the storm and the raising of a dead girl put in the shade all that has gone before. The third section is dominated by two stories concerning eating, in which human blindness is illustrated once again. Between them is interpolated a crucial dispute about the law and the example of the believing pagan (7.1–30). Beyond doubt Jesus' miracles play an important role in these chapters. In these miracles God's power and authority are revealed, but Jesus repeatedly forbids the onlookers to speak of them. Mark is saying that only he who understands what Jesus has to say in 8.31 and 8.34ff. can really recognize the power of God expressed in Jesus' miracles. Thus the entire first half of Jesus' ministry, which exhibits the blindness of the Pharisees, of Jesus' fellow citizens, even of his own disciples, is concluded with the story of the blind man whose eyes can be opened only by a miracle of God (8.22–26).

The second half of Jesus' ministry begins with Peter's confession (8.27–33). Mark does not stress the confession, with which Peter has not even attained the level of the demons that called Jesus "Son of God" in 3.11 and 5.7. Nor does Jesus hail Peter's confession; without accepting it or rejecting it, he merely tells his disciples not to speak of

[14] Thus Mark, starting from an entirely different kind of theological approach, comes to a conclusion strikingly similar to that of Paul.

[15] It is still possible to show how Mark groups his various traditional fragments in 3.20–35 around verse 23a, which states for the first time that Jesus spoke in parables. See E. Schweizer, *Good News according to Mark*, pp. 85f.

it. The focal point of the Caesarea Philippi episode, however, is Jesus' statement concerning the suffering, death, and resurrection of the Son of Man (8.31). This is the first sentence that speaks directly of God, fully revealing his nature and actions. We read in 8.32a, "He said this plainly", in contrast to 2.2, where the same phrase, but without the addition of "plainly", introduces the proclamation of victory over sin and the law, and also in contrast to 4.33-34, where it concludes the parables: "With many such parables he spoke the word to them, as they were able to hear it; he did not speak to them without a parable." With respect to the announcement of Jesus' passion, we see that Peter, like the rest of the disciples,[16] does not yet understand at all (8.32-33). Jesus' call to follow him, which is expressly addressed to all the disciples (8.34ff.), shows the way a man must take to understand Jesus. Only now can God reveal, at least to the three most trusted disciples, that Jesus is his Son, and call on them to listen carefully to him (9.7). The same series of events is repeated twice more: Jesus points to his coming passion and death, the disciples completely misunderstand him, and he calls on them to follow him (9.30-31, 32-34, 35ff.; 10.32-34, 35, 37, 38ff.). This whole second period is dominated by the notion of discipleship. Even the healing in 9.14-29 is not a miracle story, but, to Mark, a story about the faith— or lack of faith—of a disciple. Here, too, the evangelist naturally uses extant traditional material, for example an extended section in the form of a catechism concerning the proper conduct of a disciple of Jesus. This section is unified by a chain of catchwords.[17] The entire second period, and thus the entire ministry of Jesus outside Jerusalem, concludes once more with the story of a blind man whose eyes can be opened only by a miracle of God, so that he can "follow Jesus on the road" (10.46ff.). This repeats the catchwords with which the last third began in verse 32, where Jesus is "on the road" to Jerusalem and the cross, with his disciples "following" him. God's miracle, which opens the blind man's eyes and enables him to follow Jesus on the road, is the last we hear of Jesus before the passion narrative.

In the passion narrative (11.1—16.8), the sequence of events is for

---

[16] Jesus turns to address all the disciples (8.33), although he is only answering Peter.

[17] "In my name", 9.37, 38; "turn away", 9.42, 43-45; "fire", 9.48, 49; "salt", 9.49, 50. The only break in the chain comes between verses 41 and 42; at one time these were also linked by a common catchword, for Matthew 10.42 shows that the saying in Mark 9.41 once shared the catchword "these little ones" with verse 42. See Schweizer, *Beiträge*, pp. 109ff.

the most part already fixed. The very length of this section shows how crucial the passion and death of Jesus are for Mark. There have also been references to Jesus' impending death from 3.6 on. Admittedly Mark does not contain any theory to explain the passion except for the traditional saying concerning ransom in 10.45 (cf. 14.24). But one thing is clear: Jesus so identifies himself with God's side that, despite all human blindness, he goes to his death for his persistence. Only so can blind eyes be opened; only so can men find the way to discipleship.

The disciples fail Jesus again and again (14.18–21, 37–50, 66–72); their failure shows once more how impossible it is for men to know God. But this knowledge is granted even to pagans, thus eliminating all distinctions. This was brought out in chapter 7 and is here re-emphasized (11.17;[18] 12.9–10; 15.39). Of course the discourse about the coming Son of Man and the kingdom of God (ch. 13) plays an important role, but only in the same sense as in the other passage that refers to it (8.38—9.1); Jesus' Parousia gives both depth and promise to the discipleship that follows the path of Jesus' suffering. Without any euphemism Mark depicts the harshness of Jesus' death, recording only the single outcry "My God, my God, why hast thou forsaken me?" and stating that Jesus died "with a loud cry". The instructions given by the angel whom the women discover at the empty tomb, however, point toward the future: the risen Lord already goes before his disciples; they may follow him (16.7). Thus God's grace grants to those who have failed Jesus the gift to discipleship, in which they can truly recognize him, and in which Jesus' disciples, and with them the whole community of those who believe in him, will follow through the years to come the Lord who goes before them.[19]

MATTHEW

JESUS, INTERPRETER AND FULFILLER OF THE LAW

Matthew, like Luke, differs from Mark in the first place by beginning not with Jesus' baptism but with (or, in Luke's case, before) his

[18] Only Mark contains the saying about a house of prayer "for all the nations". This saying is given unusual emphasis by a profusion of Markan rhetoric, by the reinforced decision of the authorities to put Jesus to death (vss. 17–18), and by the frame, which Mark himself probably created (cf. the different arrangement in Matthew): the cursing of the fig tree as a symbol for the end of a cult restricted to Jerusalem.

[19] Cf. E. Schweizer, *Das Evangelium nach Markus* (NTD 1*, 1967), pp. 220ff.

birth. The purpose is not biographical, of course. Nowhere else do we find as many quotations from the Old Testament as in the first two chapters. What the two quotations in Mark 1.2–3 hint at is here developed in detail: this is he who fulfills and consummates the Old Testament. There is, however, no stress, as there is in Luke, on the miracle of Jesus' birth; the emphasis lies instead on Jesus' name, given him by God, which fulfills the promise of the Old Testament (1.21–23), and on his journey from Bethlehem through Rama and Egypt to the obscure town of Nazareth, and finally to Capernaum (2.6, 15, 18, 23; 4.13ff.). Thus these chapters show that in Jesus the promised bearer of salvation, the Son of God himself, has come, a fact that even the lowliness of his parentage and of his dwelling place cannot deny. At the same time, it is possible that he is being depicted as the forerunner of wandering charismatic prophets such as were typical of the Syrian communities.[20]

More important is the fact that Matthew included much more of the actual preaching of Jesus. What Jesus taught is crucial for Mark, too, but Mark 1.22 shows clearly the difference between Mark and Matthew. Mark simply informs his readers that Jesus' divine authority shone forth in "the way he taught" without at the time saying anything about its content. This authority is thus completely parallel to that revealed in exorcism (Mark 1.27). Matthew transfers the statement, not using it until 7.28, that is, after he has given in the Sermon on the Mount an example of Jesus' teaching, by which the reader can see for himself the truth of the statement. The difference is not accidental. It is a central notion to Mark that Jesus reveals God ("teaches"). This takes place with special authority, which shows itself in the unprecedented effectuality of both his words and his acts. But this authority cannot simply be observed; for man has no measure by which to weigh the words of Jesus against those of the scribes and judge between them. Therefore only he who believes can bear witness to this authority and call on others to follow Jesus. For only he who follows as a disciple will be able to understand the force of Jesus' words and deeds. It would therefore be pointless simply to set before the reader examples of Jesus' words or deeds, without insisting repeat-

[20] Cf. Krister Stendahl, "Quis et unde? An Analysis of Mt 1—2", in Walther Eltester, ed., *Judentum, Urchristentum, Kirche; Festschrift für J. Jeremias* (BZNW 26, 1960), pp. 94–105; Rudolf Pesch, "Der Gottessohn im matthäischen Evangeliumsprolog", *Biblica* XLVIII (1967), pp. 395–420; E. Schweizer "Observance of the Law and Charismatic Activity in Matthew", *NTS* XVI (1969/70), pp. 213–30.

edly from the very outset that both words and deeds can only be misunderstood apart from following the way of Jesus, which is in the first instance the way of the cross. For Matthew, however, it is possible to give Jesus' credentials, above all in the manner of his preaching. Therefore, as the interpolation of the birth and childhood narratives already shows, he transforms the Markan outline, turning it into something closer to a story of Jesus' life, from which the reader can acquire a certain picture of Jesus. Above all, as we have already noted, he includes sizable sections of discourse material, which he combines to form organized complexes. To him, Jesus is above all a teacher, who demonstrated his authority primarily through his attitude toward the law.

This shows the situation in which Matthew is writing. Whatever the details may have been, so much is clear: Matthew attaches great importance to the distinction between Christianity and Pharisaic Judaism, which had consolidated itself and become doctrinally more rigid in the years following the destruction of Jerusalem (AD 70). He has no intention of breaking the link with the tradition from which Jesus and his community derive. Matthew can record sayings like 23.2–3 or 5.17–18, which state that the scribes are absolutely right in principle, although they do not draw the proper conclusions with respect to their own lives, or that not a letter nor a stroke will disappear from the law until it is fulfilled. This shows that Matthew stands in a tradition that understood Jesus as a Jewish teacher, who, however, tightened up the law and above all called on men to practise what they preached. But of course Matthew himself no longer considers Jesus merely a teacher in the sense of a Jewish rabbi. It is Matthew who preserves sayings, mostly from Q, that distinguish Jesus most sharply from all others, who are merely teachers (4.3; 5.21–48; 11.27; 12.28, 41–42; 13.17; 25.31). It is Matthew who concludes with the statement: "All authority in heaven and on earth has been given to me. . . . and lo, I am with you always, to the close of the age." It is Matthew who records the words that promise salvation to the heathen: "Go therefore and make disciples of all nations." Jesus nevertheless proves to be a teacher and reinterpreter of the law: "Teach them to observe all that I have commanded you" (Matt. 28.18–20). What makes him superior to all other teachers is the authority with which he restates the law, even to the point of abrogating Old Testament commandments. He does not do this as though something quite new were beginning; the law rather finds its fulfillment in a better righteousness than that of the Pharisees (5.20), namely, love of God and of one's neighbor.[21] But such righteousness is possible only because Jesus is not only a teacher, but is himself the meek and humble one who fulfills righteousness (as early as 3.15!). Jesus receives those who follow him as disciples into this righteousness. Thus Jesus' lowliness strangely becomes a major theme for Matthew. Jesus' authority, which distinguishes him from all other teachers of the law and empowers him to use the words "But I say to you" is grounded in the fact that he himself walks the path of righteousness, in humility and weakness, blazing a trail for his disciples.[22]

Matthew certainly lays special emphasis on what Jesus requires. He is certainly concerned that what Jesus commands should really be performed, so that he sometimes even inserts regulations that run the risk of legalism. His Gospel has therefore been understood as a mere radicalization of the law. In fact, however, his purpose is to bear witness to the transcendent power of love, which must express itself in requirements if it would establish on earth the kingdom of God's power of love. But when one sees that the most pointed statements of the Sermon on the Mount confront each man with the needs of his

[21] In 22.39, Matthew declares that the commandment to love one's neighbor is "like" that to love God, while Mark calls it the "second" commandment; he goes on to say in verse 40 that everything in the law and the prophets is contained in these two commandments. In 19.19, Matthew adds the commandment to love one's neighbor, although it is not in Mark and does not form a part of the Ten Commandments, which are being listed (cf. 7.12 and E. Schweizer, "Matth. 5.17–20. Anmerkungen zum Gesetzesverständnis des Matthäus", in his *Neotestamentica*, p. 402; also R. A. Guelich, *Not to Annul the Law, Rather to Fulfill the Law and the Prophets*, Dissertation, Hamburg, 1967, with a summary on pp. 266–70). Matthew's scepticism toward a theology that is no longer strictly linked to the earthly Jesus is shown by Stuhlmacher, *op cit.*, pp. 238ff.

[22] Matthew 8.18–27 furnishes an excellent example. Here Matthew rewrites the story of how Jesus stills the tempest (Mark 4.35–41), interpolating between Mark 4.35 and 36 the section concerning two disciples, and reformulating Mark's general expression ("leaving the crowd, they took him with them, just as he was, in the boat") to read: "and his disciples followed him [i.e. into the boat]". The point is that in contrast to those with whom Jesus has just been speaking, they act on their discipleship, so that the miracle story becomes a presentation of what a disciple encounters when he ventures to follow Jesus. See Günther Bornkamm in *Tradition and Interpretation in Matthew*, by Günther Bornkamm, Gerhard Barth, and Heinz-Joachim Held, trans. P. Scott (NTL, 1963), pp. 52–7. Other important studies of Matthew include: Krister Stendahl, *The School of St Matthew* (ASNU 20, 1954); Georg Strecker, *Der Weg der Gerechtigkeit* (FRLANT 82, 1962); Reinhart Hummel, *Die Auseinandersetzung zwischen Kirche und Judentum* (BevTh 33, 1963); Rolf Walker, *Die Heilsgeschichte im ersten Evangelium* (FRLANT 91, 1967).

fellowman, rather than making him examine his own soul and consider his spiritual successes or failures, one realizes how Jesus' unprecedented freedom with regard to the letter of the law, a freedom that surpasses anything expected of the Messiah, leads to a new liberty in which the individual, following after Jesus, exposes himself to the power of God's love. Finally, the freedom with which Matthew himself takes the sayings of Jesus, regrouping and reinterpreting them, adapting them to his own time, is the best evidence that we are not dealing merely with a new law of Jesus that replaces the law of Moses, but with the living Lord who reigns over his community, seeking obedience of its members and granting obedience to them. This living Lord cannot be exchanged for a mere idea claiming only intellectual assent, nor for a new legalism that claims the outward act but not the heart. With the words "but I say to you", the new world of the eschaton begins—in Jesus, who dares to put himself in God's place, offering and granting men discipleship, for which he goes to his death.

Thus the Gospel concludes with the statement "I am with you always, to the close of the age", extending, as it were, the Easter experience of the disciples into the Christian community. The presence of the risen Lord, as encountered by the disciples on the mountain in Galilee, continues on in his community. Matthew is the only one of the evangelists who uses the word "community" or "church". According to 16.18, the church is to be built upon Peter, the "Rock". This can hardly have a different meaning from Paul's referring to himself as the apostle who laid the foundation for the community (e.g., 1 Cor.3.10). In like fashion, the letters written by Paul's disciples[23] consider him the sole foundation of the community. The power to bind and loose is granted to Peter (16.19) as well as to the community as a whole (18.18).[24] Above all, however, we can see that Matthew is closely related to the movement which sees in the gifts of the Spirit appearing in the community the work of the Lord, who is already present. The importance Matthew attaches to the acts of authority and power performed by the community is shown by 10.1, where the words used for such acts are the same as those used for the acts of Jesus (9.35 = 4.23). Similarly, the wonders that prove to the Baptist that Jesus is he in whom the promised eschaton has already begun are described in the present tense (11.4). That this is not fortuitous, but

[23] Cf. below, p. 174.
[24] Verses 17 and 19–20 are addressed to the community as a whole.

indicates rather that such wonders will continue, is shown by the fact that this section is not used as the conclusion to chapters 8—9, in which Jesus' miracles are collected. This is the more striking because in 9.27–34 Matthew has clearly composed and interpolated two stories in addition to the traditional material before him, in order to have a prior account of all the miracles of Jesus mentioned in 11.4. Thus his insertion of chapter 10 can make sense only as a way of indicating before 11.4 that the same miracles are to continue in the community. Finally, in Matthew 17.20–21 the saying concerning faith that moves mountains is inserted in an exhortation to the disciples, so that it becomes the point of the story of the healing of the epileptic boy, while the father's exclamation, "I believe; help my unbelief!" (Mark 9.24), is eliminated by Matthew.[25] The question of the law is important to Matthew; Jesus is introduced as a teacher of the law and of a better righteousness; it is very easy to understand Jesus as living on among his disciples simply in "all that [he] commanded [them]" (28.20). But it would be a complete misunderstanding of Matthew not to see the other side: Jesus is he who himself lived out this better righteousness to the point of death on the cross; this is the power that makes discipleship and life in the community possible. This is demonstrated in the acts of authority and power performed by Jesus' disciples, who bind and loose, heal and deliver, experiencing as they do so nothing less than the living presence of the risen Lord.

LUKE

JESUS' EARTHLY MINISTRY AND ITS SIGNIFICANCE FOR THE COMMUNITY

It was Luke's decisive contribution to see the problem posed by the passage of time. Primitive Christianity with its apocalyptic perspective could still see the resurrection of Jesus as the beginning of the events of the end and expect the imminent resurrection of all the dead together with the Last Judgment. Even Paul, who has the keenest mind for theological questions, can still say without qualification that "now"

---

[25] Cf. also 11.20; 12.28ff. Of course the theme of the law is treated expressly, that of charismatic acts only indirectly, or in any case less emphatically than in Mark 16.17–18 (not genuine, but relatively early, according to F. Hahn, *Mission in the New Testament* (SBT 47, 1965), pp. 63–5, 73–4; genuine according to E. Linnemann in *ZTK* LXVI (1969), pp. 255ff.).

is the day of salvation because the crucified and risen Jesus is now being proclaimed to the Christian community. He can, as it were, simply skip over the period of time elapsed between AD 30 and the fifties. As early as the time of Mark a Gospel must be written, referring back to Jesus' death and resurrection, which are already several decades in the past; but there is as yet no attempt to consider how the period of the church is related to the period covered by the Gospel. Matthew conceals the problem by what amounts to a timeless understanding of Jesus' commands and of the gift of discipleship. The Sermon on the Mount is as true in the seventies or eighties as it was in the twenties; the same can be said of Jesus' life of humility, which makes discipleship possible. The problem was resolved in different ways by Paul and Q, and particularly by Mark and Matthew. Luke, further removed in time from the Jesus event, felt the problem more intensely.

A Christianity with nothing more to offer than a timeless code of ethics or an equally timeless doctrine of salvation, which no longer lived in any real sense from what took place in Palestine in the twenties, would obviously no longer be the community of Jesus' disciples, living from the Gospel. On the other hand, a Christianity that lived from a glorious past without any present would be impossible. In what way, then, did Jesus' ministry and teaching, his death and resurrection, live on in the community? Were they like the actions of a hero, the consequences of which live on in the present? Were they like the teaching of a philosopher, to which one still gives an attentive ear? The claim that Jesus was with his community as its risen Lord clearly meant much more than this.

But how, then, was this presence to be distinguished from his presence in the twenties? Then, of course, he lived as a human person on earth, visible, audible, tangible. But what did this different kind of presence mean theologically? Why did he have to be present with his disciples as an earthly person before he was with them as the risen Lord?

And how is his presence in the community between Easter and the Parousia connected with his presence in the period of his earthly ministry? Should we speak in terms of a history of his operation in the community, to be understood as a process of development, as progress from a beginning towards a goal, already reached or still to come? Or do all men of all ages stand in the same relationship to the age of Jesus?

What, furthermore, is the significance of the Old Testament? How is God's presence in the earthly Jesus, but also in the post-Easter community, related to his presence in the Israel of the Old Testament? Can this be comprehended in the schema of progressive history, with the Old Testament period representing the transcended past or a mere preparation for the higher stage that was to follow? In other words, is the Old Testament period still relevant to the community of Jesus? These are the kinds of questions that arise. They concern the period of the Old Testament, the period of Jesus' life on earth, and the period of the church.

Even Q had already expressly considered the relationship between Jesus and the Old Testament; Matthew had gone into it at some length.[26] The relationship of the Christian community to Jesus had been resolved by Mark, and, more consciously, by Matthew, through his understanding of discipleship. By the time of Luke, neither question can be dealt with in the same way. The relationship to the Old Testament must be rethought, because the dispute with Judaism plays scarcely any role in the Gentile church of Luke. The law is no longer a vital force, and threatens to become a museum piece.[27] For this very reason, it is now possible to understand the law as a preliminary stage from which the transition to the gospel is easily possible. Precisely because the law is no longer an effective force in the present, hostile to the gospel, but is essentially an item of past history, Luke can accept it all the more readily as promise and preparation. He practically speaks the language of the Greek Old Testament, loves phrases from his Greek Bible, even where he does not refer to them directly or, as he often does, quote them. Not only is this true for the Old Testament as a historical book, it is also true of the law and the righteousness it requires. In a manner that is quite different from anything we find in Matthew, and above all in Paul, the religious practice of Judaism passes more or less uninterrupted into its fulfillment, the Christian faith. Jesus' parents are pictured as Jews faithful to the law, who observe its regulations precisely (2.27; cf. 2.41); and Jesus himself begins his activity programatically by participating in Jewish synagogue worship, interpreting a prophetical passage whose fulfillment he proclaims (4.16–21).[28] The temple appears at the

26 Cf. above, pp. 126 and 133.
27 Acts 28.23, for example, can speak of the "Law of Moses".
28 It appears also that the references to David and the Messiah in 1.32–33 go back to Luke's redaction.

beginning of the Gospel; it is Jesus' proper place (as early as 2.49–50)
It also stands at the end of the Gospel, now occupied by the legitimate
community as they praise God. There is equally great emphasis on
Jerusalem. The promise to Zechariah is set there; there Jesus' life is
dedicated to God (2.22) and there his ministry begins (2.41ff.)
Jerusalem is mentioned repeatedly as the goal of Jesus' travels (9.31
51, 53; 13.22, 33; 17.11; 19.11); this is a peculiarity of Luke's arrangement. Jesus' disciples must remain in Jerusalem until God's Spirit
himself sends them elsewhere (24.47, 49, 52).

The relationship of the church to Jesus must also be considered
afresh, because decades have passed since Jesus' death and resurrection, and even the destruction of Jerusalem is an event of the somewhat distant past; the coming of the Son of Man on the clouds of
heaven has not turned out to be imminent. It has therefore become
possible to survey the period between Easter and the present. Now it
is important not to misrepresent Luke. It is true that in Jesus' opening
sermon, which is placed programatically at the beginning of the
Gospel, we read: "Today this scripture has been fulfilled" (4.21)
referring to the day Jesus stood in the synagogue at Nazareth, while
Paul can say in 2 Corinthians 6.2: "Behold, now is the acceptable
time; behold, now is the day of salvation," obviously including the
whole period in which the gospel is proclaimed, as is now being done
by Paul himself.[29] It is also true that Luke dates the sacred event of
Christmas or of the Baptist's appearance by referring to contemporary
events of secular history (2.2; 3.1). But does this differ basically from
Paul's borrowing of the traditional statement "The Lord Jesus, on
the night he was betrayed" (1 Cor.11.23) and his repeated references
to the crucifixion of Jesus (1 Cor. 2.2; 2 Cor. 5.14), or from his speaking
of Jesus' being sent "when the time had fully come" (Gal. 4.4)? The
Lukan statement (4.21) goes on: "in your hearing". Luke therefore
looks upon the sacred event as a message event, that is, as an event
that cannot simply be noted objectively and made part of history; it
is an event one must confront as a listener. That this is so is shown by
19.9: "Today salvation has come to this house." Of course this statement refers to a time when the earthly Jesus was present, but the
saving event is once more understood explicitly as an event of speaking
and hearing. In like fashion, Luke can have Paul say, "To us has been
sent the message of this salvation" (Acts 13.26). In this passage it

[29] Hans Conzelmann, *The Theology of St Luke*, trans. G. Buswell (London:
Faber & Faber, 1960; New York: Harper, 1961), pp. 31–2.

might be possible to distinguish the message of salvation from salvation itself, but Acts 4.12 states unambiguously that there is no salvation in anyone but Jesus, and sets this parallel to the statement that there is no other name by which we may receive salvation. For Paul, salvation becomes a present reality "today" in the proclamation of the gospel; for Luke, salvation comes in the "name" and in the "message of salvation". This agrees with the observation that Luke looks upon the passion and resurrection of Christ, together with the proclamation of the gospel among all nations, as the fulfillment of the Scriptures (Luke 24.44–49), just as Paul juxtaposes the reconciliation of the world in Jesus Christ with the message of reconciliation (2 Cor. 5.19). Thus Luke, too, knows that the saving event cannot simply be understood as though something took place a certain number of years ago that changed the subsequent course of history, something that retains its validity whether one knows what happened or not, whether one stands in any relationship to what happened or not. A citizen of the United States is not an English subject. This has been true since the Revolutionary War, whether the citizen knows about the Revolution or not, whether he stands in any relationship to England or to the rebels or not. A message event (or an act of love, which has the nature of an unspoken message), however, can be valid for the person addressed only to the extent that he may hear it "today" and enter thereby into a relationship with the person addressing him.

But what is new here? Luke became aware that the same message cannot simply be heard in the same way in the various situations in which the community finds itself, that is, in the various periods of its history. He saw that the time of Jesus and of his travels with his disciples differs from that of the community in Jerusalem after Easter, visiting the temple as a matter of course and sharing a common life that even extended to the division of property. He saw that this in turn differs from the time of the worldwide church, when the continued advance of the Christian message to new nations represents a completely new factor. A naive equation of the discipleship practised by members of the community toward the end of the first century with that of the Galilean disciples is no longer possible. The history of half a century cannot simply be passed over, because it exhibits important developments, important also for the Christian faith. To ignore this history would lead to a purely personal piety in which two figures would confront each other: Jesus the Lord, recaptured by historical retrospection or experienced today as the exalted Christ; and the

single individual, accepting tradition and escaping into religious
enthusiasm from the world of space and time. No one would have any
place in the advance of the gospel through the nations and the decades. If it is not simply true to say that Jesus encounter seach individual afresh, that there is no continuity between this encounter and
what Jesus has meant to other believers, earlier or contemporary,
then the history of the church, that is, the history of how Jesus has
acted with those whom he has chosen, must be of crucial importance.
After the great things God has done among the Gentiles, which Paul
and Barnabas recount (Acts 15.4, 12), discipleship must be seen in a
new light. Anyone who acted as though nothing had happened since
Jesus' ministry in Galilee would be untrue to the very Jesus who
carried out his ministry in Galilee. Luke must therefore take serious
account of the history leading up to Jesus' ministry and the history
extending from Jesus' ministry to the present. It is clear to Luke that
the period of the Old Testament, like the period of the church, has its
own special quality; both are distinct from the crucial period, the
period of Jesus' ministry on earth. All three periods are essential to
the life of the community. What the essential relationship is, however,
remains the question.

The decisive question is this: how does Jesus become present today?
Luke has been understood as the creator of the concept of a continu-
ous sacred history (*Heilsgeschichte*, salvation history), extending from
creation through the period of the Old Testament down to the time
of Jesus, and thence through the period of the church to Judgment
Day.

We must remember that a similar concept can already be found in
Matthew,[30] and that Paul can also speak of the completion of a term
(Gal. 4.4). It remains true, however, that Luke devoted himself to this
problem. This is suggested by the very introduction to his Gospel, in
which he represents himself as a historian (1.1–4); in Acts 1.1–2 he
also clearly distinguishes the period of Jesus' earthly ministry from
the post-Easter period. It has also been suggested that Luke distinguishes more or less clearly between the time of the Baptist,[31]

[30] R. Walker, *op. cit.*, esp. pp. 114ff.

[31] H. Conzelmann, *op. cit.*, pp. 13ff. See especially Luke 3.19–20; here, however, Luke has merely taken the statement of Mark 1.14a and shifted it forward.
He probably did so because he, like others, was offended by the notion that Jesus
was baptized by John; he therefore reports John's imprisonment so early that the
impartial reader could hardly think of Jesus' being baptized by John. It is doubtful
whether Luke 16.16 excludes John from the time of salvation, because in 3.18, a

which is still before the time of salvation, and the time of Jesus. This seems very doubtful, however, since in chapters 1—2 of his Gospel Luke closely interweaves the stories of John and Jesus, albeit in such a way that both at the announcement of the birth and at the birth itself the story of Jesus surpasses that of John.[32] It is also doubtful that Luke uses 4.13 and 22.3 to distinguish a unique period in Jesus' ministry in which he is free of temptation by Satan.[33] All that 4.13 says is that Satan's struggle against Jesus is not yet over. Luke 22.3 is traditional, as John 13.2 shows. Above all, however, 22.28 shows that Luke assumes temptations to have taken place during Jesus' earthly life; for the statement "You continued with me in my trials" cannot refer to the temptations in Gethsemane, which come later.[34] It can also hardly be maintained that Luke distinguishes the time of Jesus emphatically from the time of the community.[35] Half a century after Easter he is aware that half a century has passed, but this has no bearing on the theological answer he arrives at. Of course Luke knows that

---

composition of Luke himself, John is said to have "preached good news" (albeit not of the kingdom of God). This particular distinction is primarily the work of Q (Luke 7.28 = Matt. 11.11). It is Luke, on the contrary, who turns the disciples of John into real Christians in Acts 18.24—19.7 ("he spoke and taught accurately the things concerning Jesus", 18.25; they had already become "believers", 19.2). It is not Luke, at any rate, who is making a sharp distinction here!

[32] Cf. 1.32: "He will be great and will be called the Son of the Most High" and 1.15: "He will be great" and 1.76: "You will be called the prophet of the Most High." Note also that Jesus is begotten by the Holy Spirit (1.35) whereas John is to be filled with the Holy Spirit (1.15). Luke 1.80 and 2.40 are very similar. They differ mainly in that nothing more is said about Jesus' "becoming strong in spirit". See also P. Minear, "Luke's Use of the Birth Stories", in *Studies in Luke-Acts* (1960), pp. 111–30.

[33] H. Conzelmann, *op. cit.*, pp. 23, 75.

[34] Mark 8.33 is omitted, but probably out of consideration for Peter; Mark 9.19, on the contrary, is used in Luke 9.41, although in much abbreviated form.

[35] Among the evidence cited is the departure of the lord in the parable (19.22); this feature antedates Luke, however (Matt. 25.14; cf. Mark 13.24). Luke 1.3 states only that he wants to tell what happened in its proper sequence, not that he wants to describe earlier and later events. The alternation between peace and persecution, which is probably behind Luke 22.35–38, is observed repeatedly in Acts. Luke 17.20–21 says only that the future kingdom is a matter being decided in the present; there is no special emphasis on the time of the earthly Jesus. See H. Conzelmann, *op. cit.*, p. 106; G. Klein, "Lukas 1.1–4 als theologisches Programm", in E. Dinkler, ed., *Zeit und Geschichte: Dankesgabe an Rudolf Bultmann* (Tübingen: Mohr, 1964), pp. 210–11; H. Hegermann, "Zur Theologie des Lukas", in . . . *und fragten nach Jesus; Festschrift für Ernst Barnikol* (Berlin: EV, 1964), pp. 30–1.

the Jesus event is the basis of all faith. Therefore all the speeches in Acts keep returning to this event instead of stopping with the church. We must also grant that he often presents this basis in the guise of a historian. But the earthly life of Jesus is never seen without the resurrection; and above all we have already noted that Luke always understands the Jesus event in the categories of a message that must be heard if one is to share in it. In other words, he never succeeded in carrying out the program formulated in theologically misleading terms in Luke 1.1–4, namely having his Gospel taken seriously as the work of a historian, like the competing projects of his contemporaries. He was too good a witness to Jesus to let this happen.

But there is more to be said. It is perhaps best to begin at Luke's weakest and most vulnerable point. The cross of Jesus does not play an essential role in his theology, except for the fact that the sufferings the community has to endure are illuminated by it.[36] But the remarkable fact remains that Luke did not fall victim to the simple schema which even Paul borrowed from tradition and gave currency to, but which, if thought through to its logical conclusion, limits the cross of Jesus irrevocably to the past. Luke never says that Jesus' death on the cross is to be understood as a ransom once paid, as a sacrifice once offered, as a death once suffered vicariously and now significant only because of its resulting consequences. He did not take the simple solution, according to which a unique event in the past, of undoubted historicity, retains the same significance through all time.[37] A man thinking solely along these lines could "objectify" the cross, that is, look back on it as something that once took place and can be ascertained as a historical fact, and can therefore be simply noted in retro-

[36] Acts 14.22; 20.19, 23–24 state that the Christian community must expect suffering; 7.59–60 makes the death of Stephen recall the death of Jesus; and Paul's journey to Jerusalem is reminiscent of Jesus' journey thither.

[37] Only in Acts 20.28 do we hear an echo of such ideas, as well as in the Eucharistic formula Luke 22.20. In both passages the phrase is a petrified formula. In Acts 20.28, "by his own blood" must refer to God, which is impossible. This means that the phrase was probably taken over automatically from a Christological formula, without any consideration on Luke's part of its meaning. Luke 22.20 is grammatically impossible: "This cup, poured out for you, is the new covenant in my blood." Making "poured out" modify "cup" is a forced rendering; the only alternative is that the phrase "poured out for you" was borrowed automatically from the Eucharistic liturgy found in Mark and Matthew, without being accommodated to the other ideas of Luke 22.20. On the other hand, Luke omitted Mark 10.45 from his Gospel and represented Jesus' death as a gracious gift to men, without repeating the cry of despair in Mark 15.34; Matthew 27.46.

ject. If a man thinks in this way, he must then consider a second, additional question, whether to accept this past event in grateful recognition or disavow it.

Such a procedure is impossible for Luke. How is Jesus, who lived at the time of Augustus and Tiberius (Luke 2.2; 3.1), present today? In his "name", Luke answers; in his "power". These are repeatedly mentioned in Acts, and we shall discuss them in the next chapter.

Of course this does not mean that all the problems are solved. But it is possible to see how the train of thought can advance from this point with some refinement. The "name" or "power" of Jesus is not simply an ascertainable historical fact that remains the same at all times when it is brought from the past into the present. "Name" and "power" suggest that the past becomes efficacious; they suggest what we have already said of the message that becomes efficacious "today in our ears", that, though always the same, must be heard differently in different situations and at different times. Luke is not really so far from what Paul meant by the righteousness of God as a "power" that blesses the community and exercises lordship over it. Luke is also concerned to present this "name" or this "power" as something that cannot simply be accepted and possessed; it becomes efficacious only where Jesus is obeyed, where he is truly accepted as Lord (Acts 9.13–20; but also 8.18–24). Lordship is not exercised in a vacuum, but in the concrete circumstances in which the community lives. For this very reason the history that extends from Easter Day to the Christian community of the present is not immaterial. This also protects against the misunderstanding that God seeks only the individual soul and not lordship over the world. We shall deal with this point particularly in the next chapter.

But what, then, is the significance of Jesus' earthly ministry? Namely this, that in it God's gracious love for the world, and the establishment of his gracious lordship over it was realized, as the Christmas angels sing: "Glory to God in the highest, and on earth peace among men with whom he is pleased" (Luke 2.14), that is, the men to whom God grants his grace. Luke does not speak in abstract theological terms of the offering of a propitiatory sacrifice or of the meteoric appearance of a heavenly being, but of God's mighty presence in the entire life and ministry of Jesus. He therefore cannot describe this life and ministry in timeless terms. Not to see that every word spoken by Jesus was filled with the Old Testament background from which he sprang would be to misunderstand everything he said.

Not to see every act performed by Jesus as taking place within t
territory of Israel and its history would be to misunderstand ever
thing he did. The parable of the prodigal son (Luke 15.11–23) or th
of the Pharisee and the tax collector (18.9–14) cannot be graspe
without a knowledge of the God of the Old Testament. Whoever do
not know the fear of the God who is absolutely superior to everythi
human—omnipotent, terrifying, and incomprehensible—will on
misunderstand the parables completely, seeing in them a pleasant a
innocuous God whose business it is to forgive.[38] Neither can God
presence in all the acts of Jesus be understood apart from the O
Testament and its prohibition of images, where God repeated
dashed to pieces all Israel's attempts to get a secure hold on its Go
to guarantee his presence in the ark or in the temple or in all kinds
images. And how can one understand correctly Luke's conception
Jesus' journey up to Jerusalem—a journey which the people thoug
would culminate with the immediate coming of the glorious kingdo
of God (19.11), while in fact the cross was waiting—without an
knowledge of the wanderings of the patriarchs and of the Israelite
who were all on the way to the promised land? In this way Luk
seeks to tell the story of God's kingdom, which begins in Israel,
fulfilled in Jesus, and, starting with Jesus, now pervades the worl
We shall study the development of this concept in the book of Acts.

THE OPERATION OF THE EXALTED LORD IN THE COMMUNITY

But how are we to understand Christ's presence as the presence
his "name", his power, his lordship? In Acts 20, Paul's farewe
address at Miletus, Luke sets down, as it were, the testament of Pau
It was demonstrated years ago that the speeches in Acts, as is true fo
all the literature of this period, were composed by the author himsel
They therefore reflect the author's situation and the author's prob
lems. He has already experienced Paul's death (vss. 22–25)—ha
already learned how leaders of new movements within the churc
have won over members of the community (vss. 29–30) by invokin
Paul's name and claiming to preach additional secret doctrines (vss
20, 27), for which they presumably were richly rewarded (vss. 33, 35)

Paul himself, however, was the greatest problem for Luke. N
doubt he was an instrument of the first order, chosen by God; ever

[38] "*Pardonner, c'est son métier*", as Voltaire is reputed to have blasphemed.

)efore Luke's time there were communities that looked on Paul's
Gentile mission as a sacred event of prime importance.[39] What could
)e said to those who, like Paul in Galatians 1, claimed to have had a
evelation of the exalted Lord and to have been sent to the Christian
:ommunities as apostles with new doctrines? Could not every vision-
ıry claim with equal right to be a teacher of the church? There is a
eal problem here. If the exalted Lord was still alive, speaking to the
:ommunities or to their teachers, was not all that really mattered
he experience of the presence of the heavenly Lord? Could not the
ıeavenly Lord impart all sorts of doctrines to the faithful in a vision?
Were the earthly Jesus and even the encounters of the disciples with
he risen Lord only a beginning, at best leading up to the essential
)oint? And could not new apostles keep appearing, with new and ever
more fantastic revelations?

What then makes an apostle? Luke does not meet this danger by theological debate, for instance
with Gnostic heresy. He does not go into the content of the true
Pauline teaching or morality anywhere in the speech; nowhere does
Luke dispute the Gnostic danger didactically. In this speech, as elsewhere in Luke, there are no special sacramental guarantees; there is
ıo reference to the Canon, which was to be so important in the next
:entury, important as Scripture is to Luke; there is no reference to
ı fixed confession of faith, although Luke summarizes this confession
ireely in the speeches of the apostles; there is no office guaranteed by
,uccession, important as the work of an apostle is to Luke. Luke in
fact emphasizes the work of an apostle in this speech.

What then makes an apostle? In Acts 1.21–22, Luke sets forth the
:onditions: an apostle must have accompanied the earthly Jesus from
ıis baptism to his resurrection. This means, of course, that Paul was
ıot an apostle, and Luke draws this very conclusion.[40] Luke also
knows, in agreement with Paul (1 Cor.9.1; Gal.1.16), that it is the
:ncounter with the risen Lord that makes a man an apostle.[41] But the

---

[39] See above, pp. 77 and 80.

[40] Only in Acts 14.4, 14 is Paul (together with Barnabas) called an apostle;
:his designation probably rests on tradition identifying Paul and Barnabas as the
apostles of the Antioch community. Nowhere else is the title applied to Paul,
which is most striking in view of the frequent appearance of the word "apostle"
(six times in Luke, twenty-six in Acts) and the emphasis on this title in the Pauline
Letters.

[41] According to Acts 1.22, an apostle must be a "witness to the resurrection" of
Jesus; in 4.33 only the apostles are witnesses to the resurrection, while the other
members of the community proclaim "the word of God" (4.31). Cf. p.61, n.21.

appearance in the church of all kinds of figures claiming to have ha
such an encounter with the risen Lord made clear limits necessar
and therefore Luke declares that having been a disciple of the earth
Jesus is an additional condition for being an apostle.[42] Furthermor
Luke clearly distinguishes the encounters with the risen Lord, wh
appeared in earthly form, which were brought to an end by th
ascension (Acts 1.9–12), from the later visions of the heavenly Chri
such as were granted Paul before Damascus (Acts 9.1–9), as well :
Peter (10.9–16). Paul, too, distinguished sharply between the ever
that constitutes the basis of his ministry (Gal. 1.15.ff) and vision
which may in themselves appear much more impressive, and can l
of great personal importance, but can by no means become a part
the Christian proclamation (2 Cor. 12.1ff.). But he, like the con
munity before him, places the appearance of the heavenly Jesus th
he himself experienced on the same plane as all previous appea
ances.[43] Now Luke in no wise seeks to deny the importance of th
present and exalted Lord. Paul's vision before Damascus and Pete
vision at Joppa decisively altered the course of church history; Paul
dream (16.9–10) brought the gospel to Europe; and the instructio
of the Spirit determined the advance of the church at every step. B
if this is not to degenerate into completely uncontrollable enthusiast
movements, the instructions of the exalted Lord or of the Spirit mu
repeatedly be measured against tradition.

The account of the Apostolic Council (Acts 15) is especially cha
acteristic of this development, particularly when we compare it wit
the account of Paul himself (Gal. 2.1–10).[44] Even taking into accou
the fact that the various participants in a conference will evaluate i
outcome differently, each according to his own point of view, critic
discrepancies remain. According to Gal. 2.1–2, Paul went to Jerusaler
of his own accord, because he had received a revelation. There certa

[42] The title "apostle" at first probably applied to every missionary, as it st
does in the Didache. Luke was not the first, however, to restrict it to the Twelve
cf. Mark 6.7, 30; Matthew 10.2; Revelation 21.14. We must remember that the
is no trace in the New Testament of our common interpretation (eleven discipl
plus Paul); that Paul calls Junius and Andronicus apostles, as well as himse
(Rom. 16.7); and that he knows of a group of "all the apostles" (1 Cor. 15.7) distin
from the Twelve. Luke gives the title only to twelve who accompanied the earth
Jesus (including Matthew; Acts 1.23ff.), not including Paul in their number.

[43] Cf. above, p. 46.

[44] Acts 11.30 is impossible in the light of Galatians 1.18; 2.1. But any attempt
reconcile Acts 11.30 with Galatians 2.1–10 is impossible for other reasons.

ham-Christians" raised the question of the freedom of the Gentile hristians, obviously in connection with the problem of circumcision; is agrees with Acts 15.5, but not 15.1–2, perhaps because of different ints of view. In Acts 15.12, however, Paul's role is reduced to thing more than recounting an edifying tale of God's miracles, hile Peter and James the brother of the Lord defend the freedom of e Gentile Christians. This at least contradicts the account in Galaans 2.5, 11–13. Acts 15 says nothing of any division of the Christian ission into different spheres;[45] verse 20, however, reports a decision the conference that cannot be squared with Galatians 2.6, 11–13, d is in fact directed towards a quite different question, that of table llowship between Gentile and Jewish Christians. It is quite imposble that Paul would have agreed to a regulation requiring Gentile hristians to observe the Jewish dietary laws; he does not even menon such a regulation in his discussions of these problems (1 Cor. 7ff.; 10.14ff.; Rom. 14.1ff.), not to speak of demanding it. Since en Acts 21.25 assumes that Paul has not heard of this regulation, it ust have been decided on in Paul's absence, as a consequence of the cident reported in Galatians 2.11ff. It was probably meant only for narrowly circumscribed group of Christian communities markedly nder the influence of Judaism.

What all these details reveal is a homogeneous Lukan perspective. aul is the chosen instrument of God. His mission to the Gentiles therere dominates the entire second half of Acts, while Peter disappears mpletely and James the brother of the Lord appears only as the ead of the Jerusalem community. But Paul is an instrument only ecause (again in open contradiction to Gal. 1.1, 12, 17–19) he was nited with the existing community by Ananias immediately after his ll, and above all was later introduced by Barnabas to the apostles t Jerusalem and legitimized by them (Acts 9.10ff.; 9.26ff.). Not he, ut Peter made the breakthrough to the Gentiles (10.1ff.). When ifficulties arise, it is the apostles alone who, together with the Jerualem leadership and the Christian community there, undertake a hange of direction; Paul functions only as a reporter. To prevent any reak in the continuity of tradition, Paul appoints elders in all of the ommunities (14.23), although there is no mention of such elders in ny of his Letters, and passages such as 1 Corinthians 16.15ff. make eir appointment impossible.

[45] The notion involved may be that of different groups of hearers rather than eographical areas.

This clearly reveals both the lights and the shadows of Luke's cc
ception. It is to Luke's credit that, in a situation of extreme peril,
linked the life of the Christian community with this history of Jesu
life, so that it could not break up into enthusiastic sectarian mov
ments, controlled by a motley assortment of spirits. Luke hims
understood best that a mere repetition of Jesus' words or recounti
of his deeds would not do the job. Far more consciously than Pa
or the evangelists before him he sensed that he was living in a differe
age. He knows better than any that communal sharing of propert
which was right for the earliest Christian community, or daily vis
to the temple were appropriate for that period of the church, but n
for other periods. Besides his emphasis on the life and ministry
Jesus, Luke also emphasizes the free operation of the Spirit. He nev
speaks of apostolic succession; and, although he probably thinks th
the elders in Ephesus, too, were actually appointed by Paul ar
Barnabas (as in 14.23), there is no mention of this in Paul's "test
ment". Only the Holy Spirit, who appointed them to their minist
(20.28), is mentioned. Furthermore, he does not picture Paul as ;
authoritative teacher, handing correct doctrine on to faithful ste
ards, but as a personal example, whose zeal for the well-being of t
community, whose humility and tears, whose public and pasto
fervor they are to emulate.

Thus the chain whose links are the earthly Jesus, the twel
apostles, Paul, and elders is not intended to guarantee the transmi
sion of unaltered tradition—the chain in fact transformed the trac
tion at crucial points (see 10.1ff.; 11.1ff.; 15.1ff.)—but the stea
advance of God.

Jerusalem is not a permanent metropolitan see, guaranteeing orth
doxy and order; the community must leave Jerusalem.[46] But Goc
history is not interrupted; it goes on from Jerusalem to new territori
Therefore Acts emphasizes so strongly that three thousand, then fr
thousand, then even more, and finally tens of thousands of Jev
believed and were added to the community (2.41; 4.4; 5.14; 21.2c
The community of Jesus is not something new, a "tertium quid"
addition to Jews and Gentiles. God had to take the measure of Isra
and exclude those who did not belong to his people. Therefore Lu
states repeatedly, to the very end of his story (28.24), that the Jev
were divided, some rejecting the gospel, but some also accepting
Luke did not forget that in Israel all the families on earth shall fir

[46] See below, p. 154.

essing (3.25), that salvation is meant for them (2.39; also in the
st speeches addressed to Gentiles: 10.36, 42; 13.16ff.), and that the
essengers of Jesus cannot turn to the Gentiles until salvation has
en offered to Israel—salvation which some have accepted, others
jected (13.46; 18.6; 28.25–28). The rejection in the missionary field
emphasized, while the accounts of mass conversions in Jerusalem
ess the continuity between Israel and the community of Jesus.[47] For
is reason also the apostles must come from Jerusalem and lay hands
the newly converted Samaritans, that they may receive the Spirit.
od's new advance into the Gentile world cannot take place without
link to his history in Jerusalem (8.14ff.). In all these instances, there
no notion of Jerusalem as a metropolitan see in the ecclesiastical
nse. For example, the money Paul collected for Jerusalem among
e Gentile congregations could easily have been made a parallel to the
mple tax paid by the Jewish Diaspora and considered a sign that
e Gentile Christian communities recognized the supreme authority
Jerusalem. Luke was acquainted with this collection (24.17), but
did not really take up the idea. On the contrary, he reported it as
purely voluntary gift, brought about by the prophetical operation
the Spirit (11.28–30).

Luke is therefore aware that neither a venerable metropolitan see
r leaders appointed by Paul can guarantee that the Christian com-
unity will adhere to the old tradition.[48] Acts therefore emphasizes
e power of Jesus' name and the abiding presence of the exalted
rd, leading his community through his Spirit. The truth that Luke
seeking to express is this: all instructions of the exalted Lord, all
velations of the Spirit, all new answers to new problems must be
dged by recollection of Jesus' words, Jesus' ministry, Jesus' death
d resurrection; God goes forward with his community, but not
ong a path that would disqualify his earlier acts.[49] On this point we

[47] Cf. J. Jervell, "Das gespaltene Israel und die Heidenvölker", *Studia Theo-
ica* XIX (1965), pp. 58ff. On the other hand, the listeners misunderstand and
ve their misunderstandings corrected typically only in the speeches addressed to
l-fledged Jews and Gentiles; this does not happen with the Diaspora Jews and the
ntile God-fearers (E. Schweizer, "On the Speeches of Acts", in L. E. Keck and J.
Martyn, eds., *Studies in Luke–Acts* (Nashville: Abingdon, 1966; London; SPCK,
68), p. 214.
[48] Otherwise the warning in Acts 20.29–30 would not be necessary. Going be-
nd Luke, there would still be the question of what tradition the leadership should
here to, that of Acts 15.1ff. or that of Galatians 2.1ff.
[49] Charles Kingsley Barrett, *Luke the Historian in Recent Study* (A. S. Peake

must agree with him, even though his formulations still appear que
tionable at certain points, and the difficulties involved in his solutio
are by no means clearly thought out. But he went beyond Paul an
the evangelists who preceded him in seeing the problems and comin
to grips with them. This was his crucial contribution to the Ne
Testament.

THE COMING OF JESUS

But does not this perspective put the history of the church in th
place formerly occupied by the Lord who comes to judgment and
establish the kingdom of God? Has not God's future been removed
such a distance that it can still be included in a final chapter of th
Christian teaching "concerning the last things", but no longer pla
any real role? It is clear that a Christian of the eighties cannot awa
the final coming of this kingdom of God in exactly the same way as
Christian of the thirties. Nevertheless, the scheme of Revelation dat
from very near the time of Luke—if anything, a decade later. He
Luke obviously represents a different point of view.

One small observation will illustrate the point. In Acts 20.31 th
elders are exhorted to be "on the alert". This phrase at one tim
referred to the attitude of faith confronting the imminent Parousi
which could come at any time (Mark 13.37; etc.). Now it refers to th
ministry of the leaders of the community, who supervise the lives o
the members of the community, ready to admonish and exhort the
in case they deviate from the Lord's will. This shift is if anything eve
clearer in Luke 12.42–46. This passage occurs in a collection of sa
ings concerning the eschaton. It begins in 12.34–38 with the parab
of the servants who wait with lighted lamps for their master to retur
from a wedding party, so that they can open the door at once whe
he comes, even if it is in the middle of the night. This expresses the o
view of "alertness", which emphasizes perpetual readiness for the sud
den and unsuspected coming of the Lord. The same attitude is reveale
in the simile, which comes from Q, of the householder who does no
know when the burglar will break in; in this latter instance, since th
arrival of a burglar is not a joyful event, the original thought probab
concerned the coming of the threatened judgment. In verses 42–4

Memorial Lectures 6, London: Epworth, 1961), p.60, points out that all th
speeches of Acts revert to Jesus, though with respect to Acts 17 we can hard
say "to the story of Jesus", as Barrett does.

owever, which also come from Q, the situation is different. Here,
ɔo, the master is absent, and the servants know neither the day nor
ie hour of his return. All the emphasis, however, has shifted to their
roper conduct during the interim, which is represented not merely as
:veral hours to be spent in waiting, but as days and probably weeks
f labor. The appearance of the Lord is still very important, but not
ierely for the moment of his appearance, when the servants must
ave the door open and their lamps already lit; it is also important
:ecause the Lord, coming unexpectedly, will find out what his ser-
ants have been up to throughout his absence.

This shift of emphasis is not typical of Luke alone; it occurs already
1 Q, in the parable of the talents preserved in Matthew 25.14–30 and
.uke 19.12–27, and in Mark 13.34–37.[50] But Luke has gone further,
irning the "faithful and wise" (Matt. 24.45) into a "faithful and wise
eward" (Luke 12.42), distinguishing him not from his "fellow ser-
ants" (Matt. 24.49) but from "the menservants and the maidservants"
Luke 12.45). By stressing the difference in status, Luke has made the
arable refer to the leader of the Christian community, to whose care
ie members are entrusted. We find here the same concern as in Acts
ɔ.31. This means that Luke takes seriously the half century that has
assed since Easter, that he looks realistically on the dangers con-
onting the community and recognizes that there must be men in the
ɔmmunity who will undertake particular responsibility. His concern,
; we have seen, is not with a succession that will guarantee legitimacy
r with a hierarchical order, but with the mere presence of leaders who
ill watch over the community.

Does this mean that the Parousia has been postponed indefinitely
nd has therefore in actual fact lost all importance? Luke introduces
ιe parable of the talents (19.11) with a strange comment: Jesus told
ιe parable, Luke says, because the crowd thought that with Jesus'
pproach to Jerusalem, the kingdom of God might dawn at any mo-
ιent. This agrees with Jesus' rejection of a very similar notion on the
art of the disciples shortly after Easter (Acts 1.6–7). According to
uke 17.20–21, Jesus declares that the kingdom of God does not come
ι such a way that its coming can be observed or calculated by obser-
ition of apocalyptic signs; one cannot even say that it appears "here"
: "there", since it is "in the midst of you". This amounts to a rejec-
ɔn of exaggerated apocalyptic expectations for the imminent future.

---

[50] Cf. above, p. 64.

The strange saying concerning the corpse around which the vultures
gather (17.37) is probably also intended to reject attempts to determine the location of the kingdom of God: when the kingdom comes,
one will see at once where it is. But what is being rejected here? An
apocalyptic expectation that awaited the coming of the end during
Jesus' lifetime or immediately after his resurrection, and in Jerusalem.
Such expectations were probably actually associated with Jesus' entry
into Jerusalem; apocalyptic circles presumably continued for quite a
while to associate such expectations with the city of Jerusalem. Luke
is of course quite right in attacking them. His actual interest can be
seen in redactional comment in 17.25; there can be no triumph of
God without the suffering preordained by God. Apocalyptic hope
must not turn into a theology of majesty and glory, overlooking the
path taken by God with his community, leading away from Jerusalem
and, through suffering, to the proclamation of the gospel throughout
the world.

Is, then, the Parousia completely peripheral? Such a conclusion
is very doubtful. At the beginning of the parable of the talents (Luke
19.12), Luke himself tells us in a redactional phrase that the master
of the servants will "return", in other words, that his present absence
will not simply continue forever.[51] Furthermore, Luke alone included
in his Gospel not one but three Parousia discourses of Jesus (chs. 12,
17, and 21). Above all, he concludes his account of Jesus' travels with
two parables that have clearly been made to refer to the Parousia and
the coming judgment by the redactional addition of 18.8, 14b, probably by Luke himself. Luke also made an interesting alteration in the
scheme of Jesus' eschatological discourse in Mark 13. Instead of a
vague reference to the time when "the abomination of desolation"
(Mark 13.14, NEB) will stand where it should not, and to battles in
Judea, Luke 21.20–24 has Jesus prophesy very clearly the destruction
of Jerusalem, which took place AD 70. This destruction is therefore
looked upon by Luke unequivocally as a judgment of God. Of course
this is not Luke's own invention; the very same thing has already taken
place in Matthew 22.7. In Luke, however, the predicted destruction
of Jerusalem leads the community to desert the city before its final
destruction; their departure is therefore traced expressly to instructions given by Jesus, and introduces a "Gentile period". Does this

[51] The word "return" occurs thirty-three times in Luke, but only two or three
times in the rest of the New Testament; its presence here is therefore surely due to
Luke himself.

distinguish the historical event from the real eschatological event of Jesus' Parousia?[52] This seems doubtful, because according to Luke himself this Gentile period, ordained by God, merges directly into the eschaton. Luke eliminates the warning against false teachers, interpolated by Mark, which delays the coming of the end (anticipating with a similar warning in 17.23). He also eliminates the statement in Mark 13.24 which distinguishes the Parousia from what precedes it ("But in those days, after that tribulation . . ."). In Luke, the Gentile period, brought on by the fall of Jerusalem, merges directly into the period of the Parousia, connected with a mere "and".

The question remains, of course, what Jesus' Parousia means. The answer must probably be as follows: it means the coming of the judge who exercises authority over all the present life and work of the community. In Acts 17.31, the appointing of Jesus to judge the world on the basis of his resurrection is led up to by a speech which otherwise speaks mostly in terms of Greek enlightenment and Jewish belief in creation. It is also emphasized in Acts 10.41, in the first speech addressed to Gentiles. The parables we have been discussing also speak of the judgment to be given by the returning master of the house.

Here, too, we see both a positive and a negative side. Luke certainly distinguishes more sharply than Paul between the earthly ministry o Jesus, his presence as exalted Lord, and his coming as judge, without seeing these events as a single whole, God's single eschatological act. The question is: Was any other approach possible toward the end of the first century? It is certainly still not settled what theological weight should be assigned to the history of the church in comparison to God's actions in the life, death, and resurrection of Jesus on the one hand and his actions in the Parousia and Last Judgment on the other. This is where the most difficult questions arise. When obedience to the law and even pagan worship (Acts 17.23) pass almost imperceptibly into Christian devotion, it is no longer possible to follow Paul in understanding the irruption of the power of God's righteousness, which justifies sinners and brings the dead to life, as God's one decisive eschatological act. Thus justification becomes merely an additional source of help (Acts 13.38–39), and Jesus' ministry becomes primarily an offer of repentance with a view toward the coming judgment (Acts 17.30–31). It is unclear what the cross is supposed to mean in

[52] This is suggested by Conzelmann, *op. cit.*, pp. 125ff., especially 134, n. 1.

all this. There are still lacunae, but at least Luke saw the problem posed by fifty years of church history. Of course an inattentive reading of Luke could easily mislead the church into drawing up a schema of sacred history in which God advances continuously and uninter-ruptedly[53] from creation through the history of Israel to Jesus, and thence through the history of the church to the establishment of his eschatological kingdom. But one must also see how this very danger leads Luke to give dominant weight to the Parousia, because the Parousia determines and controls the conduct of the Christian community now, as well as its course through history. Luke emphatically rejects any apocalyptic determination of the time and place of the Parousia; but the coming of the Lord nevertheless remains central, because it transforms the whole life of the community in the present, giving the community both responsibility and joy.

JOHN

GOD'S PRESENCE IN JESUS

John, too, takes as his theme the presence of the past, but from a quite different perspective. Writing a Gospel probably around the end of the first century, possibly in Asia Minor or Syria, or even in Egypt, he is giving an account of a period of past history; through all sorts of statements of place and time, he continually reminds us that we live in a different land and a different age. But the four whole chapters of Jesus' farewell discourses discuss the single question of his presence among his disciples after his death. Both elements are here observed together: firm commitment to the events in the life of Jesus of Nazareth, and his continuing presence in the band of disciples that survives after his death. But how can both elements be kept together? Here lies the fascination and the danger of this Gospel. There is a radical concentration on Jesus, unparalleled elsewhere. Without him no one can see God (14.6); without his coming there would be no sin, because rejection of Jesus is the only real sin (15.22). The blindness of the world becomes total and fatal blindness only when confronted with Jesus (9.41). The pre-Johannine community could still speak of

---

[53] This approach is rejected by Oscar Cullmann in his *Salvation in History*, trans. S. G. Sowers (London: SCM, and New York: Harper, 1967), pp. 48–83, and 122–6, 150–66, although elsewhere he puts great emphasis on the notion of sacred history; cf. my remarks in *TLZ* XCII (1967), cols. 904ff.

the divine Logos dwelling in the world; John concentrates everything in the figure of Jesus of Nazareth, in whom alone we encounter
God's Logos, who created the world.[54]

This notion is given what may be its most pointed expression in the
"I am . . ." statements with their appended symbolic discourses.
Even on the formal level it is clear that such a sentence as "I am the
true vine, . . . the good shepherd, . . . the light of the world" does
not belong to a parable or allegory. A parable might begin: "I am
like a shepherd; my relationship to you is like that of a shepherd to his
sheep." An allegory could have its interpretation: "I am the shepherd; you are the sheep; your opponents are the evil wolves." In a
parable, only *one* point of comparison would be important; in an
allegory, the imagery would be more obscure, and all the concepts
would be equally important.[55] In either case it would be impossible to
isolate a single concept and declare that only one was the *true* vine,
the *good* shepherd, the light of the *world*. We have here the exact
opposite of a parable: only a single individual is truly shepherd, vine,
light; everything that men call by these names is in fact only an image,
an imperfect symbol of him. Strictly speaking, therefore, the statement
is not metaphor but true discourse; the appended exposition shows
only that he alone bears this name by right and fulfills what the term
suggests. In the Old Testament, God is "truth" because he alone
fulfills what is expected of him; in like fashion Jesus is the true vine,
the good shepherd, the light of the world, the bread of life. This
means that everything men look for in vine and shepherd, light and
bread, is ultimately to be found only in him, and that the blindness
of the world consists in its being satisfied with what can at most be a
symbolic image of what it could find in him.[56]

Above all, God's presence in Jesus' miracles is so striking that it
puts all the other Gospels in the shade. In Mark, a girl who has just
died and is declared by Jesus to be sleeping is recalled to life (Mark
5.21–43); in Luke, a son who has just died is restored to his mother
(Luke 7.11–17). In John, however, a corpse that has already lain
three days in the tomb and is beginning to decay is brought back to
life (John 11.1–44). Jesus' walking on the sea is demonstrated for the
whole crowd with almost scientific precision (6.18, 22–25). Even
when we are told that Jesus is tired (4.6), he speaks with absolute

[54] Cf. above, pp. 85f., n. 45.
[55] For a discussion of parable and allegory, see above, p. 28.
[56] Eduard Schweizer, *EGO EIMI* (FRLANT 56, 2nd ed., 1965), pp. 112–24.

superiority to the woman at the well and needs neither the water she
offers him nor the food purchased by the disciples (4.7–9), because he
himself has better water to offer and better food at his disposal (4.10,
32). God's power appears even more strikingly in the Passion narrative. Jesus has foreknowledge of everything (13.1, 19, 21ff.); temptation hardly overtakes him for a moment (12.27). The police fall to
the ground before him (18.6), and he himself must give orders for his
arrest and the release of his disciples (18.8). Like a victorious conqueror he goes to the cross; like a king he gives orders for the future
of his mother and his favorite disciple; says "I thirst" only in order to
fulfill the Scriptures; and dies with the triumphal shout "It is finished"
(19.30). It is therefore not accidental that Mark calls Jesus' reference
to the rejection, suffering, death, and resurrection of the Son of Man
his first plain and open discourse (Mark 8.31, 32a),[57] while John says
the same of Jesus' statement that he came from the Father and will
return to the Father (16.29). Jesus' road to the cross is in fact his
exaltation, his exaltation on the cross and his exaltation to heavenly
glory coincide.[58]

Now it is true that the whole New Testament understands Jesus'
death as a victory. It is therefore understandable that John can speak
of "exaltation" at the point where Jesus' obedience, on which he
places great emphasis, surrenders totally and without reservation to
the father and thus attains perfection, because Jesus' will and God's
will have become one. One must keep clearly in mind, however, that
in the circles in which this Gospel was composed and copied it was
read for decades and perhaps for centuries without the corrective of
the other Gospels—Mark for example. This made it hard to comprehend what really took place in the crucifixion of Jesus. It was possible
for the misunderstanding to arise that a divine being, completely
immune to pain, was only demonstrating that men could inflict no
evil on him.[59] Mark placed distressing emphasis on the terrible and
violent aspects of Jesus' suffering, without denying that in this suffering God's mighty victory was accomplished. John placed one-sided
emphasis on the opposite perspective. This is of course also the fascination of this Gospel. Whoever reads it against the background of the
picture painted by Mark will find in every sentence a witness to the

[57] Cf. above, p.131.   [58] See below, p.164.

[59] On this point, see especially E. Käsemann, *The Testament of Jesus* (London:
SCM, and Philadelphia: Fortress, 1968), pp.4–26. For a contrary view, see W. A.
Meeks, *Union Seminary Quarterly Review* XXIV (1969), 414ff.

faith that sees the mighty operation of God as the true reality behind all human appearance.

It is clear beyond all doubt (1 John 4.2!) that Jesus is truly a human being, not, say, an angel exempt from all human frailty. Therefore men take offence at him, because he comes from the little village of Nazareth (1.46) and is the son of Joseph, someone whose parents everyone knows (6.42; 7.27). Therefore one must also overcome the temptation to judge him only "according to the flesh", that is, according to his superficial appearance (7.24; 8.15). Above all, however, one must not overlook the fact that John, too, speaks emphatically of the son's obedience to him who is greater than he (14.28), an obedience that can lead to the sacrifice of his life (10.11ff.). Even though the confusion in Jesus' soul at the prospect of his imminent Passion is resolved at once in obedience to the will of God, we note that the path to the cross is not simply a matter of course (12.27, the Johannine Gethsemane). The path taken by Jesus, into the world's hatred and ending in the sacrifice of his life for his friends, is therefore seen as an example for the path of obedience to be followed by his disciples (15.13–20). It is therefore not the path of a divine angel untouched by suffering; it is the attempt to express in a Gospel what Paul calls Jesus' divine obedience and sinlessness (Rom.5.19; Phil.2.8; 2 Cor. 5.21).

THE PRESENCE OF THE PAST

Such a perspective is no longer restricted to the period of the earthly Jesus. God's power, which shone forth repeatedly in what the earthly Jesus did or suffered, continues to shine forth, and with amazing force, in his community, whenever and wherever it may be. In a certain sense it is even true that only the Spirit will guide the community into all the truth (16.13). After Easter, the truth is no longer veiled by the veil of pure humanity, as in the earthly Jesus. His community knows the resurrected Lord. The presence of the Spirit's power was promised by Jesus as he departed; it has now been granted. Thus Jesus' complete unity with the Father is true in less paradoxical fashion after Easter than before. Of course Jesus' earthly life is fundamentally already an anticipation of his glory revealed at Easter, an irruption of heaven upon earth, a manifestation of God's miraculous power. The "glory" of the Father's only Son was seen by Jesus' disciples; the first miracle at Cana revealed Jesus' "glory", so that it was followed by faith.[60] But this must not be misunderstood. The miracles are "signs" whose purpose is to lead men to an encounter with Jesus himself. The feeding of the five thousand is completely misunderstood if men go no further than the gift, that is, the miracle itself, instead of letting themselves be guided by the miracle to Jesus himself. Therefore the story of the miraculous feeding issues in the discourse concerning Jesus, the bread of life (6.26ff.); the situation is similar with the other miracles. The most blatant of all the miracles, the resurrection of Lazarus, would not be understood if it merely reinforced Mary's traditional belief in the resurrection at the Last Judgment. Only he who understands that Jesus himself is already life and resurrection for whoever encounters him, and will therefore also be life and resurrection at the Last Judgment, understands the miracle.[61] Only he who can have such faith in Jesus as to find the power of life already present in him can really have faith that the resurrection after death is also grounded in him. And in his remarkable conversation with the royal officer (4.46ff.), Jesus bluntly rejects a faith that desires only whatever the miracle can provide and not Jesus himself, although the evangelist can say on the other hand that the very experience of miraculous help perfects the father's faith. But this is already attested by 4.42: the Samaritans believed at first because the woman had told them of a miracle; now they truly believe because they have encountered Jesus in person. In the account of the call of the first disciples (1.35–51), the witness to Jesus can respond to the doubting questions of a nonbeliever only by saying "Come and see" (1.46), and bringing the doubter to Jesus himself.

At this point we can see clearly how "transparent" the story of what happened then becomes. The earthly Jesus is already depicted in such a way that through him the coming exalted Lord of the post-Easter period can be seen. John is describing an event that repeats itself constantly in the church. No longer—as in Mark 1.16–20—are the disciples called from ship and collection table, home and family, but rather from other bearers of salvation or from false theological prejudices, from John the Baptist or from the foolish notion that the Messiah cannot come out of tiny insignificant Nazareth. Here, too, Jesus is consciously distinguished from all other figures and ideas from which

[60] John 1.14b, c is probably an interpretative gloss of the evangelist; cf. above, pp. 85f., n. 45. John 2.11 is an emphatic conclusion, which also introduces the "sign" concept.

[61] Cf. below, pp. 165f.

men might expect salvation, as the only one in whom true salvation is to be found. Therefore here, in contrast to Mark, it is no longer the Jesus who walks upon the earth that calls the disciples, but, as in the post-Easter church, the witness who testifies to Jesus: first John the Baptist, then the disciple who has been won to Jesus, who again and again calls someone else.[62] Encounter with Jesus himself is not restricted to the period of the earthly Jesus. As early as 3.1–5, Jesus says expressly that no one can come to him and encounter him with understanding unless the Holy Spirit transforms him. All this of course does away with the problem of how Jesus, a figure of the historical past, can be present in the community after Easter. On the contrary, since 7.39 states that the Spirit does not begin his work until after Jesus' death, we are compelled to say that there is no full knowledge of what Jesus is until the coming of the Spirit, that is, after Easter.

Of course this does not mean that John thought the earthly Jesus incidental;[63] it is he whom the Spirit will call to mind (14.26). It does mean that encounter with him in whom God's glory is revealed to men on earth is not restricted to the period of his earthly ministry; the believer can be brought to him at any time in the Spirit. Therefore Jesus' death cannot be understood as a severance, a departure,[64] but only as a joyous event, because it makes possible the coming of the Spirit (16.7; cf. 15.11).

According to John, therefore, we must say that one can encounter the earthly Jesus only after Easter. What does this paradoxical statement mean? It means that one has not yet really come to Jesus if one has merely encountered a man in Galilee who has performed some startling miracles and delivered some impressive speeches. The man who has really come to Jesus is he who allows Jesus' words and deeds to bring him to knowledge of what really took place in this Jesus. The fullness of this knowledge comes only in retrospect after Easter, because only from this vantage point can one see the purpose and meaning of Jesus' ministry. Thus John can even go beyond the other

---

[62] John 1.43 is a gloss (R. Schnackenburg, *The Gospel According to Saint John,* trans. K. Smyth [New York: Herder, and London: Burns & Oates, 1968], *ad loc.*) or else verse 43a originally referred to Peter.

[63] C. H. Dodd, *Historical Tradition in the Fourth Gospel* (Cambridge: Cambridge University Press, 1963), summarizing on pp. 423ff. shows that John sometimes even used Jewish–Christian traditions dating from the period before AD 70; cf. also J. L. Martyn, *History and Theology in the Fourth Gospel* (New York: Harper, 1968).

[64] Though it is a departure, of course; see 16.19–36.

Gospels, saying that discipleship in the true sense is possible only after Jesus' death. Peter is ready to follow Jesus to prison and to death, but has to be told that he will receive strength to do so only when Jesus has himself completed his way of obedience, has himself become the "way" that brings the disciples to God and to their dwelling places (13.36—14.6). It is the risen Lord who gives Peter his final call to discipleship (21.19).

This is the sense in which John's Gospel was written. In itself, it is nothing more than a description of the life, death, and resurrection of Jesus of Nazareth; but these are described in such a way that the witness, instructed by the Spirit, shows that he has learned what really took place in Jesus, who it was that encountered the world.

JESUS, GOD'S WITNESS

But how can one be a witness in this sense? Only through the living presence, in the words of the witness, of Jesus himself as God's word to us (the *Logos*, to use the Greek term).

It is the "word" or "words" of Jesus in which the disciples are to dwell, or which are to dwell in them (5.38; 8.31; 15.7). But it must be said at once that this "dwelling" depends on the "obedience" of the disciples (8.51–52; 14.23–24; 15.20; 17.6). Jesus' words do not simply convey information; they are words that set a man in motion and bring him to a specific choice: to follow or refuse (cf. also 6.60ff.). But does this mean anything more than the way Plato's or Goethe's disciples keep the words of their master? John states that the words of Jesus are nothing more or less than the words of God himself (3.34; 14.10, 24; 17.8, 14, 17), and are therefore words that cleanse (15.3) and give eternal life (5.24; 6.63, 68; 8.52). Is Jesus therefore to be understood simply as a revealer, who communicates these words? But Jesus' words are God's words, and Jesus can call on his disciples to keep and to obey them only because he himself "keeps" and "obeys" the Word of God (8.55); therefore Jesus' words at once become "commandments" for his disciples (cf. 14.23–24 with 14.21; 15.7 with 15.10). This becomes even clearer when we note the striking fact that the words "witness" and "testify" occur more often in the Fourth Gospel than anywhere else in the New Testament. These words derive from the language of the courtroom, and in fact the Gospel is permeated by the image of a legal action in which one person acts on behalf of another. We are therefore not dealing with the mere imparting of nformation—in the case of God, or Jesus, or the Spirit, or a disciple. What we are dealing with in each case is a "witness" who backs with his entire life the subject of his testimony.

In this sense God himself appears as a witness on behalf of Jesus (5.32, 36–37; 8.18). God's testimony on Jesus' behalf lives on in Jesus himself, who "testifies" primarily on his own behalf (5.31; 8.13–14, 18), but at the same time on behalf of God's "truth" (3.32–33; 7.7; 18.37). This testimony on behalf of God, which is found only in Jesus, continues to live in the testimony of the Spirit on behalf of Jesus (15.26), which is in fact identical with the testimony of the disciples on behalf of Jesus (15.27). This testimony is dependent on Jesus' own witness, as 3.11 shows, where Jesus, with a sudden transition from "I" to "we", shows his solidarity with the witnesses of all ages. In this sense John (1.7–8, 15, 19, 32, 34; 3.26), like the disciples (17.35; 21.24; cf. 4.39), can be spoken of as a witness.

But how does Jesus in fact bear witness? His words are God's word only because he keeps and obeys God's word and commandment with his whole being (8.55; 15.10). Jesus is "one with the Father"; the Father "loves" him and "knows" him, only because Jesus knows the Father, because he obeys the "commandment" of the Father and sacrifices his life (10.15, 17–18). In 15.10–13, too, it is the fact that Jesus himself obeys the commandments of the Father and lays down his life that enables the disciples for their part to obey Jesus' commandment of love, thus dwelling in him and allowing his words to dwell in them, because Jesus alone is and remains their strength (cf. 15.3–7). The categories "forerunner" and "follower" are therefore to be taken seriously. What Jesus does is more than an example: it gives his disciples the ability and the chance to follow him (13.8–11 comes before 13.14–15). The grain of wheat that dies does not die "representatively"; by its death it brings forth many grains as fruit (12.24). Therefore Jesus, being lifted up, will draw all men to himself (12.32). When Jesus chooses the image of shepherd and sheep, he does so because sheep do not imitate their shepherd, but follow him (10.11ff.). In this sense it is true to say that in Jesus one man dies for many (11.50). Therefore in John especially Jesus does not speak in long monologues; he always engages the other speakers in dialogue, encountering each individual in a different way.

Only from this vantage point can we understand the remarkable conjunction of the cross, Easter, and Pentecost. The words "cross" and "crucify" occur in John only in the actual narrative of Jesus'

crucifixion (19.6–41). Elsewhere John always speaks of Jesus' "exaltation", including his exaltation on the cross (perhaps on the basis o
Syriac usage) and his exaltation to that unity with the Father in
which the will of the Son is completely one with the Father. But no
only do Good Friday and Easter coincide—Pentecost, too, cannot be
kept apart. Probably even 7.38 should be understood as meaning tha
the Spirit "flows" into the community like streams of living wate
from the body of the exalted Jesus (on the cross).[65] The same meaning
probably attaches to the strange remark, strongly underlined by
reference to a trustworthy eyewitness, that water and blood flowed
from the body of the crucified Jesus (19.34–35), which probably refer
to the sacraments of baptism and communion that flow on and on in
the Christian community. In John, the gift of the Holy Spirit does no
take place at Pentecost, but on Easter Day (20.22–23). But ever
Christmas coincides with Good Friday, Easter, and Pentecost. Ac
cording to the famous statement in 3.16 ("God so loved the world")
God's love is shown in the sending of his Son into the world. The fol
lowing sentence runs completely parallel to verse 15, and shows that
this sending finds its goal in the exaltation of the Son of Man on the
cross for the salvation of the world, as prefigured in the Old Testament by Moses' lifting of the bronze serpent. In John, therefore, the
sending of the Son merges with his exaltation on the cross. What all
this means is that Jesus lives on as witness to the reality of God in the
community, in his sending, his obedience to God, and his sacrifice on
the world's behalf, and that the discipleship of the community can live
only by him and his testimony.

THE PRESENCE OF THE FUTURE

Among the most striking sayings in John are those that speak of
the judgment that has already taken place; 3.18 is an example: "He
who believes in [the Son] is not judged; he who does not believe is
judged already". In a certain sense, then, not only Christmas but
also Judgment Day coincides with Good Friday, Easter, and Pentecost. We find a similar statement in 3.36: "He who believes in the

---

[65] The two sentences should probably be separated: "If anyone is thirsty let him
come to me; whoever believes in me, let him drink." Verse 14.1b provides a good
formal parallel. In this case 38b echoes Isaiah 58.11. For further discussion, see
Eduard Schweizer, "Joh 7.37–39", in *Göttinger Predigtmeditationen*, XVII (1962/63),
pp. 211–12.

on has eternal life; he who does not obey the Son shall not see life."
What is John saying here? It is surely not true to say that John expected from the future nothing more than what is already present for
the believer. He distinguishes the culmination of the future from the
present of faith. When Jesus (14.2–3) goes to prepare a place for his
disciples and bring them to himself that they may be where he is, he
clearly has in mind something that differs from the present life of
faith. In 17.24, he prays to the Father that his disciples may be where
he is and look upon the glory that the Father has given him. This passage has in mind a glory transcending the glory visible here and now.
The saying concerning the grain of wheat that must die is followed by
a promise that whoever does not love life in this world will be kept
safe for eternal life, and that the servant of Jesus will be where Jesus is
(12.25–26). Both promise the disciple a life that is accorded him who
is exalted to the Father. But by placing his primary emphasis on the
sayings that speak of life in the present, John quite remarkably continued Jesus' own concern: the kingdom of God, or, as John puts it,
"life", is not merely something in the future to be looked forward to.
It comes to the man who encounters Jesus in his message. And at this
point comes the decision: belief or unbelief, "Yes" or "No" to this life.
Therefore judgment takes place in the present, and the decision rests
with Jesus.

This point is made clearly in 11.21–27. Martha represents the
orthodox belief in the coming resurrection. But how does she come to
know of the resurrection? Presumably from a teacher educated as a
Pharisee. If she had had a teacher with Sadducean tendencies, she
would have denied any future resurrection. But can this really be the
ground of her faith? Jesus replies, "*I* am the resurrection and *I* am
life." Can she find life now—not in some distant future that is still a
matter of expectation and can therefore only be passively awaited?
This alone decides the question of the resurrection. Whoever finds
life in Jesus knows that in the sending of his Son, God has become
reality, and that this reality will not be destroyed by death—neither
by guilt and misery, the harbingers of death, nor by physical death
itself: "Whoever lives and believes shall never die." But this by no
means denies the truth of resurrection beyond physical death; "He
who believes in me, though he die, yet shall he live." As in the case of
Jesus, it is the life of the future that seeks to possess man here and now.
In this sense, John can have Jesus say, "He who hears my word, and
believes him who sent me, has eternal life, he does not come into

judgment, but has passed from death to life . . . the hour is coming and now is, when the dead will hear the voice of the Son of God, and those who hear will live" (5.24–25). Both are true: the time is coming when this will happen, and it is also already here, when a man heeds the word of the coming Lord. The Jesus who is, historically speaking, a figure of the past becomes present in his words; the same holds true of the Jesus of the future. Therefore John can also repeat the traditional phrases that speak unequivocally of the future resurrection: "The hour is coming when all who are in the tombs will hear his voice and come forth, those who have done good, to the resurrection of life, and those who have done evil, to the resurrection of judgment" (5.28–29). This passage, unlike the previous one, refers concretely to those who lie in the grave: "hearing" is meant only in the physical sense, not in the sense of true hearing that understands and assents; the resurrection is therefore twofold, not merely a resurrection of those who are saved. These are of course traditional phrases,[66] and the major emphasis is on the other, typically Johannine sayings. They show, however, that John is fully capable of borrowing such expectations from ecclesiastical tradition.

This leads us to a second point. Because all emphasis is on the present act of faith, and therefore also on the present judgment, the line between Jesus' band of disciples and the world is drawn with special sharpness; the single individual and his act of faith also play an important role. Perhaps for this reason John places the story of the cleansing of the temple at the beginning of Jesus' ministry, because it effects an initial separation (2.23–25). Again, 6.60–71 emphasizes the severity and offensiveness of Jesus' words, and the separation they occasion; and a section such as 8.37–59 draws a sharp distinction between the children of the Devil (8.44) and those who are God's children (8.47), between those who belong to the world above and those who belong to the world below (8.23; 3.3, 7). Faith is seen so strongly as something that comes to a man as a gift that John comes near to making statements that trace this separation back to an act of God.[67] Everything depends so on what God does that those with

[66] Rudolf Bultmann, *Das Evangelium des Johannes* (Kritischexegetischer Kommentar über das Neue Testament, 15th ed., Göttingen: Vandenhoeck & Ruprecht 1957), pp. 196–7, suggests that they were added later by the church. But the entire section speaks of the Son of Man, which suggests that this represents a traditional stratum not a later addition. Above all, 3.3, 5 show that John is fond of borrowing such traditional ecclesiastical phrases; cf. note 68 below.

[67] See the election of the children of God in 1.12–13; but also 6.37, 44; 12.32

ight do not see, and only the blind have their eyes opened (9.39).
This reveals at the same time the limitation of the Johannine view
of the community. This absolute and imposing concentration on
Jesus, by whom alone the disciple lives, can easily reduce the disciple
to an isolated individual. Matthew 10.14 can speak of a whole city
accepting or rejecting Jesus; for John, it is always the individual person who dwells in Jesus and in whom Jesus dwells. It is therefore no
accident that Paul uses the notion of the body of Christ, in which
each member depends on the other (1 Cor. 12.14ff.). But John uses
the image of a vine, with branches connected only by a common
root, or of a flock, where sheep graze side by side with only a common
shepherd whom they follow to unite them, or of a stalk with grains of
wheat growing side by side, attached only by a common stem (15.1ff.;
10.11ff.; 12.24). Even baptism and communion, which appear only
peripherally in John,[68] where they are taken over from tradition, remain merely signs that continually remind the disciples that they live
only by Jesus' sacrifice on their behalf. These sacraments never, as
Paul would have emphasized, place the disciples in a new life open
to the needs of their brothers or bind them together in table fellowship and as the body of Christ. The danger of a sectarian community,
in which the relationship of every individual to his exalted Lord
dominates everything, is of course overcome repeatedly by the notion
of discipleship to him who sacrificed himself for others. Thus in
John, the Lord's Supper is replaced by Jesus' washing of the disciples'
feet, which is more than an example: it provides the basis that makes
it possible for the disciples to imitate their Lord's action (13.1ff.).
Thus brotherly love (which for John remains limited to the brethren) is rooted in the precedent of Jesus, who lives as witness to the
love of God, thereby likewise making his disciples witnesses to this love.

17.2. There is a corresponding blindness of the world that cannot recognize Jesus:
8.23; 14.17; 15.18ff.; 16.3.

68 John 3.5 is taken over from tradition, as is shown by the concept of the kingdom of God, which appears nowhere else in John, and by the echo of Matthew
18.3. 3.3 was composed by John himself on the basis of 3.5 (see p. 117, n. 46). Here,
as in the rest of this section, there is no reference to baptism. In view of the mention
of the bread of life, 6.51c–58 can be understood only as a later interpolation or as
the borrowing of a traditional communion mediation. The passage discussed above
(19.35) is intended only to stress that Jesus' exaltation on the cross should be kept in
remembrance within the community through baptism and communion (cf. 1
John 5.6–8). For further discussion, see Käsemann, op. cit., pp. 32ff.

More than any other New Testament writer John expects all salvation from Jesus Christ; in everything he says he seeks only to emphasize this one point, that everything is to be found in Jesus. This accounts for the fascinating power and authority of the Johannine sayings; it also gives rise to the dangers we have spoken of. The absolute significance of Jesus Christ for all men, which spans the ages, almost does away with time. It is therefore not always easy to determine why the unique historical past, in which Jesus lived upon earth, and the not yet present future of fulfillment should really be important for faith. The emphatic claim that God himself is truly to be found in Jesus is made with such consistency that it threatens to overshadow the humanity of Jesus. But the Fourth Gospel still remains gospel: the obedience of the Son, his testimony on behalf of the Father, his leadership that engenders discipleship make him what he is; recollection of the time of the earthly Jesus and anticipation of the coming fulfillment of all that has been promised to faith are not forgotten.

VII

INNOVATIONS WITH THE DAWN OF
CHURCH HISTORY

THE PROBLEM

The New Testament comprises more than books in which the message of Christ has been fundamentally pondered and expressed, as in Paul or John, or, less thoroughly, the first three Gospels and Revelation. We also find the shorter Letters, which give us a picture of the transitional period between the initial momentous statements and the early church and which show how the Christian message, formed by the crucial witnesses, was endangered, reformulated, protected, and maintained as it passed into the church, living by the New Testament and its centuries of history.

In the initial period of the community, expectation of the imminent eschaton was probably dominant. This was replaced, somewhat later, by knowledge of the presence of the exalted Lord. Especially in communities of Gentile Christians, this could easily lead men astray into an enthusiastic form of religion that left this earth behind and was interested only in the present and effectual signs of the eschaton, or, on Greek soil, in the presence of the heavenly Lord and experiences of the Spirit. To Paul, the futurity of God's kingdom was such an indubitable fact that he could never think of the Spirit except as a pledge, a kind of firstfruits pointing to what was yet to come (Rom. 8.23; 2 Cor. 1.22; 5.5). Above all, however, he identified the coming Lord with him who called him to his service on the road to Damascus and therefore remained Lord of his daily life, with all that that implied. Finally, the fact of the Messiah's crucifixion so scandalized Paul that it was always implied and could never be forgotten when Paul said "Jesus Christ". The notion of a crucified Messiah had in fact made him a persecutor of the Christian community until the exalted Lord called him. But the communities he founded had learned from him to understand the crucifixion as a saving event. Thus the cross could gradually develop into a cultic symbol. To them Palestine was nothing but an obscure corner of the mysterious eastern regions of the Roman Empire. Thus various considerations posed the question of what Jesus' earthly ministry meant for faith. If all expectations centered on the eschatological Parousia, then at most there was some importance in the miraculous powers that anticipated the end in the present. If the heavenly Lord was central, all that mattered was experiences of the Spirit. If the cross was seen as the sign of God's grace and our justification, one could ask whether other symbols and signs might not do equally well. Of course one could say that Jesus was the first to teach all this. But this remained a point of interest only within Judaism. Paul had long since translated this truth into the new situation of the Gentile world, and the people of Corinth and Rome were no longer interested in disputes with the Pharisaic interpretation of the law. Within Judaism, however, a teacher who approached the law with so radically critical an attitude as Jesus did, and was executed in the most ignominious fashion for his attitude, remained an object of greatest suspicion.

This being so, why should this new knowledge of freedom, of the law, and of God's grace not be associated in the Gnostic fashion with the myths of Attis and Osiris rather than the story of Jesus of Nazareth? This Gnostic reduction of the message of Christ into a kind of philosophical knowledge of man and the divine element within him becomes extremely dangerous at the beginning of the second century; and the dispute with this fascinating vision, which seemed to render unnecessary both the assent of faith to the crucified Jesus and the entire Old Testament, dominated most of the theological activity of the Christian community in these decades. From Revelation and from the Letters to Timothy and Titus we know how vulnerable the very communities Paul founded in Asia Minor were to this attack.

And so the Gospels had to be written. Now, of course, the converse question arose as to why the writing of the Gospels amounted to anything more than a retrospective survey of historical events disappearing deeper and deeper into the obscurity of an ever more distant past. Mark tried to counter this objection by interpreting the life of the present-day community as discipleship based on the path of suffering traveled by Jesus of Nazareth. Of course there was as yet no clear statement of why this should be anything more than the ethical example of any departed individual, which continues to influence us, although it is quite clear that this is completely different from what Mark has in mind. Matthew sees the presence of the Jesus who is, historically speaking, a figure of the past primarily in his teachings, which, as commandments, determine the life of the community. Here, too, the question arises of how Jesus differs from a teacher whose instruction is adopted by later generations. Luke probably did the most to adjust his thinking to historical categories, although he, too, understands the saving event as a process involving the Word of God, seeking men's ears and hearts. John, on the other hand, is concerned above all with the presence of the Paraclete ("Advocate"), that is, the Spirit. Even he can do no more than recall Jesus himself and his life of loving service that engenders the Christian community, the Lord who, with his testimony on behalf of God, makes it possible for the disciple to be a living witness.

From this point, developments in two directions are possible. On the one hand, the Lucan solution leads to increasing emphasis on tradition and order, as well as a steadily increasing influence of the "ancient" Jewish heritage. Thus the danger arises that an official church will gradually develop, in which the ancient traditions are automatically true. This can even raise the question whether it would not be better to return to the unaltered sacrificial cult or to the law. Then the community must struggle to distinguish proper authority and order, given by the Spirit of God, from a fixed official hierarchy that guarantees continuity but does not know the Spirit. On the other hand, the Johannine approach leads to a primary emphasis on the freedom of the Spirit, but can easily result in caprice and the sectarianism of a brotherhood withdrawn from the world. Therefore the question of the significance of the Christian community for the world must be considered and pondered. How are these dangers overcome, and how are the various approaches so far observed in the New Testament maintained in the post-Pauline and post-Johannine community?

THE EPISTLES WRITTEN IN THE NAME OF PAUL AND JOHN: COLOSSIANS, EPHESIANS, FIRST AND SECOND TIMOTHY, TITUS, FIRST, SECOND AND THIRD JOHN

JESUS CHRIST, THE SALVATION OF THE CHURCH

The Letters to the Colossians and the Ephesians are still closely associated with Paul; the former, at least, may actually have been written by Paul himself. Nevertheless, innovations appear at many points.

The dispute over the question of the law is no longer of real consequence. This is the more striking because Colossians reveals a group that is once more setting up legal requirements very similar to those postulated by the false teachers of the Epistle to the Galatians. The author is content to reject such demands, which concern feast days, unclean foods, and perhaps also unclean objects; he states merely that God has given everything of man's use (Col. 2.16–23). For Ephesians, the law is the wall or fence that had separated Israel from the Gentiles but is now broken down, because those who were dead in sins now devote themselves to good deeds (Eph. 2.5, 10, 14–15). Nevertheless the cross plays an important role in both Letters as a guarantee against any enthusiastic disregard for reality, and the author treats seriously the imperative that calls on the believer to take to heart what the indicative of announced salvation promises him (Col. 3.1–4; Eph. 6.10–20).

The law has disappeared even more completely from the theological concern of the Pastoral Letters, that is, the Letters to Timothy and Titus, which represent a non-Pauline community in Asia Minor completely under the influence of Paul and his work, and possibly date from the beginning of the second century. Jewish religious practice passes imperceptibly into that of Christianity; only in Luke do we find certain parallels to this phenomenon (2 Tim. 1.3ff.). The law was created only for evil men; it is no problem for those who are good (1 Tim. 1.8–11). In the Johannine Letters, likewise, in which we hear a community bearing the stamp of John's Gospel, presumably living as a sect, not only the problem of the law but Israel itself has vanished completely from sight. A child of God is expected to live sinlessly (1 John 3.6ff.), so that Jesus only functions as reconciler and intercessor for minor transgressions (2.1–2). The fact that legalism or trust in one's own "wisdom" can easily be a temptation for faith has here been lost sight of. The phrases in the Pastoral or Johannine Letters that speak of justification and reconciliation are merely traditional formulas that no longer possess any real power; new questions, however, have arisen and have yielded new answers, which we shall discuss in the next section. That faith rests totally on what took place in the life, death, and resurrection of Jesus of Nazareth, and cannot be degraded into an eternally valid philosophy independent of Jesus is maintained throughout. Now, however, a differently articulated schema becomes operative: the "revelation schema".[1] This means that what took place in Jesus is understood primarily according to the category of the revelation of the hidden God. Certain tendencies in this direction are found in Paul (e.g., 1 Cor. 2.6ff.), Mark (in the miracle stories), and above all in John (e.g., 1.14). Here, however, formulaic language is used to speak of the divine "secret" that lay hidden for generations, in fact from the very beginning, but is now revealed. This is the theme of Colossians 1.26ff. and Ephesians 3.3ff. This schema appears in a hymn quoted in 1 Timothy 3.16, but it is also adopted by the writer of the Letter himself. The introduction to First John exhibits a similar appearance, although the terminology differs.[2]

As a consequence of this schema, in Colossians and Ephesians the encounter with Christ can basically be understood as a grasping of God's "secret" (Col. 2.2–3; Eph. 3.3ff.). This theme is taken up in different ways by the Pastoral Epistles and by the Johannine Letters. The former speak of the "tradition" to be "kept safe" by the apostle's pupil so that it can be handed down to future generations. The latter speak of what the "anointing", that is, the Spirit of God dwelling within the believer, "teaches" the community through discourse that is constantly renewed (1 John 2.20). Throughout these Epistles the encounter with Christ that claims the total life of the believer has been replaced by the obtaining of salvation, conceived in terms of instruction, perception, and knowledge. This reduces what was originally a much broader understanding of the message-event to the domain of epistemology, with the result that the ethical consequences of the event must be discussed separately. But at this point we come to certain positive innovations that appear in this literature, pointing toward the future. We shall discuss these in the next chapter.

We have already seen that in Colossians and Ephesians the "secret" that is revealed is the mission to the Gentiles.[3] Thus statements about

---

[1] See above, p. 79.

[2] For the Pastoral Epistles, see 2 Timothy 1.10; Titus 1.2–3; also the "dawning" of Jesus in Titus 2.11; 3.4. Besides 1 John 1.2, Jesus' "appearance" is mentioned in 3.5, 8; the Letter, however, in contrast to false teachers of Gnosticism, emphasizes the reality of Jesus' incarnation (cf. below, p. 187, n. 22) and, unlike the Gospel of John, his future "appearance" at the Parousia (2.28; 3.2). For a discussion of Romans 16.25–27, see above, p. 79.

[3] See above, p. 77. Besides Colossians 1.27 (and Rom. 16.26), the most significant passage to be mentioned is Ephesians 2.13–22 (cf. 3.6, 8), according to which the dividing wall between Israel and the Gentile world has been broken down by

Christ, the Lord of the universe, become statements about Christ, the Lord and head of the church. The transfer is all the easier because "church" no longer designates primarily the community that lives as a real community of faith in a certain place, but rather the universal church. At the same time, it must be made unmistakably clear that this church can only be understood as the band of those who do obedient service for their Lord, suffering if necessary for him, if a theology speculating about Christ as the victorious Lord of the universe is not simply to be replaced by another theology that glorifies him as the Lord of an exalted heavenly abstraction, the "church".

This new approach already shows, however, that the revelation of the secret does not lead merely to a theoretical grasp of a new doctrine, nothing more than an increment in knowledge.

Neither does it lead to a withdrawal from the world on the part of those who know God, as happened at Qumran by the Dead Sea. In Colossians 2.19; Ephesians 2.21; 4.15–16, a new image is used to describe the church: the living and still growing body of Christ. Ephesians 3.10 even contemplates the church's reaching the demonic powers with its preaching. Finally, we must note that the proclamation of Christ as Lord of the universe in Colossians is a pointed counter argument against those who are not satisfied with Christ and would worship other lords besides him.

Some questions, of course, cannot be suppressed. In Colossians and Ephesians Paul is probably already a figure of the past, whom the church remembers with gratitude.[4] These questions arise even more clearly in the Pastoral Epistles. In Colossians and Ephesians, preaching to the Gentiles is still seen clearly as a miracle of God; in the Pastorals, it is an accepted fact, and therefore no longer fascinating and exciting. The challenge to the community is no longer the surrounding nations that have not yet heard the message of Christ, but false teachers who have arisen in the midst of the community itself (1 Tim. 4.1ff.; 6.20; 2 Tim. 1.15ff.; 4.3–4; Titus 3.9). Against them the correct apostolic tradition is now cited; the church is understood as the "pillar and bulwark of the truth", and faith becomes increasingly identified with assent to a body of statements that can be formu-

---

Christ. This transfers the statement concerning the reunification of the universe in Christ (1.10) in similar fashion from the mythical to the earthly realm. Colossians 1.23 has the same effect on the hymn in Colossians 1.15–20 (see above, p. 77).

[4] Cf. Colossians 1.23–25; Ephesians 2.20; 3.1–13.

lated and handed down (1 Tim. 3.15–16; 2 Tim. 1.14; 2.19; 3.14–16). In line with this change, Paul, who appears here as the only apostle (1 Tim. 1.12–16; 2.7; 2 Tim. 1.11; 4.6–8), delegates authority to his fellow-workers to appoint elders in turn and see that the church is kept in good order (2 Tim. 2.2; Titus 1.5ff.; 1 Tim. 3.1ff.; 5.1ff.). At least in Second Timothy, which refers to Paul's death, Timothy becomes for all practical purposes Paul's successor, and is so appointed. Nevertheless, despite the emphasis on the transmission of authority— transmitted by actual ordination (1 Tim. 4.12ff.; 2 Tim. 1.6–7)—the free operation of the Spirit is not restricted to the office regulated by ordination or some other form of appointment; in fact, it is the operation of the Spirit that provides the basis for the office. Only the man designated by prophetic utterance as God's chosen instrument is ordained to office (1 Tim. 1.18). In other words, the office does not guarantee the Spirit and correct preaching; it is the Spirit of God who confers the office. Here, too, the community is thought of as being ready to suffer, and is exhorted to be in a state of readiness. Not only the fellow-workers of the apostle, but also the leaders of the community in general and ultimately all the men in the community are expected always to find the right thing to say in whatever situation they find themselves.

The solution found in the Johannine Letters differs completely. Here, too, the Gentile mission is a thing of the past. There is no longer any trace of a suggestion that acceptance of Gentiles into the Christian community was ever a problem. Neither is there any hint that there are members of the community who are of Jewish origin, as well as members of Gentile extraction. Here, too, it is no longer the problem of Israel and the Gentiles that challenges the community, but false teachers in their midst. Unlike the Pastorals, however, the Johannine Letters do not have recourse to tradition and order. On the contrary, in Third John the settled official church appears as an avowed danger, against which the elder defends himself with vigor. Within the New Testament, then, the Johannine Letters exhibit the most complete devotion to the presence of Christ in the free operation of the Spirit: "You know everything . . . you have no need that anyone should teach you; as [the Spirit's anointing teaches you] about everything, and is true, and no lie" (1 John 2.20, 27). Of course, just as in the Pastorals strong emphasis on order in the community was secured by recourse to the free operation of the Spirit, so here, conversely, the almost alarming confidence in the free operation of

God's Spirit is secured by the statement that the Spirit teaches only what they had heard "from the beginning", that is, in the apostolic preaching, and that a spirit which no longer proclaims Jesus come in the flesh is a lying spirit (1 John 1.1; 2.7, 24; 3.11; 4.2–3; 2 John 5–6).

JESUS CHRIST, THE LORD OF THE CHURCH

In Colossians and Ephesians we come for the first time upon the so-called *Haustafeln*, that is, admonitions in short sentences regulating the conduct of parents and children, masters and slaves, etc.[5] Similar compilations are found in Hellenistic documents; but only in the New Testament are the persons of superior rank, the fathers or the masters, reminded as clearly of their responsibility as their inferiors. The danger lurking behind the establishment of such general rules is clear. Is faith not confused here with a kind of middle-class propriety? Paul, in his Letters, tries to see the necessary conduct in the particular situation in which the recipient of the Letter presently finds himself, and is not content until he can show how this specific conduct follows necessarily from the basic message of salvation in Jesus Christ. And is it not true in the case of Jesus himself that his preaching of the coming kingdom of God lays the foundation for all human conduct in this world, issuing in exhortations that are not simply general rules, but rather tell how the specific individual, standing before Jesus and hearing his message, is to respond to the announcement of God's kingdom? Now Colossians is still well aware of this intimate connection between indicative and imperative: only because Christ has, to an extent, already received us into his realm[6] can and must we "aspire to the realm above" (3.1–4). Within the *Haustafel* itself, Ephesians bases the reciprocal love of a married couple on Christ's love for his church (5.22–23; cf. 5.1–2, 8, etc.). On the other hand, a man must receive help and instruction in his everyday life if he is not to be tempted into retreating from the world into a religious ghetto. The community proves itself in the simple demands of family, vocation, and citizenship; they must be taken seriously.

In the Pastoral Epistles, statements concerning salvation tend increasingly to stand independently beside general ethical rules, many of which also apply in the non-Christian Hellenistic environment.

[5] The most recent discussion is that of P. Stuhlmacher, "Christliche Verantwortung bei Paulus und seinen Schülern", *EvTh* XXVIII (1968), pp. 176ff.

[6] Ephesians 2.6 goes considerably further.

The *Haustafeln* and codes of conduct for bishops (1 Tim. 3.1ff.; 6.1–2; 2 Tim. 2.1ff.; Titus 1.5ff.), as well as many general rules, borrow considerably from Hellenistic ethics. Beside these stand statements concerning Christ, who came as mediator and redeemer to save sinners or to save all men (1 Tim. 1.15; 2.3ff.; 4.10; Titus 2.11–14), and through his grace to justify men and give them hope for eternal life (Titus 3.8).

Undoubtedly the statements concerning salvation are often mere formalities, and the ethical instruction is often identical with that found outside the New Testament. Undoubtedly we no longer find here the natural growth of ethical requirements out of the special gift of the nearness of God's kingdom, as in the preaching of Jesus, or the marked theological originality that links statements of salvation with ethical demands in the Letters of Paul. We may nevertheless say that by referring the reader repeatedly to the Christ event and to the apostolic preaching, without themselves attempting to construct original new theological formulations, the Pastorals perform an extraordinarily important service for the church. And by giving central importance to everyday perseverance in family, vocation, and citizenship without wasting inflated language on the subject, they once more performed a healthy service for their church in the face of all enthusiastic or unworldly misinterpretations of Christianity. At a time when Gnosis was fascinating men with supernatural mysteries and their ethical implications, which forsook the world for enthusiasm or asceticism, the prosaic dryness of the Pastoral Epistles, which do not pretend to offer more than they can carry off, was unusually helpful.

Once again, the situation differs in the case of the Johannine Letters. Here, too, the ethical decision that is demanded at the present moment no longer follows from the basic proclamation of salvation. But neither are the universally valid ethical rules of the surrounding culture taken over. Everything is concentrated in the one commandment in which everything is comprised: reciprocal love. Here, too, the question arises whether this suffices, whether the problem of what this means in concrete instances is not simply evaded, and whether the question of where the power of such love comes from is not crucial.

But 1 John 4.7ff. emphasizes unequivocally that love is basically and comprehensively God's love for us, which took form in Jesus Christ, and that all our love can only issue from what took place in Christ. That the love which flows from the love of God or Jesus must always be a very concrete and specific act is made unmistakably clear by means of an example (3.16–17). Above all, the almost tiresome repetition of the phrase "love one another" is only the reverse side of an imposing concentration on the one thing that is really essential and testimony to an overwhelming confidence in the reality and power of God, who will give instruction in the different concrete situations to him who loves.

Thus in the post-Pauline and post-Johannine period we see how the community lives from the Christ event and from the fundamental theological labor of the so-called apostolic age. Basically it can do no more than refer back to what took place in Christ and its expression in the apostolic kerygma. The very fact that this period does not transform the kerygma into new conceptions that are up-to-date and fascinating, as the Gnostics did, thereby losing the very substance of the kerygma, gives this age its importance. It nevertheless addresses itself to the problems it faces, considers them soberly, and thus helps find the way into everyday life that leads into the world with its various tasks; this is the essential contribution of the post-apostolic Letters within the New Testament.

NEW SOLUTIONS WITHOUT DIRECT REFERENCE TO PAUL AND JOHN: HEBREWS, JAMES, FIRST AND SECOND PETER, JUDE

JESUS CHRIST, THE END OF THE CULT (HEBREWS)

The Letter to the Hebrews was probably written in the eighties by a member of the second generation; it is a parenetic exhortation addressed to an unknown readership. It has been said that what Paul did for the question of the law, Hebrews did for the question of the cult. Just as Paul presented Christ as the end of the law, Hebrews presents him as the end of the cult. There is some truth in this statement: Hebrews recognized a presumably real longing for a visible cult, representing something of the divine glory, as a serious theological problem and thought it through carefully. In actual fact, the assurance that comes through the cult would not differ essentially from that which comes through observance of the law. Thus in Hebrews the priest-king Melchizedek, mentioned briefly in Genesis 14.18ff., takes the place of Abraham, and is even clearly ranked above

Abraham (7.4); Moses and Aaron are also positively appraised. All of this is connected with the new question being asked. The approach to a solution also differs considerably from the Pauline approach. The first reason is a difference in language. The author, it is true, still lives in the sphere of apocalyptic and eschatological ideas. The community is the wandering people of God,[7] journeying to the heavenly Jerusalem under the discipline and guidance of God (12.1ff.). The goal clearly still lies in the future (9.28; 10.13, 36–39; etc.). In addition, however, the author is schooled in the thought of Hellenistic Judaism, like that found in Philo of Alexandria; this school of thought may have been represented within the community of Jesus by the group around Stephen or by Apollos (Acts 6.1—8.3; 11.19–20; 18.24–28; 1 Cor. 1.12; 3.5). In this view, the realm of God is represented as the "higher" or "heavenly" world. Even this difference of language, however, does not account for the basic contrast with Paul. Paul, too, can speak of the heavenly Jerusalem (Gal. 4.26–27), although for Paul the temporal precedence of that which comes first is primary, whereas in Hebrews spatial images dominate.

The deeper similarities and differences can be seen in the treatment by both Paul and Hebrews of the contrast between the old and new covenants.[8] Both proclaim the superiority of the new covenant. Both concentrate all their considerations on the figure of Jesus Christ, in whom alone life and salvation are to be found. Hebrews 4.14ff. and 9.11ff. are confessions of the exalted Christ comparable in their striking clarity and lucidity to many famous Pauline passages. And just as Paul maintained his emphasis on the crucified Jesus, refusing to let him simply dissolve into a heavenly figure, so Hebrews 5.5–8 recalls him who "with loud cries and tears . . . learned obedience through what he suffered". Like Paul, Hebrews is well aware that the earthly life of Jesus signifies the self-abasement of him who dwells with God from all eternity, that is, the coming into the world of God himself (2.9; etc.). There are also parallels in the author's refusal to restrict himself to a single category in order to represent the significance of Jesus' death for the community. Besides the image of atoning sacrifice (9.11ff.), we find above all the notion of the forerunner, who opens the way and makes it possible for the community to follow as his disciples (2.10; 5.8–9; 6.20). We also find the image of the heavenly

[7] See E. Käsemann, *Das wandernde Gottesvolk* (FRLANT 55, 1961).

[8] See U. Luz, "Der alte und der neue Bund bei Paulus und im Hebräerbrief", *EvTh* XXVII (1967), pp. 318ff.

intercessor (7.25; 9.24), which appears only rarely in Paul (Rom. 8.34).

But how is the salvation of this new covenant related to that of the old? For Paul, the key figure who represents the unity of God's action in both covenants is Abraham. He is the symbol of God's completely free and unmerited grace, which is vouchsafed in Jesus Christ to those who are justified in him. For Hebrews, Melchizedek plays the same role. But in actual fact this Melchizedek is no longer merely the Old Testament figure from Genesis 14, but a heavenly high priest appearing upon earth. Thus in parallel to him Jesus is depicted as he who performs priestly service in heaven. Judaism said much the same, for example, of the archangel Michael. The Qumran sect also pictured Melchizedek thus as a heavenly being.[9] Just as in Paul, the connection between the old and new covenants is not observable on the historical level; it is ultimately found only in "heaven". When Paul speaks of the completely free act of God in the old covenant and Hebrews speaks of a heavenly figure appearing in the old covenant, they both mean something very similar: the unity of both covenants is brought about by God himself; it is not historically demonstrable.

The crucial difference between Paul and Hebrews lies in their negative appraisals of the old covenant. For Hebrews, the old covenant contains merely shadows and copies that pass away; they are left behind, now that what is truly real has come (8.2, 5; 9.23; 10.1). Ever since Plato, the Greeks have sought in the world the transitory image and shadow of what is truly divine and eternal. Using these categories, Hebrews seeks to comprehend both the allusive nature of the Old Testament and its insufficiency for knowledge of God. Paul could never speak in this fashion; to do so would be to say both too much and too little. On the one hand, Paul considers the law to be the good and holy Word of God. On the other hand, as such it had the function of bringing sin to its fullness and revealing man as what he really is even at the highest stage of his righteousness: a being never in the right before God, but totally dependent on grace. Thus Christ is not only the end of the law in the sense that what is perfect spells the end of what is temporary and shadowy, but also in the sense that in him the kingdom of God's righteousness has replaced that of sin and death. Paul would therefore hardly equate faith in Christ structurally

[9] A. S. van der Woude, "Melchisedek als himmlische Erlösergestalt in den neugefundenen eschatologischen Midrasschen aus Qumran Höhle XI", *Oud-testamentische Studiën* XIV (1965), pp. 369ff.

with the faith predicated of a whole "cloud" of Old Testament witnesses; he would hardly be able to define it as a certain hope for what is not yet seen, because here, too, he could not think exclusively in terms of what is provisional and what is perfect (11.1—12.1). On the other hand, one could not imagine Paul stating the impossibility of a second repentance, as in Hebrews 6.6.

We must not forget, however, that Hebrews attacked a problem not even considered by Paul, that of the status of the Old Testament cultic laws and, in its own way, subjected the problem to rigorous analysis. The author fell victim neither to the Gnostic tendency to place the Old Testament completely in the background, refusing to consider it any longer the Word of God, nor to the Jewish Christian tendency to seek salvation through cult and law. He illustrated thereby the allusive character of the Old Testament, how it points to the God who speaks and acts in it, and thus to him who is the goal of the entire old covenant, Jesus Christ. Hebrews made its contribution to guiding the community between the twin dangers of rejecting the Old Testament as heretical and accepting it legalistically. It could do so because when the community faced a very specific problem, it issued a clear word of warning. Despite its use of currently popular modes of thought, it never lost sight of the critical problem within the community that needed to be solved. Just as Paul repeatedly turns from declaring the message of salvation to exhorting the community, so Hebrews, too, in everything it says exhorts a community confronting danger. It does so, however, without turning into a moralistic tract and forgetting that Jesus Christ alone is and will always be the focus of all evangelical discourse.

JESUS CHRIST, THE TEACHER OF THE LAW (JAMES)

We have seen how the question of the law loses all significance in the Letters written in the name of Paul and John. In the Letter of James, this question becomes the central and indeed almost the only theme. In it we hear once more the voice of an outspokenly Jewish Christianity, albeit stamped with the Hellenism of the Diaspora. The very address to "the twelve tribes [presumably of the true Israel] of the dispersion" betrays the origin of the Letter.[10] This leads in

[10] We also find expressions from elevated Greek speech and echoes of the Greek translation of the Old Testament. It is hardly possible to say more than this with assurance about the date and authorship of the Letter, except that the author cannot

2.14ff. to what is actually a dispute with Paul; before Paul, no one had made the claim attacked by the author, namely that man is justified by faith alone. Certainly the author of the Letter would not have chosen what is probably the least favorable text of the entire Old Testament as the point of departure for his argument (Gen. 15.6, "Abraham believed the LORD, and he reckoned it to him as righteousness"), if Paul (Rom. 4.3) had not compelled him to do so. Of course when he says that a faith without works is dead, and that to tell those who have nothing to eat or wear to keep warm and have plenty to eat without giving them anything at all is not a saving faith, Paul himself could hardly have disagreed. Paul never claims that faith is without works; he states only that it does not issue in works of the law, by which he means works based on the law, performed only because the law requires them and because they are expected to yield a reward. On this point the Letter of James can no longer see the crucial difference, although it still preserves an echo of this difference when it speaks of "the perfect law, the law of liberty" (1.25), a phrase without parallel in Judaism.[11]

The problem of the law could only reappear in this fashion, and probably necessarily so, because the wealth and fullness of Paul's statements concerning God's righteousness in the community could no longer be maintained. The call to faith and to a life based on God's righteousness rather than one's own righteousness had ceased to be an invitation to undertake a journey, and was understood instead as a theological proposition to be accepted. This being so, a man brought up in the sound school of the Old Testament would be forced to ask apprehensively whether the community had not fallen victim to the danger of a dead faith, whether it was not on the brink of falsely turning "costly grace" into "cheap grace". James brings together a wealth of admonitions, often without internal continuity, rather like what we find in Wisdom literature, for example, the book of Proverbs. At first glance this resembles the exhortations to persevere in daily life that we find in the post-Pauline and post-Johannine Letters. But much related material also occurs in the hortatory sec-

---

be identical with James the brother of the Lord, and that 2.14ff. presupposes a period in which Paul's major theses have been largely accepted.

[11] A possible parallel from Qumran has been cited, probably without justification (Wolfgang Nauck, "Lex insculpta (חוק חרות) in der Sektenschrift", *ZNW* XLVI [1955], pp. 138ff.).

tions of the Pauline Letters. When 2.1ff. uses colorful imagery to warn against overestimation of the rich or 3.1ff. uses elaborate metaphors to describe the damage the tongue can do, we are not far from what Paul calls everyday worship. When 5.12–14 encourages prayer and common intercession in special cases of need,[12] or 5.7–11 urges patience in suffering, looking forward to the "Parousia" of the Lord, we are confronted with nothing that differs basically from Paul's exhortations to his communities. Above all, the warning against self-assurance and boasting (4.13–16) is closely related to similar warning in Paul, just as the summarizing of the law in the "sovereign commandment" to love one's neighbor (2.8) is closely related to Romans 13.8–10. Like 1 Corinthians 1.18ff., the Letter of James also acknowledges that true wisdom is not "earthly", but is vouchsafed from "above" (3.15–17).[13]

Nevertheless, the purpose of this Letter is completely different. Even externally, we note that the name "Jesus Christ" occurs only in 1.1 and 2.1, and could just as easily be omitted. This has even led to the suggestion that James is a purely Jewish document later adapted for Christian use. This cannot be true, as the peculiarities just mentioned show. It is correct to say, however, that no mention is made of Jesus' earthly ministry, nor of his death and resurrection; certainly there is no trace of the pre-existence and incarnation of Jesus Christ. The writer considers Jesus important only as an ethical teacher[14] and coming judge (2.12; 3.1; 5.9). This leads immediately to what sets him completely apart from Paul: not only does he warn against a dead faith without works; he also expressly maintains that man will be justified by works (2.21, 24–25; cf. 2.10). A proper and necessary reaction against a Paulinism that has reduced living faith to a set of propositions has here become so exaggerated that Paul's crucial message, which is fundamentally identical with that of Jesus, has been lost. This Letter is therefore good to read as a warning against mortal oversimplification of Pauline principles, as an arresting and

---

[12] The anointing mentioned here is intended to aid recovery, not to serve as last rites. This is also the only passage that speaks of a confession of sins after profession of faith.

[13] James 3.15 also shares with Paul (1 Cor. 15.44–49) the peculiar usage that equates "sensual" with "earthly", in contrast to what is "heavenly", "spiritual", or "above".

[14] James 5.12 probably contains the earlier form of Jesus' saying that is also preserved in Matthew 5.34–37.

beneficial exhortation to live the life of faith in all its practical consequences, as a mirror in which the community can repeatedly recognize itself. But it can be properly understood only against the background of the central affirmations of the New Testament, which furnish a corrective.

JESUS CHRIST, WHO IS TO COME, LORD OF THE COMMUNITY'S LIFE (FIRST AND SECOND PETER, JUDE)

In the Pastoral and Johannine Letters, future expectation tended to be replaced by a mode of thought that divided the world into a heavenly and an earthly realm, and expected salvation from "above" rather than in God's future action. Hebrews and James place more emphasis on God's action expected in the future. The two Letters of Peter go even further, maintaining that faith always involves hope in God's finishing and perfecting action.

The First Letter of Peter[15] does draw on the schemata of rebirth (1.3) and of the Christ event and the Christian community as the goal of Old Testament prophecy (1.10–12), both of which actually emphasize the present reality of salvation; but it keeps its gaze fixed on the "revelation of Jesus Christ" (1.7) that is yet to come.[16] This concentration on the Lord who is to come derives its force and authenticity from the situation of the community, which is being subjected to persecution (4.12–19). It is true that here, too, we find the notion that the salvation to come is already prepared for the community "in heaven" (1.4; but cf. also Gal. 4.26; Heb. 12.22; Col. 1.5; etc.). In fact, however, this notion expresses the certainty of the future and its significance for life in the present. On the other hand, the juxtaposition of present distress and eschatological rejoicing (1.6; 4.13) is reminiscent of Pauline formulations, the more so because the suffering is understood as participation in the suffering of Christ.[17] Present suffering and future joy are much more sharply distinguished, however, than they are in Paul, and less paradoxically combined. In the meantime, the enthusiasm that ignores the distresses and chal-

---

[15] The First Letter was probably sent from Rome, for which "Babylon" in 5.13 is a cover. It was surely not written by Peter himself, as its good Greek and use of the Greek Old Testament show. In all probability it was not even written at Peter's request by a contemporary (5.12), but by a later author.

[16] Perhaps 1.21 should be translated: "so your faith may also be hope in God".

[17] Cf. above, p. 101.

lenges of the present has emerged more clearly as a danger. As a contrast to this enthusiasm, the sobriety with which persecution is interpreted as the beginning of God's eschatological judgment of the community is extremely valuable. This approach overcomes the temptation to view the church as a triumphant entity in which the Christian can live far from the earth and its distress.

Thus here, too, as in Paul, the Christian community is understood as a community of service. It is true that the image of the body and its members is replaced, as in Ephesians 2.20–22 (but cf. also 1 Cor. 3.16–17), by the image of a building, which does not so much depict life "in" Christ as life based on his action in founding the community. But the building stones are described as "living stones" that "come to" Christ, the cornerstone (2.4–5), so that we are not dealing with the concept of a static and finished "institution". Thus even 4.10–11 thinks of the members of the community as "good stewards of God's valued grace", albeit the division of God's grace into oracles and service no longer reflects the wealth of the Pauline charismata. The rules for elders mentioned in 5.1–5 emphasize the examples set by the leader of the community, warn against arrogance and greed, rank the apostle in whose name the Letter is written as a "fellow-elder" rather than a superior, and, finally, base their admonitions to the shepherds on their sharing in the suffering of Christ and their hope for the coming of Christ, the "chief Shepherd". The Letter thus illustrates a later period, but seeks to meet its dangers in a way that is thoroughly Pauline.

The crucial point, however, is the Letter's adoption of the Old Testament view of the people of God, traveling its way through the world under God's guidance as "God's scattered people" (1.1, NEB), as "a chosen race, a royal priesthood" (2.9).[18] Here we come upon the first mention of the vision of a universal priesthood. This is especially important in that it refers not to service within the community, as the passages mentioned above, but to service to the pagan world (2.12). The description of this service is introduced by a sentence that recalls Philippians 2.3b and Ephesians 5.21, "Submit yourselves to every human institution" (2.13, NEB), and then goes on using *Haustafeln*[19] to elaborate the details of this service in highly personal and idiosyncratic fashion. The Christian exercises this universal priest-

---

[18] Cf. John Hall Elliott, *The Elect and the Holy* (Supplements to *Novum Testamentum* 12, Leiden: Brill, 1966), pp. 146 ff.

[19] See above, pp. 176.

hood daily in his life as citizen, servant, or spouse. A more serious attempt is made here than in other uses of *Haustafeln* to ground this conduct in the Christ event. Jesus' suffering and death are admittedly thought of primarily as an example (2.21–23; 3.18); but we can see in 2.24–25 and 4.1–2 how the author is still aware that one should go further, maintaining that Jesus' death actually created the possibility for new life. The first of the two passages borrows formulas from the Old Testament, especially Isaiah 53, that speak of substitution and atonement, while the second presumably echoes Pauline statements to the effect that dying with Christ is dying to sin (cf. Rom. 6.1ff.). The decisive contribution of these passages, however, is their recognition that the total life of the community must be understood as proclamation of the gospel to non-believers, as a message of salvation to others that is, as a missionary enterprise (2.12; 3.15; 4.4).

The Second Letter of Peter[20] is the only New Testament document showing that the delay of the Parousia became a serious problem. It holds resolutely to its expectation that the world will end, even suggesting concrete features of the end by borrowing the Stoic concept of a universal conflagration in which all the elements are consumed. It answers doubters by saying that for God a thousand years are like a day, and that God wants merely to give sinners an opportunity to repent (3.3–13). Here, then, the author revives the old apocalyptic perspective of Judaism, which expects God's final creative act to produce a new heaven and a new earth (cf. 3.5); but we must not overlook the Greek and Stoic dress in which this conception appears. Ancient statements are repeated, but we see at once that they no longer really put their stamp on what the community believes. The relationship of the Christian community to God and Christ is understood primarily as "knowledge" (1.2–3, 5–6, 8; 2.20; 3.18); above all, faith is conceived of as coming to "share in the very being of God" (1.4, NEB). The church is here seen as the place where man's natural being is made divine. The middle chapter, which incorporates the Letter of Jude without too extensive changes,[21] shows that this divine host is threatened by false teachers who are reminiscent of second-century Gnosticism. The Letter meets this danger by recourse to the

[20] This Letter makes its first appearance around AD 200, and has been a matter of dispute for centuries. It has nothing to do with the apostle Peter, and is probably the latest document in the New Testament.

[21] That the dependence is not in the other direction is shown, for example, by Feine-Behm-Kümmel, *op. cit.*, p. 303.

official ministry, the canon, and the confession of faith; this became the basic position of the entire church in the second half of the second century. The official ministry, it is true, is not yet represented by a bishop standing in apostolic succession, but only by the apostle himself. He is emphasized as an eyewitness, who reminds the community that all tradition has a historical beginning (1.12–16).[22] The whole Epistle is in fact conceived as the testament of the apostle, who will soon suffer martyrdom according to Jesus' words (John 21.18). The guarantee provided by Holy Scripture is strongly emphasized (1.20–21); the words of the Old Testament prophets and the New Testament apostles are placed on the same footing (3.2). Of course the author is aware that the Letters of Paul contain difficult passages, on which the false teachers clearly rely. Therefore Scripture still needs legitimizing interpretation, which is here guaranteed once more by the apostolic authority of Peter (as eyewitness, which Paul was not!), in order that the community may understand correctly what "our beloved brother Paul wrote to you according to the wisdom given him" (3.15–16). In this sense, our Letter can conceive of faith as a body of "truth" that the community "knows" and in which it is "well grounded" (1.12, NEB). In similar fashion, Jude 3.20 exhort the reader to hold fast to the ancient faith and to live blamelessly. In this way the coming of the Last Day can even be hastened (2 Peter 3.11–12). That faith can be described not only as "piety" (1.3, 6–7, NEB; 3.11) but even as "virtue" (1.5) shows how much the author is influenced by Greek thought.

The Letter is thus an interesting document of the recourse to tradition that was abundantly necessary to combat the Gnosticism of the second century, but could nevertheless not keep the author safe from a totally different mode of thought, which he shared in large

---

[22] 2 Peter 1.17–18 refers to the transfiguration of Jesus, so that the author interprets "eyewitness" in the Lucan sense; see above, p. 148. How urgent it became to have recourse to the earthly Jesus in a period when Gnosticism (see above, p. 170) was trying to eliminate him entirely is shown by other New Testament passages. Many exegetes find even in 1 Corinthians 12.3 the battle-cry of those who reject Jesus, viz., Jesus the earthly human being, in order to serve only the heavenly Christ. Paul, however, would argue quite differently against this position. First John 4.1–3 certainly attacks the theory of a heavenly "Christ" who no longer had anything to do with Jesus. In later Gnostics we find detailed exposition of the view that "Jesus" or "Christ" is only a symbol, a "cipher", for the truth that God seeks man or the divine spark in man, so that one could equally well take as one's symbols the divine figures of Hellenism and their myths.

measure with his opponents. If we ask what Jesus Christ really signifies in this Letter, we discover that in fact only his divine power and majesty, and above all his future office as judge, are emphasized (1.3, 16; 2.3ff.; 3.7). Urgently necessary as reference to Jesus himself and the apostolic preaching to counter the dangers that appear in the second chapter, the question nevertheless remains whether Jesus Christ is in fact really still central here, or has not been replaced by the deification of man and his proper conduct in the face of threatened judgment. There is no trace of Jesus' humanity, of his suffering and death; this shows that the completeness of the New Testament message of Christ has been lost. Nevertheless, it was both beneficial and necessary to rivet the community's attention on the new heaven and the new earth, as well as to remind them of Jesus and his disciples, in a period that was rejecting everything historical and finding interest only in the divinization of man. The Letter is an attempt to return to the original message under the threat of Gnosticism. On the one hand, it too often merely repeats ancient formulas without really transposing them into the new situation; on the other, it falls victim to the language and thought of its time even where these cannot be reconciled with the gospel of Jesus Christ. This shows that neither firm adherence to tradition nor modern open-mindedness guarantee the authenticity and vitality of the testimony. Nevertheless, the approach taken by this Letter served to dam the Gnostic flood, which had no room for either God's acts in past history or his creative act at the end of time.

James and Second Peter show how Jewish-Christian and Gnostic thought infiltrate parts of the New Testament and set their stamp on its message. This is not just a matter for negative appraisal. The mere repetition of sacred formulas in a language of the past would reduce the gospel to a museum piece. One can of course say that in these Letters the message of Christ did not make use of the language of the times as effectively as it did, say, in Romans or the Gospel of John. But they did see critical problems, which they met in one-sided but effective ways, and brought them to the attention of the community.

RETROSPECT

We have followed Jesus' band of disciples from the days they spent with their Master in Galilee to the beginning of the second century. Within this period they had to make clear both to themselves, and to the world to which they proclaimed Jesus, who he actually was. To do so they naturally had to use the language and imagery with which they were individually familiar and which was significant to them. At first glance, the result was a confused tangle in which one could scarcely find one's way. What a confusing wealth of ideas appear— the Son of David, who will come as eschatological Messiah; the Logos of God, who comes down from heaven as God's Son; the exalted Lord, exercising his authority from his throne beside God; the Son of Man, coming on the clouds of heaven; and many more. But how could it be otherwise? The knowledge of the community grew as its members learned how Jesus' power and influence affected new questions, problems, duties, areas of life. This implied not only new, additional insight into the significance of Jesus, but also a retreat from much that had been central in an earlier situation but was now without significance. At a time, for instance, when the imposing accomplishments of Jewish obedience to the law were familiar to all, Jesus had to be proclaimed as the end of all legalism. At a time, however, when the unrestrained freedom of man—already divine in his inmost soul—to reject the claims of marriage, human society, and the state was being proclaimed, a community that steadfastly repeated the old formulas of Jesus as the end of all legalism would have been denying Jesus and misleading those who heard its message. Therefore the church must continue to make fresh statements of who Jesus is. It can never reduce these statements to a single final formula that would define Jesus for the rest of time. If it did so it would be lord over Jesus, and he would no longer be Lord of the church.

But when the community accepted him as Lord and listened to him humbly, he showed himself again and again to be the risen Christ. This might take place when the band of Jesus' disciples, despite their resignation and despair, recalled his resurrection, experiencing and proclaiming him as the living Lord who already rules over them and brings the entire world to its consummation. It might take place when, recollecting Jesus' earthly ministry, they were moved to some new course of action, say by his association with the poor and despised, by his unflinching insistence on summoning men to the freedom that is also absolute responsibility before God, or by his easy readiness to help whoever had need of him at the moment. Above all, it took place repeatedly in the shadow of what distinguished this Jesus from all the gods and saviors of other cults and religious groups: his death on the cross, to which God had said "yes" at Easter, making the message of the cross part of the proclamation of Jesus' witnesses. Many other discoveries were able to add their bit to the significance of what took place in Jesus. The community could speak of Jesus' incarnation, of his exaltation, of his Parousia; but the cross and resurrection remained the focal point at which Jesus Christ proved himself again and again to be Lord of his community and the salvation of the world. For only the post-Easter community can tell us who Jesus really is; Jesus without Easter would be a dead Jesus, a figure of the past. Without the testimony of faith, Jesus would be a personality of past history. On the other hand, the totality of Jesus' life and death always bring the affirmations of faith back to earth when they threaten to become too enthusiastic, too restricted, or too one-sided. This duality is implicit in the total history of the community. In a certain sense, it is already present in what took place on the very first day when Jesus summoned men to follow him: he lived with them totally as their traveling companion, and yet they knew that, from the very first summons of him who called them to discipleship, in him God himself was calling them. When the community remained the community of Jesus Christ, it could never forget that Jesus was wholly man, to the point of an ignominious death on the cross. Neither could it forget that God had recalled this crucified Jesus to life and appointed him Lord. This duality determined the entire story we have been following, which often seems so confused.

In a certain sense one can say that the unity in the New Testament stands at the end, not the beginning, of its development, at the point where the documents that make up our New Testament today take form. In those days there were other writings concerning Jesus, in plentiful supply. There were some in which he was only one teacher among many, but above all others that turned him into a fantastic heavenly being who transcended this earth and soared high above mankind, without entering into mankind. Many documents were long a subject of dispute, such as Second Peter and Revelation, or the First Letter of Clement, which was finally excluded. On the whole, however, the various documents of the New Testament won the day on their own behalf, because they had proved their power in the life of the church and had maintained themselves as God's word to his people through the sufferings of the age of persecution. On the whole, then, there was no doubt where this word was to be heard. When everything from that period that has since come to light is brought together, there may perhaps be a few isolated sayings of the Lord that would deserve to be included in our New Testament, and it is still possible to debate whether the Letter of Jude really belongs there. Here, too, we have no absolute guarantee that the contemporary church came to the right decision. But apart from these peripheral passages, it remains clear today that what is authoritative has been brought together in the New Testament.

This unity is of course not without its tensions, but tensions must be preserved, because they lead us back vigorously to Jesus. Many have been resolved in the course of church history, bringing about new understanding; many still divide the confessions, and compel them not to be satisfied with their confessional position, but to inquire again and again after Jesus himself.

INDEXES

INDEX OF MODERN SCHOLARS

SELECTIVE INDEX OF NEW TESTAMENT REFERENCES